Cultivating Peace

TRANSITS:
LITERATURE, THOUGHT & CULTURE 1650–1850

Series Editors
Greg Clingham, Bucknell University
Kathryn Parker, University of Wisconsin—La Crosse
Miriam Wallace, New College, Florida

Transits is a series of scholarly monographs and edited volumes publishing beautiful and surprising work. Without ideological bias the series seeks transformative readings of the literary, artistic, cultural, and historical interconnections between Britain, Europe, the Far East, Oceania, and the Americas during the years 1650 and 1850, and as their implications extend down to the present time. In addition to literature, art and history, such "global" perspectives might entail considerations of time, space, nature, economics, politics, environment, gender, sex, race, bodies, and material culture, and might necessitate the development of new modes of critical imagination. At the same time, the series welcomes considerations of the local and the national, for original new work on particular writers and readers in particular places in time continues to be foundational to the discipline.

Since 2011, sixty-five Transits titles have been published or are in production.

For a list of selected titles in the series, see the last page of the book.

To S.r William Bowyer Baronet of Denham Court in the County of Bucks.

Geor: 2. L.1.

Frontispiece John Dryden, *Georgics* plate 6, Rare Book Collection, Howard Gotlieb Archival Research Center

TRANSITS

Cultivating Peace

THE VIRGILIAN GEORGIC IN ENGLISH, 1650–1750

MELISSA SCHOENBERGER

Bucknell | BUCKNELL
UNIVERSITY | UNIVERSITY
| PRESS

LEWISBURG, PENNSYLVANIA

Library of Congress Cataloging-in-Publication Data

Names: Schoenberger, Melissa, 1987- author.
Title: Cultivating peace : the Virgilian Georgic in English,
    1650-1750 / Melissa Schoenberger.
Description: Lewisburg, PA : Bucknell University Press, 2019. |
    Series: Transits: literature, thought & culture 1650-1850
Identifiers: LCCN 2018044226| ISBN 9781684480487 (cloth) |
    ISBN 9781684480470 (pbk.)
Subjects: LCSH: Virgil. Georgica. | Virgil—Influence. | English
    Poetry—Early modern, 1500-1700—History and criticism. |
    English Poetry—18th century—History and criticism. | Peace in
    literature.
Classification: LCC PA6804.G4 S34 2019 | DDC 871/.01—dc23
LC record available at https://lccn.loc.gov/2018044226

A British Cataloging-in-Publication record for this book is available
from the British Library.

♾ The paper used in this publication meets the requirements of the
American National Standard for Information Sciences—
Permanence of Paper for Printed Library Materials, ANSI
Z39.48-1992.

www.bucknell.edu/UniversityPress

Manufactured in the United States of America

For my parents, my first and best teachers
For my sister, my first and best friend

CONTENTS

Unless otherwise specified, all translations are my own. I render passages from Virgil more or less literally, and therefore sometimes diverge from idiomatic English usage. I have sometimes consulted modern translations, including Fairclough, Greenough, Williams, and Ferry.

Cultivating Peace

IN 1713, QUEEN ANNE DECLARED PEACE. Addressing Parliament on 9 April, she announced the impending Treaty of Utrecht, which concluded the protracted and costly War of the Spanish Succession. Although many welcomed the resolution of a conflict that had spanned eleven years, the Whig opposition had resisted an agreement with France, citing secret peace talks carried out by the Tory ministry, as well as possible threats to English mercantile interests.[1] Well aware that these ideological divisions would not disappear after the ratifications were finalized, Anne urged Parliament to repair domestic discord:

> Now we are entering upon Peace Abroad; let Me conjure you all, to use your utmost Endeavours for calming Men's Minds at Home, that the *Arts of Peace may be cultivated*. Let not groundless Jealousies, contrived by a Faction, and fomented by Party Rage, effect that which our Foreign Enemies could not.[2] [my emphasis]

By urging that the "Arts of Peace" be "cultivated," Anne underscores the significance of the processes whereby peace is created and sustained. Understanding the vast difference between declaring and perpetuating peace, Anne admits the limited power of the monarch to impose tranquility from on high. This speech marks a dramatic departure from earlier conventions; up to this point, the phrase "arts of peace" had not typically been associated with the toil and productivity of agricultural labor. Instead, it had more often meant either diplomacy abroad or domestic pursuits such as music, poetry, or philosophy—"arts" generally thought to flourish in the absence of war. In either case, the "arts of peace" stand in opposition to the arts of war. In her speech, however, Anne proposes a closer relationship between peace and war: the "arts of peace" are in fact the arts of perpetuating peace and of preventing resurgent conflict. The British, she implies, cannot assume that stability will emerge in the absence of war, just as a farmer would never expect crops to erupt spontaneously from the soil.

In contrast to Anne's vision of cultivation, seventeenth-century politicians and panegyrists had generally conceived of peace and war as opposing and mutually exclusive states, rather than mutable spaces fundamentally linked by their malleability. The early years of the century had ushered in the reign of King James I, sometimes referred to as the Rex Pacificus, who built his monarchial identity around the central goal of brokering peace at home and abroad; at the end of the period, in 1697, William III signed the Treaty of Ryswick, which concluded the yearly cycle of battles that had characterized the Nine Years' War. Despite the promises of peace that framed the century, the decades between the death of Elizabeth I and the accession of Anne saw a series of brutal conflicts. The Thirty Years' War marked a drastic acceleration in the European capacity to inflict devastating violence upon soldiers and civilians alike, and its memory haunted art and literature long after its resolution at Westphalia in 1648. As battle receded abroad, English factions struggled violently during a long series of civil wars. Despite the renewed peace and prosperity that the restoration of Charles II seemed to promise in 1660, the final third of the century included two disastrous naval wars with the Dutch and eight costly campaigns against the French. From the vantage point of 1713, Anne could understand well the flimsiness of peace declared and celebrated, but not maintained.

In striking contrast to the perpetual threat of battle, many artistic productions of the period reinforced a model of idealized tranquility in which central powers provide security by imposing stability understood to exist wholly apart from war. The masques performed at the Stuart and Caroline courts famously depicted the power of the monarch to transform the world itself, initiating a golden age and eradicating the forces of chaos. The paintings adorning the ceiling of the Banqueting House at Whitehall, where some of those masques were performed, were commissioned to celebrate the peaceable interests of James I, and exemplify the iconography of peace so common in this period: warm, shimmering light bathes olive branches, caducei, cornucopias, and other symbols of idealized peace and plenty (Figure 1). This aesthetic blends classical art and literature with images drawn from biblical prophecy and mythology, combining the peace of the Greco-Roman golden age with the Christian promise of a second Eden, two spaces in which peace and plenty persist effortlessly. Most important, this vision of peace depends on an oppositional relationship between states of peace and war: where one takes hold, the other cannot exist.

In a letter to Justus Sustermans dated 12 March 1638, the painter and diplomat Peter Paul Rubens, who had executed the Whitehall paintings, offers a rare description and analysis of one of his own canvases, *The Horrors of War*, completed a few years after he retired from active political work. In his description, Rubens explains the collapse of what both monarchs and poets would have understood,

Figure 1 Peter Paul Rubens, *Peace Embracing Plenty*, oil sketch, between 1633 and 1634, Yale Center for British Art, Paul Mellon Collection

in the century before Anne's speech, as the "arts of peace," or intellectual and creative pursuits that cannot coexist with war:

> There is also a mother with her child in her arms, indicating that fecundity, procreation, and charity are thwarted by War, which corrupts and destroys everything. In addition, one sees an architect thrown on his back with his instruments in his hand, to show that which in time of peace is constructed for the use and ornamentation of the City, is hurled to the ground by the force of arms and falls to ruin. I believe, if I remember rightly, that you will find on the ground under the feet of Mars a book as well as a drawing on paper, to imply that he treads underfoot all the arts and letters. There ought also to be a bundle of darts or arrows, with the band which held them together undone; these when bound form the symbol of Concord. Beside them is the caduceus and an olive-branch, attribute of Peace; these also are cast aside.[3]

Here, the world of the "City" represents the human capacity to create "all the arts and letters": works of visual art, architecture, literature, music, philosophy. Rubens emphasizes movement from high to low as he dramatizes the power of war to demolish such achievements and the foundation of peace upon which they rest; they are "hurled to the ground," they "fall to ruin," they are caught "under the feet of Mars." The artist also pairs these striking, classicized images with highly conventional allegorical symbols of peace. In addition to the olive and caduceus, the "bundle of darts or arrows" lies in disarray, grounding the more abstract idea of a state in chaos by reversing the image of the Roman fasces. At the same time that Rubens describes the realms of peace and war as opposed to one another, he also suggests that they are unequal: what peace makes, war destroys, and when they interact, the forces of destruction overwhelm those of creation.

The actual phrase "arts of peace" appeared frequently in the poetry of the seventeenth century, perhaps most memorably in Andrew Marvell's *Horatian Ode*, in which the restive Oliver Cromwell cannot remain content with the "inglorious arts of peace."[4] By the time Marvell used this phrase to contemplate a burgeoning republican government, it had come to be associated with questions of civic organization and monarchial power. In the dedication to *The First Part of the Elementarie Which Entreateth Chefelie of the right writing of our English tung* (1582), the schoolmaster Richard Mulcaster, whose pupils included Edmund Spenser, proposes a direct relationship between a standard orthography and a stable government, arguing that upright learning stands as "the Art of peace," which when practiced well creates a good life for everyone "from the highest diuine to the lowest infant." In his *Hypercritica, or, A Rule of Judgement, for Writing or Reading our Histories,* largely written during the reign of James I,[5] the antiquary Edmund Bolton distinguishes the "Foundations" that eventually gave rise to the English state of his own period, "whether we consider Piety, force of Arms, or Arts of Peace."[6]

In 1625, Hugh Holland found the phrase valuable as he joined the poetic chorus lamenting the death of James, describing the late king as a man who harbored disdain for all that belongs to the war god Mars—even the month of March, during which he met his end: "This is the moneth of Mars to him so bloudy, / Because he still the arts of peace did study" (73–74). At the same time that Holland eulogizes James as a ruler averse to battle and committed to peace, he also warns that the loss of such a king portends the threat of renewed war, as he indicates by turning to the subject of the sustained attacks made on Breda by Spain in the months before and after the king's death. These affronts portended the continuation of war in Europe, and therefore reinforced the need for sustained efforts to avoid further involvement. At the end of a passage describing James as a lifeless flower, Holland makes a sharp turn into these topical concerns, posing an urgent question in a couplet: "Yet hath Breda thrice three months siege endured, [*sic*] / [I]s life no more in peace then warre secured?" (37–38). Although poets would for many more decades invoke "the arts of peace" in panegyrics celebrating strongman rulers of the middle and later seventeenth century,[7] this early moment of hesitation suggests a nascent dissatisfaction with the notion of perpetual peace as the natural result of war concluded. Perhaps distantly recalling Jove's prophecy of peace in the first book of Virgil's *Aeneid*—in which Furor broods, seething and wrapped in chains, within the Temple of Janus—Holland imagines peace as a condition of contained war. Recognizing the persistent conflicts in Europe, Holland conceives of peace in negative terms: at least while fighting persists on the continent, English peace can be understood only as a state of war prevented. The responsibility for such prevention falls upon the monarch, who forges political peace through his relations with other kings, either by defeating them in battle or by succeeding at diplomatic negotiations. The ominous generality of Holland's formulation is striking: he rather resignedly asks whether "life" during peacetime must not always be defined in terms of war, but seems to settle on a definition of peace as the absence of war. His question betrays the logical difficulty at the heart of seventeenth-century models of peace miraculously sprung from the end of war: these representations elide the processes that lead from war to peace. Implicit in Holland's question are several others: Where do the energies of war go when peace is declared? How do we know we are living in peace? How can we be sure war will not return?

Despite the glaring problems attached to the dream of a golden age restored, idealized representations of peace, like those adorning the ceiling at Whitehall,

Figure 2 Medal struck in celebration of the Treaty of Breda, John Roettier, 1667, © The Trustees of the British Museum

persisted even at times of political instability or in the wake of serious military loss. In 1667, for instance, the English produced a medal to celebrate a treaty ratified at Breda to bring the calamitous Second Anglo-Dutch War to an end (Figure 2). The design is attributed to John Roettier, whose designs were praised in the diaries of both John Evelyn and Samuel Pepys. The medal features a laurelled bust of Charles II on its obverse, while the reverse portrays the national goddess Britannia, posed for by Frances Stuart, later Duchess of Richmond. Only two years earlier, Roettier had revived the figure of Britannia—featuring her on a pattern farthing—with a design recalling coins made during the reign of the Roman emperor Commodus in the second century CE.[8]

The medal places the goddess on the far right, where she sits on the shore, gazing over her right shoulder at the British navy. She holds an olive branch in her left hand, with its leaves draped across her knee. Her right hand wields a javelin, held erect. Roettier divides the scene along a diagonal line running from the edge of the rocky ledge in the upper right section, down to the shoreline in the lower left, below the largest battleship. Running along the upper quadrant of the left side, the phrase "Favente Deo" appears, meaning "with God favoring" or "supporting" England. The word "Deo" is placed in direct vertical alignment with the word "Britannia" at the bottom of the frame, perhaps suggesting that a nearly equal partnership between God and England has returned the world to a state of peace. This golden object reflects the ideals that had long motivated Stuart mythology: like a court masque, the Breda medal suggests that the end of war—even war that ends in defeat—marks the commencement of a new golden age, radiating downward from a benevolent tyrant.

In April 1713, poets eagerly heaped the same tropes onto Anne, in celebration of her political success. In his panegyric *Windsor-Forest*, the best of the poems written in praise of the peace, Alexander Pope exalts the queen in terms recalling the omnipotent God of Genesis. Yet by this point, the glorious machinery of Stuart mythology offered little more than idealized fictions, and Anne's words in her speech to Parliament suggest her awareness of this shift. By the early decades of the eighteenth century, poets and politicians alike had begun to realize that peace and war could not be conceived in mutually exclusive terms, and that the monarch could not necessarily impose lasting stability from on high.

In her speech, Anne relinquished some of the authority to make peace that her ancestors had so often claimed, emphasizing instead the communal duties that the English needed to accept: "It affords Me great Satisfaction," she pronounced, "that My People will have it in their Power, by Degrees, to repair what they have suffered during so long and burthensome a War." There is certainly a measure of shrewdness here; the queen distances herself from faction, suggesting instead that although she has overseen international diplomacy, the responsibility for full recovery lies with Parliament and the greater populace. Yet the subjunctive quality of her hope "*that* the Arts of Peace *may be* cultivated" fixes her focus on what could be, rather than on what is. Anne's address stresses the process of sustaining concord, rather than the ideal product of those efforts. Crucially, the burden of this maintenance falls largely upon the shoulders of the people, whom the queen charges with the shared task of making and keeping peace.

As it had for the Treaty of Breda, the Royal Mint produced a medal for the agreement at Utrecht; this commemorative object, however, echoes the queen's speech in striking ways (Figure 3). Joseph Addison was perhaps recalling that speech when in July 1713 he wrote in the *Guardian*, "I am informed [. . .] that we shall have several Farthings and Half-pence charged on the Reverse with many of the glorious Particulars of her Majesty's Reign. This is one of those Arts of Peace which may very well deserve to be cultivated, and which may be of great use to Posterity."[9] Groundbreaking recent work by Joseph Hone has illuminated the carefully orchestrated and dramatically increased production of medals under Anne, demonstrating the hitherto unrecognized influence of Isaac Newton—master of the Royal Mint for nearly thirty years—on the propagandistic valences of medal design, and providing new evidence showing the close creative relationship between Newton and John Croker, chief engraver when the medal for Utrecht was struck, and the man traditionally credited as its primary designer.[10]

The obverse side of the medal features a bust of Anne; on the reverse, the seated figure of Britannia holds an olive branch in her right hand and a javelin in her left. A shield adorned with the crosses of St. George and St. Andrew leans

Figure 3 Medal struck to commemorate the Peace of Utrecht, John Croker, 1713, © The Trustees of the British Museum

against her left thigh. Britannia sits in the foreground, her body bisecting the scene in the background. The British navy sails behind her right shoulder—although one very small ship floats under her left arm. Over her left shoulder, farmers plow and sow their fields. Britannia's body both divides and unites two ostensibly disparate realms: to her right, held in check by the suspended olive branch, the world of naval war; to her left, protected by the javelin and shield, the world of cultivated peace. Her body separates peace from war at the same time that it emphasizes their inextricability from one another.

In contrast to the totalizing vision of peace depicted on the Breda medal, the one designed for Utrecht suggests a dynamic relationship between war and peace. With much of the Breda imagery reversed and realigned, this medal offers what might seem like a more balanced—and therefore more certain—portrayal of peace, but it nevertheless evinces lingering threats.[11] In this vision, the materials of war mix with those of peace: read from left to right, the medal displays four naval masts running parallel to one another, but then, where the eye might otherwise have expected a fifth, the vertical olive branch appears. Whereas the Breda medal leaves the olive branch lying in a passive position, the olive rendered here supports itself in parallel alignment with the masts of the ships. In its authoritative position, the olive branch appears to hold sway over the vessels, as though commanding them to remain at rest, at the same time that it creates a visual echo of the structures of war in the realm of peace, reinforcing the mutable relationship between war and peace urged by the queen in her speech. Continuing to the right, we encounter the body of Britannia, after which we begin to pass into the realm of peace. Here one more warship appears—a tiny vessel floating in the distance, just above the shield and below Britannia's elbow—before the scene of agricultural labor begins. On the Breda medal the goddess holds her weapons upright in parallel vertical positions, but in this instance her javelin tilts to the right side of the frame, her shield leaning in the opposite direction and resting against her leg. These inactive weapons frame the scene of labor; the javelin divides the field from the rest of the medal, and the word "Armis," or "weapons," nearly touches the land. The imagery on the right side of the frame gestures toward the lingering memory of war; after battle, javelins and spears are not destroyed, but simply laid aside, and to look upon them is to recall the time when they were taken up to destroy enemy forces.

A time of peace should require agricultural tools, not implements of war, but the medal leaves us doubting whether the weapons have been put aside forever. Spanning the top half of the frame, the words "Compositis Venerantur Armis"—taken from the odes of Horace, book 4, poem 14—unite the two halves of the image.[12] The poem, addressed to Augustus, celebrates military victories achieved on the emperor's behalf by Drusus and Tiberius. Over the course of fifty-two lines, Horace enumerates the various peoples and places that have ceded to Roman imperial power, saving the brutal Sygambri for last:

> Te caede gaudentes Sygambri
> Compositis venerantur armis.[13]
> (The Sygambri, delighting in bloodshed,
> venerate you, their weapons set aside.)

Horace means primarily to praise Augustus, so he chooses his final image carefully: because these warriors revel in carnage, to conquer them is to quash the very heart of war. Yet in typically Horatian fashion, this final image also betrays a distinct sense of irony and uncertainty. The poem does not suggest that the Sygambri have ceased to delight in bloodshed; rather, it presents their enjoyment of battle as a kind of permanent or static trait. In other words, we might understand *caede gaudentes* in the same sense that we would understand such phrases as "The Sygambri, who live in the North," or "The Sygambri, who train horses." If the Sygambri love, have always loved, and will always love slaughter, then chances are good that Rome may very well go to war with them again. In its final moments, the ode offers a single image indicating at least two meanings: both an illustrious victory in war and the possibility that such a victory may not guarantee peace in perpetuity. The Sygambri represent violence subdued and contained, but not eradicated.[14]

Of course, the medal struck for the Treaty of Utrecht expresses hope for a peaceful future, but it also suggests a sharp turn away from the idealized representations of peace typical of Stuart iconography, and, fulfilling its purpose as a piece of state propaganda, corroborates Anne's call for the cultivation of peace. No one labors in the scene struck for Breda: warships rest on a calm sea as the English goddess gazes tranquilly upon them. Half a century later, however, the figure of Britannia appears as an emblem of the permeable boundary between the implements of war and the tools of peace. The medal offers the image of retired weapons to recall the recent end of war, as well as to signify the possibility that further efforts will likely be required to achieve lasting peace. In commemorating the Peace of Utrecht, the medal celebrates labor of many kinds: the peacetime labor that provides food for Britain, the labor that contains and orders impulses toward war, and the labor that stands vigilant against the consequences of history.

Yet it also depicts the monarch as a mediating force rather than an absolute one. In Roettier's scene, the serene national goddess gazes upon a calm sea, representing total and inviolable stability. The medal for Utrecht, however, corroborates the queen's speech: work, as it were, remains to be done, and the work of peace must remain in permanent conversation with war. According to this model of peace, the monarch yields some of her power; she does not preside over an achieved state of peace, but rather introduces a set of favorable conditions within which citizens can cultivate stability from the ground up.

VIRGIL'S *GEORGICS* AND POLITICAL PEACE

The primary aim of this book is to show how the notion of peace as a cultivated and mutable state informed the work of several poets who refused to partake in the myth of golden-age peace and plenty, but who were nevertheless committed to envisioning peaceable ways of life, and especially the processes whereby these peaceable ways persist. Such writers imagine peace not as a permanent golden age imposed from above and somehow ignorant of war, but rather as a mutable state grounded in perpetual conversation and tension with war. My major claim in the chapters that follow is that this vision of peace derives largely from the *Georgics* of Virgil, a poem in four books organized according to the cycle of agricultural labors required for successful production. Scholars of British literature have long recognized the profound significance of this ancient Roman poet for the development of English-language poetry; yet they have also often replicated the long tradition of misreading Virgil as a poet who wrote in the service of empire. Some late seventeenth- and early eighteenth-century poets, however, betrayed in their work a more nuanced understanding of Virgilian attitudes about war, peace, and political power; the factional politics of their own age likely predisposed them to detect the darker shades not only of the *Georgics*, but also of the *Eclogues* and the *Aeneid*.

Of Virgil's three major works, the *Georgics* speak most directly to the political tensions following the English civil wars and the age of party faction that developed over the ensuing decades. Composed during a long decade in which escalating tensions between Antony and Octavian would finally culminate in civil war, and completed in 29 BCE, not long after Octavian had defeated his rival at Actium,[15] the *Georgics* are everywhere marked by deep reservations about the possibility of lasting peace.[16] In the poem, Virgil finds many ways to describe the constant cycles of labor necessary for sustaining a successful farm. This emphasis on processes extends beyond the world of agriculture to the uncertain time that follows civil conflict: the *Georgics* insist that lasting peace must be constantly created and maintained.[17] In the same way that a farmer must work unceasingly to preserve the health of his cattle or crops, secure his farm against pests, and recover from unexpected storms, people who desire peace must tend it with vigilance and diligence, at the same time that they must accept the possibility of renewed conflict wrought by forces beyond their control. Neither the farmer nor the peacemaker can expect to control the wider world, but both can learn to mitigate its destructive power.

The most important lesson imparted by the *Georgics*, however, is that states of war and peace derive from the same materials: for Virgil, war and peace exist only as mutable versions of one another. He deems agricultural tools *arma*, or weapons; he instructs a farmer to follow the order of a military regiment when drawing the rows of his vineyard. Early in the poem's first book, the Roman army calls agricultural laborers to war. At the same time that this conscription leaves fields untended, *curuae rigidum falces conflantur in ensem* (I.508), "curved scythes are smelted into stiff swords":[18] the same metal shaft wielded as an implement of peace is melted down and reshaped as an implement of war. The medal struck for Utrecht envisions exactly such mutability between the tools of the agricultural and the military worlds. Moreover, the Latin word *falx*, here in its plural form *falces*, indicates not only a scythe or pruning hook, but also a scythe-like weapon intended for dismantling enemy stockades.[19] Thus, even when it signifies an agricultural tool, this word always carries with it a military significance.

The doubleness of this word, and many others Virgil uses in his poem, suggests an intertwined relationship between war and peace dramatically unlike the oppositional iconography of the golden age restored. Although this relationship may seem pessimistic—perhaps implying that peacetime is somehow fallen or scarred by war—I prefer to read it as a more measured representation of the threat of war. So long as the scythe remains a scythe and is used to reap, it remains a symbol of peaceable labor; yet at any moment it may be melted down and forged into a deadly weapon. To ignore this possibility is to remain deliberately and dangerously unaware of the processes whereby peace turns into war, and vice versa.

In this book, I focus my attention on four poets writing between the English civil wars and the rise of the British Empire who understood the fundamental concerns of the *Georgics* better than those seventeenth- and eighteenth-century writers who tended to take the agricultural subject matter of the poem at face value. The poems discussed in the following chapters exemplify what I call the "Virgilian georgic mode," in which peace appears as a mutable state of continuous, laborious cultivation. The creators of these poems—Andrew Marvell, John Dryden, Anne Finch, and John Philips—each had reason to doubt the promise of peace imposed from above, and although they work in different styles and in response to different historical problems, each shares with the others and with Virgil an interest in exploring the nebulous space between peace and war. Two of these writers, Marvell and Finch, did not write poems we would recognize as "georgic" in any traditional sense; yet they turn to Virgilian images of mutability and contingency to contemplate the possibilities for making peace in the midst of intense political debate and conflict. The other two poets might come more readily to mind when we imagine georgic poems in English: Dryden translated the *Georgics* as part of his complete *Virgil* of 1697, and Philips's *Cyder* stands as the first formal imitation of the Latin poem in English. As I will show, however, *Cyder* also marks the moment when this earlier Virgilian georgic mode begins to give way to the conventionally recognized genre of eighteenth-century English georgic poetry. Together, Marvell, Dryden, Finch, and Philips represent a wide range of creative responses to Virgil occurring during this period.

The works of Virgil remained widely known in the centuries following his death in 19 BCE, and extensive scholarship has demonstrated their immense influence upon writers of the medieval, Renaissance, Restoration, and eighteenth-century periods. Alongside biblical texts, Virgilian poetry, especially the epic *Aeneid* and the pastoral *Eclogues*, was of central significance for these literary cultures. It provided material for school texts and prose romances, and the poet's creative trajectory, the *cursus Virgilianus*, provided a model for others who hoped to reach the heights of epic. Yet despite the fact that Virgil's poems often betray serious concerns about the violence of state power and imperial conquest, subsequent readers tended to conflate his work with the ideologies of empire. In the twentieth century, classicists began to read more skeptically, detecting the subtle political criticisms woven through Virgil's body of work, though these readings usually focused on the epic and pastoral poems. Moreover, scholars of classical reception have shown that many poets working before the twentieth century detected and exploited these more ominous strains; in other words, poetic engagements often anticipated shifts in scholarly thinking, sometimes by hundreds of years. Although much of this renewed consideration has primarily involved the *Aeneid*, the *Georgics* have perhaps even more to tell us about the Roman poet's profound concerns about the consequences of war and the likelihood of peace. Happily, within the past fifty years, classicists have devoted much more attention to Virgil's middle poem: initially, a debate arose over the degree to which the *Georgics* supported the Roman civil wars, the victorious Octavian, and the crystallization of imperial power. By now, arguments about the poem's fundamental optimism or pessimism have largely given way to other questions, but no classicist would describe the *Georgics* as decidedly idealistic or patriotic.[20]

In contrast, scholars of English poetry have tended to assume that the *Georgics* extol rural peace and rustic morality, reinforcing nationalism and imperialism. Certain specific habits of reading have crystallized this limited sense of the poem. For instance, Virgil's famous passage on the bliss of rural laborers, made resoundingly English in Dryden's translation, has too often been read as emblematic of the *Georgics'* vision of agricultural life:[21]

> Oh happy, if he knew his happy State!
> The Swain, who, free from Business and Debate,
> Receives his easy Food from Nature's Hand,
> And just Returns of cultivated Land!
> (2.639–642)

The most cursory reading of the Latin poem makes clear that this brief, idyllic moment offers only a respite from a world marked by incessant and brutal toil, as well as by the constant threat of failure.[22] To read this passage alone is to misunderstand the world of struggle and uncertainty that Virgil builds across the four books of the *Georgics*. Even more significant is the fact that this passage appears as part of a meditation on the labors of the poet himself, who reflects here on the bliss of rural life as a way of recalling what he has already done—writing the pastoral *Eclogues*—and imagining what he might yet do: dare to compose an epic.[23] Virgil's description of the act of writing georgic poetry is itself highly contingent; whereas the *Georgics* everywhere reflect deep political uncertainty, the turn from the second to the third book—the very center of the work—poses the problem of creative uncertainty.[24] In this middle section, the work of the farmer—which requires both sustained human efforts and favorable conditions in the natural environment—more specifically comes to represent the work of the poet.[25] At their very core, the *Georgics* negotiate the problem of being in-between, caught perpetually in process, unsure how to realize an end. Perched between success and failure of all kinds—agricultural, political, poetic—this poem is marked by the fullest hope, but also, like the queen's speech of 1713, by the fullest recognition of contingency. It insists on process as a viable state of being.

Perhaps more deleterious than the overemphasis on rural happiness is the notion that Virgil necessarily handed down to the English a ready-made set of justifications for empire. A recent essay reflects this tendency:

> In Virgilian georgic, labor naturalizes and legitimates imperial expansion, because the military flowing-out of the Roman nation into heroic conquest is imagined as similar to the rich superfluity of its agriculture. The farmer subduing the soil with the plow, and the soldier subduing the rebellious border province with the sword, provide metaphors for each other. . . . The teleology of natural resources finds its fulfillment . . . in military and political aggression.[26]

This could hardly be more wrong. The Latin poem, completed before the commencement of Augustan rule and almost exactly at the same time that the Roman civil wars came to an end, cannot accurately be said to "legitimate" empire; in fact, the *Georgics*, like the *Aeneid*, betray deep ambivalences about war, empire, and the role of the poet in relation to the vicissitudes of power. Whereas scholars have often understood the *Georgics* to be working in one direction—toward subjugation, dominance, control—the poem itself offers image after image of the mutable, bidirectional relationship between peace and war. Most formal English georgic poems of the middle and later eighteenth century are Virgilian only at the level of verbal and structural imitation.[27] Moreover, they borrow poetic authority from a flawed tradition that conflates Latin poetry with the Roman Empire.

Joseph Addison's seminal *Essay on the Georgics*, affixed to Dryden's translation of 1697, profoundly influenced the development of the English georgic as a specific literary type—one that eventually proved amenable to imperial attitudes.[28] Noting that "the *Georgics* are a subject which none of the *Criticks* have sufficiently taken into their Consideration,"[29] Addison argues for the poetic beauties of georgic poetry, and distinguishes it from pastoral by explaining that whereas eclogues feature the voices of shepherds, georgics filter "the Precepts of Husbandry" through the voice of the teacher-poet. One belongs to a tradition of competitive song; the other descends from the didacticism of Aratus, Lucretius, and other ancient writers.

In Addison's eyes, georgics elevate lowly agricultural subjects to the heights of well-crafted poetry; in his words, "*A Georgic therefore is some part of the Science of Husbandry put into a pleasing Dress, and set off with all the Beauties and Embel-*

lishments of Poetry."[30] By this time, the conception of poetic language as a kind of clothing was not a new one, but the conventional formulation shifts as Addison applies it specifically to the georgic, which seems to possess a particular power to dress any naked or unbeautiful subject in the clothing of poetry, and therefore render it art. Carefully avoiding the problem of why Virgil does not treat all aspects of "*the Science of Husbandry*" in his *Georgics*, Addison supposes that the Roman poet chose only those precepts that would most lend themselves to poetic beautification.

Addison is thinking in typically eighteenth-century terms of high and low style, and as a result finds the georgic attractive for its capacity to raise everyday subjects into this higher register.[31] Significantly, Addison's formulation suggests a poetic form, or frame, entirely separable from content and identifiable by certain words and patterns that mark good writing—what he calls the "*Beauties and Embellishments of Poetry*"—doubtless including the Latin hexameter line, or, in English, the heroic couplet or blank verse, and Miltonic diction. From this perspective, the value of georgic poetry derives not from its ancient connections to civil war, but from its capacity to render the most basic of human activities worthy of expression through ornate poetic filters.[32]

The specific terms of real agricultural practice, on the other hand, remain distinctly beyond the bounds of Addison's georgic poetry:

> I think nothing which is a Phrase or Saying in common talk, shou'd be admitted into a serious Poem: because it takes off from the Solemnity of the expression, and gives it too great a turn of Familiarity: much less ought the low Phrases and Terms of Art, that are adapted to Husbandry, have any place in such a Work as the *Georgic*, which is not to appear in the natural simplicity and nakedness of its Subject, but in the pleasantest Dress that Poetry can bestow on it. Thus *Virgil*, to deviate from the common form of words, wou'd not make use of *Tempore* but *Sidere* in his first Verse, and every where else abounds with Metaphors, *Grecisms*, and Circumlocutions, to give his Verse the greater Pomp, and preserve it from sinking into the *Plebeian* Stile. (149)

The keen sense of high and low that dominates the poetics of this period primes Addison, a great reader and writer of literary language, to sense such a distinction in the *Georgics*. An English georgic poem, imitating the Roman model, would demonstrate literary achievement by translating the details of agricultural labor into elegant poetry that imitates the decorum of Virgil. In advocating for the georgic as a poetry of elevation, however, Addison teaches other English writers that Virgil aimed primarily to celebrate agriculture in his *Georgics*. This celebration of British agricultural products and productivity, combined with the period's tendency to remember the writings of Virgil as central to the Roman imperial project, grad-ually gave rise to what has often been called the "imperial georgic."[33]

Yet the dominant conception of the georgic as necessarily linked to empire is surprising, since over the course of four books, the *Georgics* linger at the tail end of war, envisioning a world that has only just begun to tilt toward peace—hence Virgil's choice of subject, the precarious and contingent processes of agricultural work. These darker strains persist in many English agricultural poems written dur-ing the late seventeenth and early eighteenth centuries by poets who fostered Vir-gilian doubts about political stability.[34] By reading from antiquity forward into this period, a time often marked by vicious factional politics, I aim to expand our sense of how the *Georgics* fit into the history of British poetry; before it was plun-dered for its ostensible visions of Roman greatness, this poem offered alternative ways of imagining lasting peace.

In this book, I am also advocating a specific way of reading; in contrast to the currently prevailing practice of considering British georgics alongside con-temporary scientific or agricultural texts, I read English-language poems next to a Latin one: most of the writers I discuss would have been educated to read Latin quite easily, so any intervention in or manipulation of an ancient text betrays a deliberate act of making meaning. Those English poets who enter into conversa-tion with the *Georgics*—by translating and rewriting, and sometimes by imitating—find a landscape rich with images and forms through which to contemplate ques-tions of mutability and contingency. I consider all the major poems treated here to be related, however distantly, to the practice of translation, which, as several scholars have argued, is a crucial channel through which to understand how writ-ers of various historical periods comprehended and represented their own moments.[35] In this book, I approach poets' conversations with Virgil by focusing closely on specific words, phrases, and forms.

Some of the most important forms for *Cultivating Peace* are the markers of a didactic poetic voice. Typically, the idea of didactic georgic poetry in English brings to mind the imitative poems of the middle and later eighteenth century.[36] Yet scholars have paid little attention to the ways in which the didactic stance itself can communicate significant meaning, which becomes apparent when we keep the historical situation of the Latin *Georgics* in view. In claiming to teach, a didac-tic poem occupies an abstract, imaginary space, and therefore reinforces the dis-tance between saying and doing. This distance undercuts the certainty implied by declarations of stability or success: for Virgil, writing in an age marred by decades of civil war, the prospect of lasting peace, no matter how gloriously or fully prom-ised by the soon-to-be emperor, would likely have seemed precarious. To describe fully realized peace would have been a hollow task; instead, Virgil speaks through the language of agriculture to imagine not what is, but what could be, as a result of consistent effort. In the same way that no farmer would expect a continuous harvest, no Roman citizen—or emperor—should expect to enjoy easy peace in perpetuity. At the same time that we gaze upon the ripened olive as a symbol of peace, Virgil asks us also to see the process that gave rise to the product.

Relating the arduous labors necessary to maintain a successful farm, Virgil establishes a point of departure for meditating on the process of making a peaceful life in a world deeply aware of war and failure. The *Georgics*, completed when the remnants of war were only beginning to transform into the rudiments of peace, blend agricultural subject matter with a didactic stance in order to model peace as a constant negotiation of discord and violence, not a circumscribed utopia. Within the *Georgics*, agriculture represents a fundamental awareness of the interconnectedness of destructive and constructive forces—an awareness that should inform human action of all kinds.

Marvell, Finch, Dryden, and Philips all experiment with formal and generic elements to dramatize the very processes of containing and ordering history, and of cultivating peace. They write in relation to political and social forces that sometimes proceed with the same regularity as the march of the seasons, and at other times inflict all the unpredictable damage of an early frost; in confronting these forces, each writer creates a distinct aspect of the Virgilian georgic mode. The poets of Chapters 1 and 3 draw conceptual lessons from the *Georgics*: we can better understand Marvell's interest in mutability, specifically the mutable relationship between peace and war, by reading his poem *Upon Appleton House* in conjunction with the Latin poem. For Finch, the most valuable concept from the *Georgics* is contingency, which informs her Virgilian representation of herself, in *The Petition for an Absolute Retreat*, as a vine ripped from its prop during a storm. In Chapters 2 and 4, we encounter the crowning translation and first English imitation of the *Georgics*—two key moments in the history of English poets' conversations with Virgil. Dryden's translation is an active rewriting of the Latin that capitalizes on that poem's political uncertainty to consider the prospect of peace at the end of the brutal seventeenth century. Philips's imitation, on the other hand, marks both a serious conversation with Virgilian uncertainty and a permanent departure from the Roman poet, since it inspires a wave of imperial georgic poetry that is not supported by the classical model.

The making of peace has often engendered and exposed deep political conflict, and continues to do so in the twenty-first century. In the centuries with which this book is concerned, diplomatic accords with Spain under James I and Charles I were thought to threaten social, political, and religious stability in England; the ostensible calm of Charles's personal rule encouraged faction and sowed the seeds of civil war; and attempts at concord with France in the later years of the War of the Spanish Succession were understood by Whigs to threaten English mercantile interests. Perceiving the tendency of peace to dissatisfy, Queen Anne urged Parliament to *cultivate* it, suggesting that the ratification of a political treaty could only determine a point of origin from which lasting stability might proceed.

By the early decades of the eighteenth century, the idea of peace as a stable entity, mutually exclusive with war, rang patently false. In this book, I am suggesting that idealized visions of easy peace were in some instances replaced by a Virgilian georgic model: depicting peace and war as highly mutable states derived from the same fundamental materials, the Virgilian georgic mode interprets a declaration of peace as nothing more than a set of conditions from which further peace must be actively, continuously, and laboriously cultivated. This model breaks down, however, the more decisively the British move toward global empire: within an imperial, capitalist agricultural system, the tools and processes of farm labor necessarily connote national products, profit, and pride. Images of agriculture cease to represent the transition from war to peace. Yet the idea that we would do better to attend to the processes, not the products, of peace persists beyond the life of the Virgilian georgic mode in English poetry.

Today, the Perpetual Peace Project, an initiative created by institutions and organizations from several countries and primarily located in the Centre for Humanities at Utrecht University, supports projects devoted to forging lasting peace on a global scale. Its organizers observe that current conversations about peace do not acknowledge the sustained work that must follow declarations of concord:

> The Perpetual Peace Project begins from the understanding that for many politicians and policy experts, today "peace" is a poorly defined word that has many meanings in different contexts. Similarly, when used in public discourse peace is often dismissed as an empty rhetorical gesture, or as an abstract and unsustainable concept. It persists more pragmatically through short-term processes to mitigate suffering or end ongoing hostilities, or as the desired outcome of supposedly necessary wars. Yet this resigned acceptance of strife, and this dismissal of peace as an esoteric or irrelevant exercise, seems paradoxical in a world that has long dreamed for things to be otherwise.[37]

The project is grounded in Immanuel Kant's *Perpetual Peace: A Philosophical Sketch* (1795). In a curatorial statement appended to the essay, republished by the Slought Foundation and the Syracuse University Humanities Center in 2010, Aaron Levy, Gregg Lambert, and Martin Rauchbauer note that for Kant, lasting peace was "unnatural," and therefore needed to be created and maintained.[38]

Like the vision of constructed peace that appeals so strongly to the organizers of the Perpetual Peace Project, the forms of peace that arise in this book all depend on continuous cultivation. The following chapters tell the story of how four poets explored alternative models of stability—not secured from on high, but raised from the ground up—during a period of intense political, social, and literary transition. Each asks questions about war and peace that transcend the categories of genre, poetry, and even literature itself, however broadly construed. As the lines of a poem accumulate on the page, we are invited to sense the process of creating and sustaining a miniature world made of words. This process is especially palpable within a Virgilian georgic poem, which deliberately inhabits a space somewhere between knowledge and action. In the poems that follow, we are made to feel the work of georgic poets as they imagine the making of peaceful worlds. We are made to feel the work of georgic peace.

NOTES

1. For an extensive account of the factional politics surrounding the War of the Spanish Succession and the Treaty of Utrecht, see "To Fix a Lasting Peace on Earth," chap. 10 in James A. Winn, *Queen Anne: Patroness of Arts* (Oxford: Oxford University Press, 2014).
2. *British History Online, House of Lords Journal*, vol. 19.
3. Ruth Saunders Magurn, ed., *The Letters of Peter Paul Rubens* (Evanston, IL: Northwestern University Press, 1991), 408–409.
4. Around the same time, Thomas Hobbes wrote in his *Leviathan* that "[d]esire of knowledge and arts of peace inclineth men to obey a common power" (IV.46.6). All references to the poetry of Andrew Marvell are cited by line number and taken from *The Poems of Andrew Marvell*, rev. ed., ed. Nigel Smith (Harlow, UK: Pearson Longman, 2007). The "arts of peace" followed Cromwell into Edmund Waller's *Panegyric Upon My Lord Protector*—"Your never-failing sword made war to cease,/And now you heale us with the arts of peace" (109–110)—and persisted into the eighteenth century, when Samuel Johnson would recall the "useful violence" by which Cromwell brought the "arts of peace" to Scotland (*A Journey to the Western Islands of Scotland*, in *Samuel Johnson: The Major Works*, ed. Donald Greene [Oxford: Oxford University Press, 2009], 505–506).
5. Likely begun by 1618, but not published before Bolton's death. D. R. Woolf, "Bolton, Edmund Mary (b. 1574/5, d. in or after 1634)," in *Oxford Dictionary of National Biography* (Oxford University Press, 2004; online ed., 2011).
6. Section VII.
7. See Warren Chernaik, *The Poetry of Limitation: A Study of Edmund Waller* (New Haven, CT: Yale University Press, 1968); Roger Pooley, "The Poets' Cromwell," *Critical Survey* 5, no. 3 (1993): 226–227; Laura Lunger Knoppers, *Constructing Cromwell: Ceremony, Portrait, and Print, 1645–1661* (Cambridge: Cambridge University Press, 2000); Timothy Raylor, "Waller's Machiavellian Cromwell: The Imperial Argument of 'A Panegyrick to My Lord Protector,'" *Review of English Studies* 56, no. 225 (2005): 386–411.
8. Leonard Forrer, "Roettiers (Roettier or Rotier), John (or Jan)," in *Biographical Dictionary of Medallists* (London: Spink and Son, 1912), 5:161–173.
9. No. 96, 1 July 1713. In *The Guardian*, ed. John Calhoun Stevens (Lexington: The University Press of Kentucky, 1982).

10. Joseph Hone, "Isaac Newton and the Medals for Queen Anne," *Huntington Library Quarterly* 79, no.1 (Spring 2016): 119–148. Pointing even more directly to the politics of the moment, Hone also articulates the influence of Robert Harley, "a lifelong medal enthusiast" (139).

11. See James Winn, "'Like Her Britannia's Self': Mythology and Politics in the Life of Queen Anne," *Swift Studies* 30 (2015): 31–70, as well as *Queen Anne*. Winn also treats the Breda and Utrecht medals, describing an earlier and ultimately rejected design for the latter. Strikingly, that version would have divided the scene in half, like Roettier's, with Britannia to the side. Whereas Britannia's weapons stand erect on the Breda medal, the early design for Utrecht depicts the goddess with the spear and shield in the tilted position, anticipating the way they would finally appear on the circulated version.

12. Reference to Horace observed in Augustus W. Franks and Herbert A. Grueboer, *Medallic Illustrations of the History of Britain*, Medallic Illustrations of the History of Britain, 2 vols. (London: Trustees of the British Museum, 1885), 399–400.

13. Horace, Ode 4.14.51–52, in *Odes and Epodes*, rev. ed., ed. Paul Shorey and Gordon J. Laing (Chicago: Benjamin H. Sanborn, 1919). The translation that follows is my own.

14. There is likely a connection to more immediate politics in Croker's choice of inscription as well. In a speech to Parliament advocating peace in 1711, Anne had derided "the Arts of those who delight in War," likely gesturing toward the Whig opposition; the possible origins and ensuing Whig responses to this phrase are thoroughly discussed in Winn's biography.

15. R. J. Tarrant, "Poetry and Power: Virgil's Poetry in Contemporary Context," in *The Cambridge Companion to Virgil*, ed. Charles Martindale (Cambridge: Cambridge University Press, 1997; online ed. 2006), 175.

16. Richard F. Thomas describes the poem as marked by "the utmost political uncertainty" in the introduction to his edition of the *Georgics*, 2 vols. (Cambridge: Cambridge University Press, 1988). All quotations of the *Georgics* taken from this edition.

17. Of course, the *Georgics* are not in themselves a stable point of reference. Deeply interested in Greek literature and well aware of his Roman predecessors and contemporaries, Virgil drew heavily from other sources in all of his works, and made no exception in writing this poem. For extensive documentation of Virgil's engagement with other writers, see Richard F. Thomas, *Reading Virgil and His Texts: Studies in Intertextuality* (Ann Arbor: University of Michigan Press, 1999). The *Georgics* are most directly modeled on the *Works and Days* of Hesiod and the *De Rerum Natura* of Lucretius. Although poets of the seventeenth and early eighteenth centuries were generally more familiar with Roman poets than Greek ones, Homer and Hesiod were available in English translations by George Chapman. Complicating matters, Chapman's version of the *Works and Days* was titled *The georgicks of Hesiod*.

18. I have translated *ensem*, a singular noun, as the plural "swords" here, following the usual practice of translators as disparate as H. T. Rushton Fairclough and David Ferry, but it is significant that the line could also be rendered to depict *many* scythes melted down into a *single* sword. None of the major commentaries—Conington, Mynors, or Thomas—addresses the strangeness of the nouns in this line, but I am grateful to Aaron Seider for directing my attention to a similar formulation in the *Aeneid* (7.635–636). Strikingly, there the situation is reversed: the scythe takes a singular form, whereas *ensem* appears as the plural *enses*.

19. "*falx, falcis*" in *Cassell's Latin Dictionary*, revised by J.R.V. Marchant and Joseph F. Charles (New York: Funk and Wagnalls, 1957).

20. Christopher Baswell (*Virgil in Medieval England: Figuring the "Aeneid" from the Twelfth Century to Chaucer* [Cambridge: Cambridge University Press, 1995]) traces the ecclesiastical, pedagogical, and aristocratic interests that solidified the primacy of the *Aeneid*. L. P.

Wilkinson (*The Georgics of Virgil: A Critical Survey* [Cambridge: Cambridge University Press, 1969]) provides an early and important schematic summary of the *Georgics*. Michael Putnam (*Virgil's Poem of the Earth: Studies in the Georgics* [Princeton, NJ: Princeton University Press, 1979]) argues for a pessimistic reading, whereas Llewelyn Morgan (*Patterns of Redemption in Virgil's Georgics* [Cambridge: Cambridge University Press, 1999]) considers it a form of political propaganda, not unlike the poems Dryden would compose at the Restoration or during the Exclusion Crisis. Thomas connects the *Georgics* to contemporary political insecurity, whereas Christine Perkell (*The Poet's Truth: A Study of the Poet in Virgil's Georgics* [Berkeley: University of California Press, 1989]) explains the poem's generic and narrative disunities as an extension of its aim to raise difficult literary and political questions. For Monica Gale (*Virgil on the Nature of Things: The "Georgics," Lucretius, and the Didactic Tradition* [Cambridge: Cambridge University Press, 2000]), the *Georgics* participate in an "intertextual dialogue" with Lucretius and other poets writing in the didactic tradition. Avoiding the term "allusion," Gale diverges from Joseph Farrell (*Vergil's "Georgics" and the Tradition of Ancient Epic: The Art of Allusion in Literary History* [Oxford: Oxford University Press, 1991]).

21. Maren-Sofie Røstvig's exhaustive study *The Happy Man: Studies in the Metamorphoses of a Classical Ideal* (Oslo: Norwegian Universities Press, 1954–1958) has long been appreciated as a foundational source of information about early modern poems of rural happiness and retirement. Yet it has also led many to believe that Virgil's brief praise of the blissful husbandman was a blanket endorsement of agricultural labor as a source of moral purity, material abundance, and true happiness. The genre studies of Dwight Durling (*The Georgic Tradition in English Poetry* [New York: Columbia University Press, 1935]) and John Chalker (*The English Georgic: A Study in the Development of a Form* [Baltimore: Johns Hopkins Press, 1969]) strengthened the tradition of misunderstanding the passage on the blissful rural life as emblematic; this tendency has limited the ways in which we understand the georgic mode in English.

22. Scholars of African American literature more often sense the ways in which agricultural poetry can capture painful struggle and toil. For instance, Margaret Ronda makes a convincing case for the points of connection between Virgil's *Georgics* and *Lyrics of Lowly Life* (1896) by Paul Laurence Dunbar. Taking as a point of departure the fact that the classical georgic insists on the fundamental state of lack against which the rural laborer struggles, Ronda describes the Dunbar's bleak vision of agricultural labor performed under the subjugating forces of a racist culture ("'Work and Wait Unwearying': Dunbar's Georgics," *PMLA* 127, no. 4 [2012]: 863–878). See also Sarah Wagner-McCoy, "Virgilian Chesnutt: Eclogues of Slavery and Georgics of Reconstruction in *The Conjure Tales*," *ELH* 80, no. 1 (2013): 199–220; and Ronda, "Georgic Disenchantment in American Poetry," *Genre* 46, no. 1 (2013): 57–78.

23. Virgil, *Georgics*, ed. Thomas, Volume I: 253–254.

24. Ibid., 252.

25. Ibid., 250.

26. Robert P. Irvine, "Labor and Commerce in Locke and Early Eighteenth-Century English Georgic," *ELH* 76, no. 4 (2009): 974. David Fairer has offered the strongest alternatives to and criticisms of the imperial georgic to date; his readings are informed by a deep understanding of the historical conditions that gave rise to the *Georgics*. See especially "Georgic," in *The Oxford Handbook of British Poetry, 1660–1800* (Oxford: Oxford University Press, 2016), and "'Where Fuming Trees Refresh the Thirsty Air': The World of Eco-Georgic," *Studies in Eighteenth Century Culture* 40 (2011): 201–218.

27. Courtney Weiss Smith reads such poems in new and productive ways in *Empiricist Devotions: Science, Religion, and Poetry in Early Eighteenth-Century England* (Charlottesville:

University of Virginia Press, 2016), attending closely to verbal and grammatical particulars. Clare Bucknell has articulated the range of responses to Virgil among those eighteenth-century readers who accepted the *Georgics* as primarily an agricultural treatise, linking midcentury poems to capitalistic ambition. See "The Mid-Eighteenth-Century Georgic and Agricultural Improvement," *Journal for Eighteenth-Century Studies* 36, no. 3 (2013): 335–352.

28. Juan Christian Pellicer puts it so strongly as to say that Addison "establishes the eighteenth-century orthodoxy" for georgic poetry ("John Philips [1676–1709]: Life, Works, and Reception" [doctoral thesis, University of Oslo, 2002], 216). In contrast, Annabel Patterson, Alastair Fowler, Anthony Low, and Andrew McRae have each resisted the teleological account that locates the commencement of English georgic poetry in 1697. Instead, they situate the georgic in relation to political, scientific, moralistic, and economic contexts.

29. John Dryden, *The Works of John Dryden*, ed. H. T. Swedenberg et al., 20 vols. (Berkeley: University of California Press, 1956–2000), 5:145.

30. Ibid., 146.

31. As Patricia Meyer Spacks reminds us, admiration for the "elevated diction" of Homeric and Virgilian epics was widespread in the period. *Reading Eighteenth-Century Poetry* (Chichester: Wiley-Blackwell, 2009), 58.

32. Addison's conceptions continue to inform scholarly approaches to the georgic; for instance, see Kevis Goodman, *Georgic Modernity and British Romanticism: Poetry and the Mediation of History* (Cambridge: Cambridge University Press, 2004), 22.

33. Karen O'Brien offers one of the most explicit articulations of this term, writing that during the late seventeenth and eighteenth centuries, the "georgic, more than any other literary mode or genre . . . assumed the burden of securing the aesthetic and moral links between country, city, and empire" ("Imperial Georgic: 1660–1789," in *The Country and the City Revisited: England and the Politics of Culture, 1550–1850*, ed. Gerald MacLean, Donna Landry, and Joseph P. Ward [Cambridge: Cambridge University Press, 1999], 161). The notion of the imperial georgic is rooted in the work of Anthony Low, whose book *The Georgic Revolution* (Princeton, NJ: Princeton University Press, 1985) characterized the *Georgics* and English georgic poetry too broadly and nationalistically.

34. Stephanie Nelson finds in the *Georgics* "not a pastoral escape from contemporary history," but rather a palpable engagement with it; the poem "holds that history just under its surface, only occasionally allowing it to break through, but always aware of its latent presence" (*God and the Land: The Metaphysics of Farming in Hesiod and Virgil* [Oxford: Oxford University Press, 2008], 88).

35. Three books in particular have advanced sophisticated notions of translation as conversation: Paul Hammond, *Dryden and the Traces of Classical Rome* (Oxford: Oxford University Press, 1999); Paul Davis, *Translation and the Poet's Life: The Ethics of Translating in English Culture, 1646–1726* (Oxford: Oxford University Press 2008); and David Hopkins, *Conversing with Antiquity: English Poets and the Classics, from Shakespeare to Pope* (Oxford: Oxford University Press, 2010). For these scholars and the writers they discuss, translation is never, in Hopkins's words, "a lone encounter between two parties," but rather a rich conversation that "always involve[s] the recollection, invocation, and questioning of *other* conversations" (11, 13). And as Charles Martindale has put it, "antiquity is constantly changing as ever-changing modernities engage in dialogue with it" ("Reception—a New Humanism? Receptivity, Pedagogy, the Transhistorical," *Classical Receptions Journal* 5, no. 2 [2013]: 171). See also David Quint, *Epic and Empire: Politics and Generic Form from Virgil to Milton* (Princeton, NJ: Princeton University Press, 1993), 8, and Nigel Smith, *Literature and Revolution in England, 1640–1660* (New Haven, CT: Yale University Press, 1997), 3.

36. This interest in the didactic aspect of georgic as a locus of scientific knowledge develops from debates that begin at least as early as the writings of Plato and Aristotle, extend through the Renaissance, and persist across the eighteenth century. See, for instance, Robert M. Schuler, "Francis Bacon and Scientific Poetry," *Transactions of the American Philosophical Society* 82, no. 2 (1992): 1–65; Andrew Wallace, "Virgil and Bacon in the Schoolroom," *ELH* 73, no. 1 (2006): 161–185; Low, *Classical Receptions Journal* 5, no. 2 (2013): 169–183; Annabel Patterson, "Pastoral versus Georgic: The Politics of Virgilian Quotation," in *Renaissance Genres: Essays on Theory, History, and Interpretation*, ed. Barbara K. Lewalski (Cambridge, MA: Harvard University Press, 1986). For the history of reading the *Georgics* alongside agricultural manuals, see Alexander Dalzell, *The Criticism of Didactic Poetry: Essays on Lucretius, Virgil, and Ovid* (Toronto: University of Toronto Press, 1996), 111, as well as the work of Frans De Bruyn, who demonstrates how intensely eighteenth-century agricultural experts debated the value of the *Georgics* as a scientific text. See De Bruyn, "From Virgilian Georgic to Agricultural Science: An Instance in the Transvaluation of Literature in Eighteenth-Century Britain," in *Augustan Subjects: Essays in Honor of Martin C. Battestin*, ed. Albert J. Rivero (Newark: University of Delaware Press, 1997); "Reading Virgil's *Georgics* as a Scientific Text: The Eighteenth-Century Debate between Jethro Tull and Stephen Switzer," *ELH* 71, no. 3 (2004): 661–689; and "Eighteenth-Century Editions of Virgil's *Georgics*: From Classical Poem to Agricultural Treatise," *Lumen* 24 (2005): 149–163.
37. redraftingperpetualpeace.org.
38. Strikingly, this definition agrees with the oldest senses of the word "peace"; it derives from the Indo-European root "pag-," which suggests the act of fastening or binding things together (*The American Heritage Dictionary of Indo-European Roots*, rev. and ed. by Calvert Watkins, 2nd ed. [Boston: Houghton Mifflin Harcourt, 2000], 61).

MUTABILITY

Cycles of War and Peace

I N THE SUMMER OF 1651, Andrew Marvell was employed as tutor to Mary Fairfax, who would turn thirteen that July. The poet resided with the Fairfax family on one of their estates, Nun Appleton, in the northern county of Yorkshire. His employer, the recently retired Lord General Thomas Fairfax, had commanded the New Model Army during the English civil wars, but ceded his post to Oliver Cromwell in 1650, refusing to lead a preemptive strike into Scotland where the exiled Charles II was living. Politically moderate, Fairfax had also objected to the execution of Charles I in 1649. Upon retiring from military service, Fairfax hardly returned to idle country pleasures: in addition to overseeing the normal labors of his rural properties, he needed to mend damage that had been wrought by the civil wars.[1] Moreover, Fairfax had removed himself from war, but war threatened to follow him: Scottish troops were assembling near the border with England, and, closer to Nun Appleton, the English army remained poised for battle. Also gaining momentum nearby were protests by the populist Levellers.[2]

Amid these conditions, Marvell composed a country house poem: *Upon Appleton House, to my Lord Fairfax*. Adhering to the conventions of the genre, the poet praises the Fairfax family and their tranquil home; simultaneously departing from tradition, however, he refuses to idealize the peace of rural life. In fact, Marvell distinctly resists the notion that ideal peace exists at Nun Appleton—or anywhere on earth. He mounts this resistance in part by drawing from the *Georgics* of Virgil, which insist on a fundamental mutability between the circumstances of war and peace. If we read *Upon Appleton House* as a poem written not at a distance from conflict, but rather on the verge of renewed violence, then its meditations on peace become all the more urgent, and all the more proximal to Virgilian georgic. Like Virgil's poem, *Upon Appleton House* is fundamentally rooted in a sense of mutability: one of Marvell's most comprehensive biographers observes that the "house" to which the title refers is most likely a defunct convent located on the grounds of the estate, which was in the early 1650s being converted into a residence.[3] This long poem, then, takes as its point of departure a vision of renewal, process, and transformation. More specifically, Marvell points to the alteration of physical space as a representation of the material continuities that accompany historical shifts. During the summer of 1651, as Marvell lived and wrote among the rural labors of Nun Appleton, external unrest threatened to reprise the violence of a barely concluded war. The only way to imagine lasting peace in these conditions must have been first to accept the continuous efforts required both to recover from and to prevent war.

Upon Appleton House has sometimes been read alongside the Georgics because it includes many scenes of agricultural labor. Scholars have connected the idea of the georgic with representations of peace in the poem, but most of these readings seek to detect Marvell's interest in golden-age and postlapsarian visions of peace. According to this view, the frequent scenes of violence in the poem represent intrusions into the otherwise ideal peace possible on the estate.[4] I maintain, however, that in this poem the golden age has abandoned Appleton—and England—altogether, and that Marvell accepts the constant negotiation of war as a permanent condition of peace. Some scholars have observed that the poem rewrites the conventions of the country house genre,[5] but I would propose an even stronger distinction: whereas such a poem as Ben Jonson's To Penshurst describes an ideal and stable retreat, Upon Appleton House does not assume that any stability exists to be described; instead, it dramatizes the ordering and shaping of peaceful spaces, which always threaten to transform again into warlike ones.

I read Upon Appleton House as an instance of the Virgilian georgic mode: like its classical model, it uses images of agriculture to envision the creation and maintenance of peace in perpetuity. The poem depends on a fundamental awareness of the mutable relationship between peace and war, and I suggest that this focus on mutability can be better understood by reading Marvell and Virgil in conversation with one another. Of course, the poem also reflects the depth and breadth of Marvell's learning, and can be linked productively to many other classical, biblical, and European texts. Yet Virgil and Marvell illuminate one another well, and by reading them together, we can better sense the lasting, but mutable, peace imagined in this poem. Here Fairfax appears as a mediating force who accepts disorder and violence and "tame[s]" them (766). This vision cuts against the period's dominant ways of envisioning peace as gloriously and permanently stable. The first Virgilian georgic poet to appear in these chapters, Marvell crafts Upon Appleton House in part to consider the sort of peace that was possible in the middle of a contentious summer that followed fast on the end of a contentious decade. With subtle didacticism, the poem demonstrates how worlds of peace and war derive from the same fundamental materials, and instructs the makers of peace never to assume perfect isolation from, or immunity to, the forces of war.

ON MUTABILITY: VIRGIL'S FIRST LESSON

The first book of the *Georgics* begins and ends with two dramatically different scenes:

> Quid faciat laetas segetes, quo sidere terram
> uertere, Maecenas, ulmisque adiungere uitis
> conueniat, quae cura boum, qui cultus habendo
> sit pecori, apibus quanta experientia parcis,
> hinc canere incipiam.
> . . .
> uicinae ruptis inter se legibus urbes
> arma ferunt; saeuit toto Mars impius orbe,
> ut cum carceribus sese effudere quadrigae,
> addunt in spatia, et frustra retinacula tendens
> fertur equis auriga neque audit currus habenas.
> (1.1–5. 510–514)

> (What makes the grain fields happy, when to turn the earth, Maecenas, and bind the vines to the elms, what care of oxen, how to breed cattle, how much experience [have] the economical bees, from here I begin to sing.

> . . .

> Neighboring cities take up arms, the laws between them having been ruptured; impious Mars rages over the whole world, as when the four-horse team rushes out from the start, accelerating in the course, and the driver, clutching the reins to no effect, is dragged on by his horses, nor does his chariot obey the curbing bridle.)

Better known to students of British literature is the opening invocation, leading to the word *incipiam* or "I begin," in which Virgil announces the agricultural scaffolding upon which he will build his intricate middle poem. In the eighteenth century, nearly all formal, imitative georgic poems would begin with a poet's translation or rewriting of this passage. Less discussed but in dire need of our attention are the concluding lines, in which the poet laments the deleterious conditions of the Roman civil wars that raged during the 30s BCE as he composed the *Georgics*. This passage concludes the first book by dramatizing the beginning of war.

Carceribus, meaning "from the starting gate," and used here to describe the commencement of a violently swift horse race, can also mean a prison or jail—it provides the root of our term "incarceration." These double senses derive from the similarity between the cells of prisoners and the gates that enclose racehorses. By choosing this word to describe the rages of Mars across the land, however, Virgil also gestures toward the Roman practice of symbolically imprisoning the energies of war inside the Temple of Janus during peacetime, and acknowledging their release by opening the temple's doors during times of battle. The early lines of the *Georgics* portray the poet about to begin his song, but the final image of the first book depicts war about to be unleashed. Together, these two moments represent the strange and brilliant project of the *Georgics*: to articulate the problems of war and peace through the language of agricultural instruction.

Between these passages, Virgil establishes the terms according to which the rest of the poem will proceed, advancing a series of preliminary agricultural precepts, celebrating the power of rural gods to help or hinder the farmer, and relating the transition from the Saturnian golden age to the days of lack and strife—and agricultural labor—under the iron reign of Jupiter. The second and third books of the *Georgics* treat various aspects of agricultural life, pausing at times to consider questions of poetry, history, or religion more broadly. The fourth book largely turns away from precepts, and offers two narratives in their stead, beginning with an account of a society of militant bees, and concluding with the myth of Orpheus and Eurydice, whose lives were changed forever by the error of the impulsive and ignorant Aristaeus, who in turn must set the world right again by recognizing and atoning for his missteps. The multiplicities of the poem are knit together by Virgil's recurring interest in mutability, from the progression of the seasons to the transition from golden to iron age, and on to the gods' order that Aristaeus visit Proteus, the shape-shifter, in order to understand the harm he has unknowingly wrought. Within the world of the *Georgics*, no state is permanent, all success remains contingent, and human survival depends on continuous labor.[6]

Virgil makes this point many times, but one of its clearest iterations appears shortly after the poet has described how Jupiter imposed want upon human beings, necessitating agricultural labor. To survive in such a world, the farmer must accept an unending cycle of toilsome effort:

> quod nisi et adsiduis herbam insectabere rastris
> et sonitu terrebis auis et ruris opaci
> falce premes umbras uotisque uocaueris imbrem,
> heu magnum alterius frustra spectabis aceruum
> concussaque famem in siluis solabere quercu.
> (1.155–159)

> (Since unless you will pursue the weeds with an incessant rake, and frighten the birds with noise, and press back the shade plants of the shadowy field, and with prayer summon rain, then alas you will look at the great store of another in vain, and relieve your hunger shaking an oak in the forest.)

Virgil insists upon the urgency of agricultural labor by offering a glimpse of failure; like the charioteer grasping the reins of his car *frustra*, or in vain, here the idle homesteader will glance, *frustra*, at his neighbor's cultivated plenty before sulking off to gather sustenance in the woods. The verbal echo between this passage and the dramatic scene at the end of the first book suggests a link between the overpowering forces of nature and those of war. These connections become more explicit as the poem proceeds; in the line that follows this passage, the poet commences a catalogue of the agricultural tools necessary for preventing the scene of loneliness and lack suggested in this passage. He describes these implements as *agrestibus arma*, or "the weapons of the farmer."

Within the world of this poem, then, agricultural work is itself a perpetual battle. A little further on, Virgil describes mowing in military terms, noting that grain about to be reaped sways in the wind like soldiers in *proelia*, or battles (1.318). Given the frequent connections between agricultural and military images in book 1, its chaotic and violent ending seems all but inevitable. Just before concluding the book, Virgil explicitly laments the civil wars in Rome, where *fas uersum atque nefas* (1.505), or right things (*fas*), are turned around (*versum*)—suggesting they have turned into monstrous things—at the same time that monstrous things (*nefas*) are converted to seemingly right things. The concision and passivity of these Latin phrases makes them difficult to render in English; even more elusive is the chiastic quality of *fas . . . nefas*. Such pairings are not uncommon in Latin; a more famous example might be *otium*, "rest" or "leisure," and *negotium*—"non-rest," or, more familiarly, "business." As a larger group, however, word pairs like these are particularly fascinating in that they expose the dialectical relationships inherent in language generally. *Fas* and *nefas* are particularly apt for Virgil's purposes at the end of the first book: quite literally versions of one another, these words capture the dangerous mutability that marks civil conflict, and reinforce the poet's sense of war as a sweeping and transformative force that recasts peace as violence. Even more dramatically, the words as arranged here suggest the deadly, recursive patterns of war: when we reach the word *nefas*, we are reminded of its link to *fas*, and as a result are dragged backward as helplessly as Virgil's charioteer.

Heightening the specificity of what he means by *fas versum atque nefas*, Virgil presents a series of images—wickedness with many faces, agricultural fields abandoned, and, finally, *curuae rigidum falces conflantur in ensem* (1.508), or "the curved scythes are smelted into stiff swords."[7] This image makes concrete the sense of transformation that pulses through the first book. With relative alacrity the farmer converts his scythe, a tool of peaceable labor, into a weapon. A similar, though reversed, image appears of course in the biblical book of Isaiah: "He shall judge between the nations, / and shall arbitrate for many peoples; / they shall beat their swords into plowshares, / and their spears into pruning hooks; / nation shall not lift up sword against nation, / neither shall they learn war any more" (2.4).[8] Mynors's commentary on the *Georgics* suggests that the pairing of the sword and the share was potentially "proverbial" by the 30s BCE.[9] It is significant, though, that the biblical prophecy envisions a permanent future state, whereas for Virgil the image makes explicit the idea that a peaceable object already bears within itself the potential for war. Furthermore, as I noted in the Introduction, the very word *falx* can be used to mean either a scythe or a scythe-like weapon that a soldier might use to destroy an enemy barricade. In a sense, then, the farmer's tools are always *arma*, in that they share a material base with swords and grappling hooks. Yet the metaphor works in the opposite way too; swords and grappling hooks can be recast as scythes again when the war ceases. In either state, the metal shaft evokes both peace and war, suggesting hope in times of conflict, and insisting on vigilance in times of tranquility. With these ideas in mind, then, we might understand the transformation from scythe to sword as both less sudden and less negative than it seems.

The *Georgics* ask us to think less about states of war and peace independently, understanding instead the processes whereby one can become the other. This poem dramatizes both positive and negative mutability, allowing that plenty may collapse into lack, but also that a barren field may come to be fruitful; mowing may give way to battle, but in turn, the terms of battle inform those of mowing. Virgil handed down many lessons to the poets who wrote in the centuries after him, not the least of which was the *Georgics'* sense of threat and possibility forever intertwined, and forever in flux.

BEFORE MARVELL: GEORGIC MUTABILITY IN ENGLAND

The fundamental mutability coursing through the *Georgics* was not lost on seventeenth-century readers and writers. Thomas May, for example, appended to his translation of 1628 a note recounting the origins of these associations:

> *The Fable is thus; When the famous City of Athens was founded, and* Neptune *and* Minerva *were in great contention who should have the honour of naming the place, it pleased the gods to appoint it thus, that the honour should*

accrow to that deity, who could bestow the greatest benefit upon mankinde. Vpon which sentence Neptune *with his trident striking the shore, immediately a furious horse provided, and armed for the war, was created by that stroke:* Minerva *casting her javelin from her, of that javelin produced an Olive tree; which being a fruitfull and good plant, and the embleme of peace, was iudged more usefull and profiable to mankinde.*[10]

Here the javelin, an implement of war, gives rise to the fruit highly praised by the *Georgics* for its relative independence; unlike grapevines and other crops, the olive requires little tending, and therefore represents the closest possible alliance between the farmer and the serenity of the land. Like the image of the scythe that straightens into a sword, the metamorphosis of the javelin into an olive tree reinforces the tendency of the *Georgics* to suggest the uncomfortable proximity between peace and war derived from their mutual material origins.

In the year after May's translation appeared, Peter Paul Rubens began a new piece for King Charles I, titled *Minerva Protects Pax from Mars*, and sometimes referred to as *Peace and War*. In that year, 1629, Charles I had prorogued Parliament and initiated what would become eleven years of personal rule, accelerating tensions that would eventually erupt into civil war. At the same time, the Thirty Years' War had been raging in Europe for over a decade, and while Charles was proffering glittering representations of tranquility and abundance with masques and other artistic works, his court was increasingly involved in complicated military matters abroad. These actions were provoked by extensive English military failures under the command of the Duke of Buckingham.[11] Ultimately, the English sought to extricate themselves from international conflicts; peace with France was achieved with relative ease, but agreements with Spain proved more difficult.[12] Aware of the king's predilection for the visual arts, the Spanish sent Rubens to the English court. Among historians of art and politics alike, Rubens is well known for his dedicated interest in peace—as a subject for his creative work and as a central aim of his diplomatic service under the Infanta Isabella.[13] The painting Rubens created for this occasion—which featured the likenesses of the children of his host, Balthasar Gerbier—dramatized the making and keeping of peace (Fig. 4).[14]

Although the allegorical content of *Minerva Protects Pax from Mars* cannot be attached to any single literary source,[15] the painting is nevertheless deeply implicated in the same questions of mutability and contingency that mark the *Georgics'* engagements with peace and war. The canvas lacks some of the more obvious symbols of agriculture—wheat or corn, for instance, or a scythe—but some historians of art have suggested a connection between this painting and the *Works and Days* of Hesiod.[16] Moreover, the plentiful pile of fruit—like the satyr figure

Figure 4 Peter Paul Rubens, *Minerva Protects Pax from Mars (Peace and War)*, oil on canvas, 1629–30, © The National Gallery, London

offering it—establishes a loose connection to the georgic.[17] The appearance of Pan and Minerva together also suggests a more direct connection to the *Georgics*; the juxtaposition of these two figures recalls early lines in which Virgil invokes the favor of *Pan, ouium custos . . . oleaeque Minerua inuentrix*—Pan, guardian of sheep, and Minerva, inventor of the olive (1.17–19).

In this arresting scene, figures of idealized peace revel in a luminous foreground, while Mars and the fury Alecto look down upon them from the dark and churning background. Between the two stands Minerva, repelling Mars with her shield. Some scholars have found in the painting not a clear distinction between peace and war, but rather a suggestion of future stability, which will be possible only after the threat of war has been dispelled. In the immediate context of international diplomacy, this interpretation makes a great deal of sense, since the peace was not finalized until after Rubens departed from England.[18] Yet I believe that the painting also depicts peace and war as locked into a perennial dialogue, wherein a mediating force perpetually preserves peace by dispelling the energies of war. Such mediation is embodied in the image of Minerva, who represents here the same mutability that May sensed in his translation of the *Georgics*.

In other words, whereas this work, completed in the midst of attempts to broker political peace, can indeed be understood to represent the contingency of the peace process, it also suggests peace itself as a continuous and contingent process. According to this view, the painting does not figure the path to peace: it *is* peace. Rubens's canvas forces into uneasy proximity the ostensibly opposite realms of shimmering, idealized peace and raging, nebulous war. The figure of Minerva situated between them troubles conceptions of war and peace as stable and dichotomous states. Attended by a putto presenting the olive wreath and caduceus, the goddess establishes a diagonal boundary between the plentiful happiness in the foreground—marked by teeming fruit; a playful leopard; a tamed satyr; and the female figure Pax[19]—and the swirling rage of Mars in the background.[20] Rubens paints the goddess so that she blends into the upper half of the image, seeming to belong more to the world of war than of peace, but nevertheless struggling to protect the figures of innocence and plenty from bloodthirsty Mars.

Perhaps the most threatening aspect of the painting is the way it forces these two worlds into a single frame; although the goddess attempts to separate them, they remain frozen in dialogic tension with one another. Split almost perfectly into diagonal halves, the work makes no promise of eradicating war by pushing it beyond the frame, nor does it suggest that the scene of peace intends movement outward or upward, expanding into the space left should war disappear. With her back turned to the scene of rural peace and plenty, Minerva embodies vigilant efforts to subdue threats of rupture and destruction, but the ravages of war do not return her gaze; Mars wrenches his head back over his shoulder to stare with intensity down upon the idyllic scene the goddess defends. The direction of his gaze forces the painting inward and downward. Indeed, Rubens imbues this painting with a pervasive sense of recursion and cyclical motion; even its title, *Minerva Protects Pax from Mars*, suggests that both peace and war will survive in perpetuity, and that the question is not whether war will be destroyed but rather how it will be prevented from devouring peace.

It is according to these terms that I find in the painting a visual analogue for the dynamic relationship between the peace of the agricultural world and the violence of battle that the Virgilian georgic mode attempts to communicate. In *Minerva Protects Pax from Mars*, the goddess embodies malleability—anticipating the figure of Britannia on the medal that would be struck for the Treaty of Utrecht several decades later. The glittering world she guards represents unfettered innocence, plenty, and tranquility; its figures betray no awareness of the threats lurking above them. The shadowy world she repels epitomizes the rage, disorder, and violence of war. Taken separately, the depictions of these two realms stand in heavily allegorized and deeply dramatic opposition. Yet they are linked by the figure of Minerva, goddess of wisdom and military strategy, a mediating force connected both to war and to peace. Near the center of the painting's top edge, to the left of Minerva's helmet, the olive wreath and caduceus, a section of the goddess's javelin, and her arm appear in close proximity to one another, perhaps suggesting the same links that May noted in his translation. In this very small section of the canvas, the materials of peace and war are united through the physical body of Minerva.

Moreover, her elbow, the most luminous part of her body, appears to jut into the scene of peace below, connecting the worlds of war and peace even more overtly. What this painting does in miniature, I suggest it does in a larger sense as well: it depicts peace not as the mere absence of conflict, but as a constant process carried out in close proximity to war. Although the scene of plenty in the foreground most immediately attracts the eye, Rubens urges us to acknowledge the processes occurring behind or beyond that world, troubling the viability of easy peace and accepting the efforts required for lasting stability. This painting was meant to address tensions among warring countries, but its cyclical vision of the relationship between war and peace finds special resonance when applied to the particular concerns of civil discord.

THE TRAP OF WAR AND THE MAP OF PARADISE: MARVELL'S VISION OF PEACE

A generation later, as the Second English Civil War dragged on, John Milton composed a sonnet that reproduces the sense of monstrous volatility that marks the particular struggles of violent conflict in Virgil's *Georgics*. Yet this poem, "On the Lord General Fairfax at the Siege of Colchester," likely written in the late summer of 1648,[21] also implores the commander of the New Model Army to turn his efforts more directly toward peace—to act, perhaps, like Rubens's Minerva. Although written only a few years before *Upon Appleton House*, this poem presents General Fairfax as a drastically different man: Milton's panegyric pen praises the commander as a nearly omnipotent public force, potentially capable of setting England on a course of peace. The first eight lines of the sonnet praise the general's military victories, but its final sestet raises the daunting problem of bringing the war to a peaceful conclusion:

> Fairfax, whose name in arms through Europe rings,
>> Filling each mouth with envy or with praise,
>> And all her jealous monarchs with amaze
>> And rumours loud, that daunt remotest kings,

Thy firm unshak'n virtue ever brings
    Victory home, though new rebellions raise
    Thir Hydra heads, and the false North displays
    Her brok'n league, to imp their serpent wings.
O yet a nobler task awaits thy hand;
    For what can War, but endless war still breed,
    Till Truth and Right from Violence be freed,
And Public Faith clear'd from the shameful brand
    Of Public Fraud. In vain doth Valor bleed
    While Avarice and Rapine share the land.
                      (1–14)

Milton uses only present and future tense verbs, suggesting the urgency of the situation at hand and imploring Fairfax to resolve it. Yet although the speaker attends to what could or should be, he also reaches back through poetic time to make sense of the present age: the sonnet's Horatian echoes have long been noted, particularly in the figure of the Hydra heads rearing again and again as "new rebellions" continue to erupt.[22] The terrible recursiveness of the self-perpetuating Hydra is mirrored by the structure of the tenth line, in which Milton asks, "what can War, but endless war still breed"; like the mythical monster, this line functions circularly. Its rhythmic structure, with stresses on "what," "war," "end," "war," and "breed," offers no solution other than further battle; "endless," flanked on either side by "war," sits trapped in the middle of the line, which reaches its own ending by landing on "breed." Although Milton's contorted syntax reflects his career-long preference for Latinate patterns, its particular function here is to heighten the sense that war alone never brings peace: when we reach the word "breed," we must turn back to the second "war" to locate its grammatical object. The line forces us back into the middle of the line, back into the nest of constantly sprouting Hydra heads. The effect here also recalls the recursive pattern of Virgil's *fas versum atque nefas*: for both poets, the terms of battle offer little guidance about the path to peace, and consequently, both poets envision civil war as a dangerous trap.

    Notably, the same backward movement marks the conclusion of Virgil's *Aeneid*, a poem that also casts deep doubt upon the idea that the conclusion of war guarantees the return of peace. The epic arrives at its infamous ending by depicting the death of Turnus at the hands of Aeneas, who cannot bring himself to show mercy to his enemy. Observing that the final line of the *Aeneid* repeats exactly the words used to describe the death of Camilla in book 11, one scholar has suggested that the repetitive nature of Virgil's poem precludes the possibility of envisioning a golden age to come; instead, the problems of history persist into the present moment.[23] Others have pointed out the significant way in which the verb *condere* links the beginning and end of the epic: in the poem's conclusion it expresses the plunging motion of Aeneas's sword into the body of Turnus (12.950), whereas in the opening lines it suggests the founding of the Roman Empire (1.5). In this way, the death of Turnus lends devastating irony to the very words with which the imperial state might be glorified. Even more fundamentally, a striking idea emerges from the patterns that appear in both the epic and the sonnet: historical cycles of violence perpetuate because the terms of war persist. Such terms cannot be recruited to articulate lasting peace. For both Virgil and Milton, the smallest verbal and grammatical details can expose the illogic of believing that battle might realize anything other than destruction.

Unlike Virgil, however, Milton imagines a solution. The depiction of self-perpetuating war appears nestled between two more hopeful lines; as the octave cedes to the sestet, the poet suggests that "a nobler task awaits" the general. Although Milton does not explicitly use the word "peace," he attempts to redirect the course of history away from war by condemning the reign of "Avarice and Rapine," hoping they will be replaced by "Truth and Right" and "Public Faith." He beseeches Fairfax to transcend the world of battle, restoring stability and expelling the monstrous civil strife. General Fairfax occupies here a crucial position between war and peace. His engagements with the world of war, hopes Milton, have equipped him with the wisdom to subdue conflict and usher in stability.[24]

Political realities, however, would not bear out Milton's hopes that Fairfax could bring peace to England. In the wake of Fairfax's retirement, Marvell addressed his replacement, Oliver Cromwell, with another, more overtly Horatian poem written during a time of especially indeterminate political transition. Although Marvell, like Milton, contemplates the idea of peace, he makes a darker proposal about the power of one man to bring England out of war, suggesting that the triumphs of a soldier hardly indicate his readiness to rule in peacetime.[25] In a manner quite similar to Milton's recursive question, "For what can War, but endless war still breed," Marvell's *An Horatian Ode upon Cromwell's Return from Ireland* arrives at its notorious conclusion by suggesting that the English may well experience a state of perpetual militarization:

> But thou the War's and Fortune's son
> March indefatigably on;
>   And for the last effect
>   Still keep thy sword erect:
> Besides the force it has to fright
> The spirits of the shady night;
>   The same arts that did gain
>   A pow'r must it maintain.
>   (113–120)

The final verb, "maintain," sends us back to "it," and then further back to "power," since as we hear a pronoun we want subsequently to recall the noun it replaces. Moreover, as with all rhymes, the sound of "maintain" recalls its sonic precedent, "gain." As progeny of Mars, Cromwell recognizes only the glory of military victory, and as a result Marvell makes little attempt to envision peace as anything other than the tenuous stability that might attend perpetual armed vigilance, or perhaps perpetual military aggression. Treading carefully around loss, violence, and rule by brute force, the ode concludes with a more subtle version of Milton's gesture, casting doubt upon the capacity of a warrior to create a form of peace that would truly transform the energies of war into constructive action.

The *Horatian Ode* also evinces Marvell's interest in the closeness of peace and war. In one of its more controversial passages, the poem eulogizes the executed king, then links his beheading to early Rome:

> So when they did design
> The Capitol's first line,
> A bleeding head where they begun,
> Did fright the architects to run:
> And yet in that the State
> Foresaw its happy fate.
> (67–72)

Here Marvell invokes an ancient legend in which Roman "architects" found a human head—*caput* in Latin—buried at the site where they had begun to build the Temple of Jupiter, and, deeming the event an auspicious one, named the site Collis Capitolinus, or the Capitoline Hill. Marvell exploits the wordplay between "Capitol" and "head" with devastating irony, criticizing not only English violence but also the very long tradition of building upon brutal foundations. The very name of the central seat of government is forever attended by the memory of violence and loss, but this moment shares with Milton's sonnet and Virgil's writings a deep pessimism about declarations of military greatness: for all their glory, they offer very little to support the making of peace. The rhyme of "state" with "fate" in the trimeter lines is quite jarring here, since it suggests with suspicious ease a transition from war to a time when the "state" will enjoy a "happy fate." Almost half a century later, "state" and "fate" would be one of the most frequent rhymes in Dryden's couplet translation of the *Aeneid*—along with, remarkably, "cease" and "peace." Yet Marvell distinguishes "the state," or political authority, from "the architects," who perhaps wisely see the discovered head as ominous. Creative minds respond differently than political ones; this distinction suggests another layer of critical irony, as Marvell—not unlike Virgil before him and Dryden afterward—implicitly separates the worlds of artistic achievement and political power.

Marvell's poem for Fairfax takes an interest in the work of architects as well, though *Upon Appleton House* begins by acknowledging a very different kind of builder—one unconstrained by state pageantry:

> Within this sober frame expect
> Work of no foreign architect;
> That unto caves the quarries drew,
> And forests did to pastures hew;
> Who of his great design in pain
> Did for a model vault his brain,
> Whose columns should so high be raised
> To arch the Brows that on them gazed.
>
> Why should of all things man unruled
> Such unproportioned dwellings build?
> The beasts are by their dens expressed:
> And birds contrive an equal nest;
> The low-roofed tortoises do dwell
> In cases fit of tortoise-shell:
> No creature loves an empty space;
> Their bodies measure out their place.
>
> (1–16)

The opening lines of the poem are perhaps best known for their praise of Fairfax's modest taste, which follows the proportions of nature rather than the whims of fashion. The sense of balance suggested by specific phrases here—as in the images of "birds contriv[ing] an equal nest" and the tortoise with his aptly fitted shell—also indicates the careful work of the poetic architect: these lines anticipate the conclusion of the poem, in which fishermen will "hoist" their vessels, tortoise-like, over their heads. These mirrored images reinforce the aesthetic balance of the poem at the same time that they indicate the sense of moderation and upright morality that Fairfax shares with local laborers.

In contrast to the ambiguous representation of the shift from warmongering to governing that marks the *Horatian Ode*, Marvell's *Upon Appleton House* praises Fairfax for cultivating peace, at least within the bounds of his rural retreat. The specific verbal links between these poems have moved some readers to find in them clues to Marvell's complex political attitudes, since both poems appear to prefer qualified over explicit praise.[26] In the reading that follows, however, I want to make clear a shift in Marvell's engagement with questions of peace: whereas in the *Horatian Ode* he troubles the idealized representation of peace as possibly the product of victory in war, in *Upon Appleton House* he suggests that lasting peace results from the continuous process of reshaping violent materials into harmless and productive ones. It may be the case that with *Upon Appleton House*, Marvell was reconsidering whether peace was possible at all, and whether that peace could be made to agree with what had become a seemingly endless cycle of war and political strife in England.

The poem has long been recognized for conjuring up images of war, which seem everywhere to intrude upon the estate; one of the best-known examples is the poet's observation of Fairfax as he arranges his garden in military formations (ll. 345–352).[27] Scholars have debated the significance of this and similar images, but many have explained them to some degree as obstacles impeding "the central dream of the time: the return to a state of Edenic innocence."[28] I am suggesting, however, that the interplay between images of war and peace in the poem exposes the fundamental impossibility of this dream, and supports a model of cyclical georgic peace—the same model represented visually in Rubens's painting. Although the poem might seem to advocate vigilance,[29] I find its representation of peace to be less a form of watchfulness than one of continuous engagement with violence. At Nun Appleton, there is no stable or idealized peace; the estate is vulnerable to invasion because all the materials of the world harbor the potential to be turned toward peace or toward war.

By holding up and then rejecting various forms of ostensibly perfect peace, Marvell suggests that the stability of the estate, continuously made and maintained, offers the most viable form of lasting peace in a time of grave uncertainty. Unlike Milton's recursive line, or the conclusion of the *Horatian Ode*, *Upon Appleton House* concludes with a representation of peace sustained by a cycle of labor. In further contrast to the *Horatian Ode*, which proceeds outward from a private, "inglorious" georgic world to the world of military victory, *Upon Appleton House* moves backward and inward, confronting its own violent history as well as the violence that continues to emerge from the agricultural work carried out on its lands.

Like the *Georgics* of Virgil and the formal georgic poems of the eighteenth century, *Upon Appleton House* takes a keen interest in history. Although its primary aim is to praise Fairfax and his peaceful estate in the present, it achieves that aim by dredging up past events, particularly the story of how the general's ancestor William Fairfax won his bride by releasing her from confinement in a convent. Aside from providing an early channel through which to extol the virtues of the Fairfax family, this episode also establishes a false—and even threatening—form of peaceful retreat that contrasts with the more viable model of peace Marvell finds in the present. In other words, the poem first moves backward in time, examining the deceptions lurking within the convent, whose inhabitants claim to have retreated into an impenetrable space immune to the ills of the outside world. Then, the poem returns to the present time, studying Fairfax's own retreat from politics and battle; this kind of retreat, however, makes no attempt to deny the world without or to claim perfection for the world within. It succeeds because it absorbs the terms of war in order to cultivate peace.

Early in the episode, one of the "subtle nuns" (94) attempts to persuade the young Isabel Thwaites to join the sisterhood by claiming that the convent is a place of secluded peace, where

> These walls restrain the world without,
> But hedge our liberty about.
> These bars inclose that wider den
> Of those wild creatures callèd men.
> The cloister outward shuts its gates,
> And, from us, locks on them the grates.
> (99–104)

The nuns claim to maintain an unadulterated retreat: such verbs as "inclose," "shuts," and "locks" establish a firm boundary between "the world without" and their internal "liberty." While of course the poet disagrees, suggesting that the convent is anything but unadulterated, I find more here than allegations of sexual duplicity and general anti-Catholic sentiment. *Upon Appleton House* offers peace first as a smug retreat, in which the nuns pride themselves on keeping absolute control over their secluded space. Yet the rupture and defeat of this space by the elder Fairfax punctures this illusion.

The sequence takes an absurd turn as it depicts the invasion by Fairfax and the nuns' attempts to repel him:

> Some to the breach against their foes
> Their wooden saints in vain oppose.
> Another bolder stands at push
> With their old holy-water brush.
> While the disjointed abbess threads
> The jingling chain-shot of her beads.
> But their loud'st cannon were their lungs;
> And sharpest weapons were their tongues.
> (249–256)

To be sure, the militarized language of this stanza heightens the emotional tenor of the rescue scene, yet as the nuns scream, curse, and fling beads for "chain-shot," they also fulfill the earlier stanzas' expectations that they share more traits with grotesque harpies than with women of upright virtue, and that their alleged peace is built upon nothing more than idolatry and idle talk. The rapidity with which the nuns devolve into farcical, pseudo-militaristic caricatures emphasizes the poem's resounding disapproval of oblivious retreat: to claim circumscribed peace is, paradoxically, to invite its rupture.

Although the appearance of military imagery begins in the past with the nuns' transformation into raging warriors, it takes root most meaningfully in the present, as the younger Fairfax makes a new life in retirement. Famously reversing the "cease"/"peace" rhyme applied to Cromwell in the *Horatian Ode*, Marvell suggests that the transition from war to peace has not been a simple one for Fairfax,

> Who, when retirèd here to peace,
> His warlike studies could not cease;
> But laid these gardens out in sport
> In the just figure of a fort;
> And with five bastions it did fence,
> As aiming one for ev'ry sense.
> (283–288)

Despite having given up his post as commander of the New Model Army, Fairfax persists in militarizing his surroundings, blending the work of the gardener with that of the general. Whereas the *Horatian Ode* praises Cromwell as a fighter, *Upon Appleton House* praises Fairfax as a thinker, heir to the intelligence of Minerva, not the wrath of Mars. In choosing the word "studies," Marvell elevates Fairfax's skill in war to the level of intellectual pursuit; unable to cast off such learning, the general cannot help but impose it upon the plants of his own garden. Although the "peace"/"cease" rhyme typically works by recalling the idea of something that must "cease" to make way for "peace," here the experience gained during a military career persists.[30]

Of course, the poem also suggests that the land would be a militarized space regardless of its owner's peculiar gardening methods. Bees buzzing through the garden beat the drums of war and act as pollinating "sentinel[s]," flowers hoist "silken ensigns," and each species grows as a "regiment in order" (292, 318, 294, 311). By applying military language to even the smallest creature, the poem seems to reinforce the idea that the present time is a fallen one. These images anticipate and contrast with the vision that follows, a lament for a lost garden paradise isolated from other places. Here, *Upon Appleton House* entertains the idea of a prelapsarian age, but refuses fully to distinguish the golden age from the current, less perfect time.

Oh thou, that dear and happy isle
The garden of the world ere while,
Thou paradise of foúr seas,
Which heaven planted us to please,
But, to exclude the world, did guard
With wat'ry if not flaming sword;
What luckless apple did we taste,
To make us mortal, and thee waste?
                    (321–328)

This lost paradise appears as a garden in which humanity was "planted"; such an image suggests that before original sin human beings were part of a unified landscape. The stanza asks how this world could have fallen into "waste," then answers its own question. The images of defending and excluding that pervade this passage transform the idyllic garden island into a militarized stronghold, and therefore expose this paradise too as a false hope. In casting the "happy isle" as distinctly separate from other spaces, guarded by the "watery . . . sword" of the seas in order "to exclude the world," the poem suggests the same conditions that precipitated the failure of the convent to shun the external world.

More specifically, the paradise Marvell invents here is bound within a linguistic paradox: although he attempts to articulate a time free from war, he can only use militarized language, and as a result constructs a long metaphor in which a time without war finds expression as a militarized space:

Unhappy! Shall we never more
That sweet militia restore,
When gardens only had their towers,
And all the garrisons were flowers,
When roses only arms might bear,
And men did rosy garlands wear?
Tulips, in several colours barred,
Were then the Switzers of our guard.

The gard'ner had the soldier's place,
And his more gentle forts did trace.
The nursery of all things green
Was then the only magazine.
The winter quarters were the stoves,
Where he the tender plants removes.
But war all this doth overgrow:
We ordnance plant and powder sow.
                    (329–344)

In these stanzas, the poem reverses the classical trope of the *beatus ille*, or the "happy man." Rather than suggest happiness so complete as to be imperceptible to those who enjoy it, the speaker laments the burden of remembering, yet never returning to, a lost world of peace. The catachresis of the "sweet militía" punctures the expectation of idyllic peace established in the first line. The imposition of militarized language over this ostensible scene of golden-age peace indicates a permanent lens fixed over the eyes of the onlooker: by concluding with a sudden shift back into the present, in which the language of gardening now applies to real warmongering—"We ordnance plant and powder sow"—these stanzas suggest that the poet can see the world *only* in terms of war. To claim an imaginative position outside these terms, he admonishes us, is at best simply useless, and at worst arrogant and irresponsible: violence endures, so the horrors of war demand attention even when regarded from a position of retired safety.

This violence, of course, infiltrates even the happy labors of the swains hired to mow the grounds of Nun Appleton. One of the mowers, "with whistling scythe, and elbow strong," proceeds to "massacre the grass along"—language that perhaps distantly recalls Virgil's grains poised for *proelia*, and the military reverberations of *falx*—until he inadvertently strikes a small bird nesting in the field. He rues the accident, depicted in the poem as an inadvertent murder: "The edge all bloody from its breast / He draws, and does his stroke detest, / Fearing the flesh untimely mowed / To him a fate as black forebode" (393–394, 397–400). The tragedy of this moment lies in the mower's late realization of and subsequent recoiling from the death wrought by his own hand: the normal chores of the agricultural year have made an executioner of him. Centuries later, Jean Toomer would rewrite this scene with gruesome intensity in his short poem "Reapers" (1923), in which a field rat suffers a similar fate under the unfeeling blade of an early mechanical mowing machine drawn by horses. Both poets point to the perpetual threat of violence symbolized by the implements of farm labor, as well as the history of weaponized scythes; for instance, ancient charioteers would attach scythe blades to their wheels in order to cut down their enemies on the battlefield. For Marvell this memory would have been more immediate: the English club-men had fought with scythes and other agricultural implements during the civil wars of the 1640s. Crucially, however, Marvell condemns neither the reaper nor the blade, lamenting instead the vulnerability of both low-lying nests and those perched high in trees. The problem is the environment itself, which offers no positions of complete safety. Of course, during the civil wars, even the highest office had failed to protect Charles, but here Marvell suggests that the land retains a degree of that undiscriminating danger. Finally, the poem compares the mowers to "Alexander," as if to suggest that the completion of their work in the fields resembles a conquest (428). At every turn, *Upon Appleton House* both laments and accepts violence as a fact of life and work on the estate.

Although the poem makes contact with the *Georgics* through images of mutability, Marvell was not, of course, writing a georgic poem in any formal sense. In fact, as he shifts his focus from agricultural work to a forest landscape, he refuses the overtly Virgilian—and Lucretian—project of using poetry to contemplate knowledge itself. Whereas Virgil praises the *felix qui potuit rerum cognoscere causas*, or the "happy" person "who knows the causes of things" (2.490) and expresses his own wish to gain comprehensive knowledge, Marvell turns away from such aspirations:

> Let others tell the paradox,
> How eels now bellow in the ox;
> How horses at their tails do kick,
> Turned as they hang to leeches quick;
> How boats can over bridges sail;
> And fishes do the stables scale.
> How salmons trespassing are found;
> And pikes are taken in the pound.
> (473–480)

The repetitions of "how" here recall both the opening lines of the *Georgics* and the long passage on the "how" and "why" of natural processes that follows the initial praise of the *felix* in that poem's second book. Retreating from the task of teaching, however, Marvell turns the poem toward the dense shades of the forest. Yet traces of work and war remain in his sights. He sees "Timber" that Noah might have used for the Ark as he looks upon the trees, and he imagines that animals labor like the mowers: in the forest, "all creatures might have shares, / Although in armies, not in pairs" (487–489). This image arises and departs quickly, but its strangeness is worth noting; here, figures of the nonhuman world not only work, but their labor is couched in military terms, again suggesting that Marvell cannot see a scythe without also imagining the glimmer of a sword.

More than two centuries after Marvell's death, the American artist Francis William Loring—who had served in the American Civil War—painted *The Army of Peace* (1893), now held by the Museum of Fine Arts, Boston. The canvas depicts several mowers with scythes slung over their shoulders, walking in a row as though in a loosely ordered military regiment, apparently ceasing work for a midday break. Although this striking image likely gestures most immediately toward the biblical vision of swords turned to plowshares, we might consider Loring's image to be even more powerful if we read it alongside the connections between civil war and agricultural imagery that so preoccupied Virgil and Marvell. Whereas the prophecy of Isaiah looks forward to a state of perpetual peace, Loring's painting knits together visions of concord and conflict in the present moment. The word "Army" troubles the entire scene, demanding that we, like Marvell, see weapons where others might see simple tools. Having come into close contact with the mutable and tense relationship between tranquility and violence necessitated by civil war, Virgil, Marvell, and Loring create works of art that do not allow us to rest with easy visions of peace unencumbered by history.

Yet none of these pieces is the work of a cynic. Marvell's poem praises Fairfax's daughter—shaped by her parents' "discipline severe" (723)—for her power to "hush / The world" (681–682), and concludes by settling into a peace that professes neither an idealized nor an ascetic retreat:

> 'Tis not, what once it was, the world;
> But a rude heap together hurled;
> All negligently overthrown,
> Gulfs, deserts, precipices, stone.
> Your lesser world contains the same,
> But in more decent order tame;
> You, heaven's centre, Nature's lap,
> And Paradise's only map.
>
> (761–768)

The nuns eschew the external world, the island paradise "exclude[s]" it, and in similar fashion Marvell appears to reject the space beyond Nun Appleton as a "rude heap" fallen into disorder. The poet explains this heap largely in terms of geography, but the harshness of the landscape he describes connotes social discord as well. Although the phrase "what once it was" may seem to suggest nostalgia, Marvell does not explain where he locates this ostensibly better past; the drama of a global landscape "hurled" into chaos suggests potent forces that precede human history.

Regardless of when or where the rude heap began to take shape, the very banality and imprecision of the phrase indicates the current and future state of things; in other words, Marvell urges acceptance of these conditions and places no real hope in returning them to golden-age perfection. With a dramatic shift away from the earlier models of ostensibly pure peace, Marvell concedes that this "lesser world contains the same": the estate offers respite, but not total isolation or immunity. The final couplet of the penultimate stanza would not have been out of place at the end of a court masque: "You, heaven's centre, Nature's lap, / And paradise's only map." Yet whereas the masque would have meant these lines as flattering praise for the king, here they find resonance in the contrast between Nun Appleton and all the false paradises the poem has exposed in earlier passages.

Such paradises promise an impossible life unpolluted by the rude heap of violence, corruption, suffering, or any other maladies plaguing the world beyond their borders. The grounds of the estate foster the makings of these woes as well, but under Fairfax they have been made "tame." Yet, like the leopard in *Minerva Protects Pax from Mars*, a tamed beast is a beast nonetheless: it has simply been trained to sublimate its wild impulses into "decent order." From its first depiction of General Fairfax arranging the plants of his garden as though they were soldiers, *Upon Appleton House* makes clear the limits of such sublimation. After all, in its oldest root forms, the word "paradise" suggested limits, signifying a walled garden, not a boundless utopia. In subtle ways, Marvell continuously reminds us that a wall always indicates a sense of threat, no matter how beautiful or tranquil the space it encloses. As in the *Georgics*, the materials of war rupture Marvell's poem at every turn, but they do so to suggest that viable peace seeks conversation with war, both as a fact of the past and a possibility for the future. Perpetuating this conversation, the peace of *Upon Appleton House* places no stock in a renewed golden age. Rather, it insists on fully occupying the present time, in which peace and protection come to those who labor to maintain them.

Perhaps reaching back into Virgil's tenth eclogue—in which sheep return home from their pasture, shadows fall, and Hesperus rises in the evening sky—the concluding moments of *Upon Appleton House* invite us to take shelter at the end of the day:

> But now the salmon-fishers moist
> Their leathern boats begin to hoist;
> And, like Antipodes in shoes,
> Have shod their heads in their canoes.
> How tortoise-like, but not so slow,
> These rational amphibii go!
> Let's in: for the dark hemisphere
> Does now like one of them appear.
> (769–776)

The curved image of the salmon-fishers' boats grounds the stanza as it moves from a concrete scene of labor to one of sweeping imaginative space. The "dark hemisphere" begins to cover the earth, which of course means that night is falling, but this phrase also connotes a more general threat, resonating with the "rude heap" of the previous stanza. A sense of threat also emanates from the urgency of the imperative "Let's in"—especially if Marvell was remembering this phrase as uttered by Shakespeare's King Lear before Poor Tom's hovel.[31] In any case, whatever is coming at the end of Marvell's line should propel us toward refuge.

By now, we should know better than to think that by going into the house with Marvell we will completely escape the dangers outside, but the poem ensures we make no such mistake. It does not settle comfortably upon "Let's in," concluding with an image of stillness. Instead, its final lines enact the same recursive motion as Milton's sonnet and Marvell's own *Horatian Ode*. But rather than fall backward again and again into war, this poem reaches its conclusion by casting its gaze upon a cycle of labor, suggesting a cycle of peace akin to the circular motion suggested in Rubens's painting. On its surface the final line hardly seems like the work of a poet as skilled as Marvell. Constructed from a string of rather vague words, the line only perks up in its final verb, "appear." Yet Marvell does not expect this line to succeed on its lexical merits: the work performed by its syntax is far more important. In order to parse the line, we must tread back to earlier lines in the stanza, seeking a referent for "one of them." In doing so, we return to the scene in which fishermen draw their boats from the water and carry them overhead as they return home. Now reminded of the meaning of "one of them," we arrive again at "appear," remembering that Marvell is comparing nightfall to the movement of the boats as they are hoisted overhead. This comparison defuses the threat of the "dark hemisphere," rendering it as nothing more sinister than an overturned fishing boat. Nevertheless, the poem still commands us to seek shelter. After all, the fishing boat only serves as a point of comparison, and the "spirits of the shady night" that haunted the *Horatian Ode* have found their way into this poem as well. But like Minerva protecting Pax from Mars, Nun Appleton counters the threats lurking in the darkness.

Created in the middle decades of a century in which battles raged all over Europe, the works of art discussed here confront the urgent problem of transforming the energies of war into those of peace. Both Rubens and Marvell locate peace in the georgic *labor* churning between the *otium* of pastoral and the *bellum* of epic. They and Milton find ways of articulating this peace in the specific practices of visual and verbal art, and at the very end of the seventeenth century, John Dryden would use poetic translation to contemplate the many failed forms of peace he too had witnessed. He would find in the *Works of Virgil*, and specifically in the *Georgics*, a means for advancing a fraught conversation about the way to lasting peace.

NOTES

1. Nigel Smith, *Andrew Marvell: The Chameleon* (New Haven, CT: Yale University Press, 2010), 82.
2. Derek Hirst and Steven N. Zwicker, *Andrew Marvell: Orphan of the Hurricane* (Oxford: Oxford University Press, 2012), 13–18. Hirst and Zwicker locate this poem firmly in this

intense and uncertain summer, noting that in this particular year, "neither radicalism nor war could be confined to the past" (17). David Norbrook heightens the stakes of the poem's topical engagement, noting that during the same summer, "the government was in agony of indecision over whether to execute the Presbyterian minister Christopher Love, who had been found guilty of intriguing with the king" (*Writing the English Republic: Poetry, Rhetoric and Politics, 1627–1660* [Cambridge: Cambridge University Press, 1999], 288).

3. N. Smith, *Andrew Marvell*, 95.

4. See M.J.K. O'Loughlin, "This Sober Frame: A Reading of 'Upon Appleton House,'" in *Andrew Marvell: A Collection of Critical Essays*, ed. George deF. Lord (Englewood Cliffs, NJ: Prentice-Hall, 1968), 122; Rosalie Colie, *"My Ecchoing Song": Andrew Marvell's Poetry of Criticism* (Princeton, NJ: Princeton University Press, 1970), 244; Judith Haber, *Pastoral and the Poetics of Self-Contradiction: Theocritus to Marvell* (Cambridge: Cambridge University Press, 1994), 145–146; Robert Markley, "'Gulfs, Deserts, Precipices, Stone': Marvell's 'Upon Appleton House' and the Contradictions of 'Nature,'" in *The Country and the City Revisited: England and the Politics of Culture, 1550–1850*, ed. Gerald MacLean, Donna Landry, and Joseph P. Ward (Cambridge: Cambridge University Press, 1999), 90. Ryan Netzley reads the poem in apocalyptic, though still hopeful, terms in *Lyric Apocalypse: Milton, Marvell, and the Nature of Events* (New York: Fordham University Press, 2015), 152–92.)

5. See Norbrook, *Writing the English Republic*, 289, and Donald M. Friedman, *Marvell's Pastoral Art* (Berkeley: University of California Press, 1970), 214.

6. Exploring Roman conceptions of farmland, Christopher Nappa observes that "if the farm is a particularly Roman symbol for the gentleman's self-sufficiency and ability to control nature and himself, the battlefield is the symbolic space where Roman dominion is realized. In the *Georgics*, they are the same place, as they often have been in history." Even more crucially, Virgil's poem offers for Nappa multiple visions of Roman life after the civil wars. Its structural variety, he argues, begets "ideological variety." This sense of mutability and multiplicity motivates my conception of the Virgilian georgic in English—for writers responding to the civil wars, the terms of agricultural production anchor their distinct conceptions of lasting peace. (*Reading after Actium: Vergil's "Georgics," Octavian, and Rome* [Ann Arbor: University of Michigan Press, 2005], 19). See also Philip Thibodeau's *Playing the Farmer: Representations of Rural Life in Vergil's* Georgics (Berkeley: University of California Press, 2011), 5.

7. For discussion of the singular and plural nouns in the Latin, see note 19 in the Introduction to this book.

8. *The New Oxford Annotated Bible*, 3rd ed., edited by Michael D. Coogan et al. (Oxford: Oxford University Press, 2001).

9. Virgil, *Georgics*, ed. R.A.B. Mynors (Oxford: Clarendon Press, 1990), 98.

10. Virgil, *Virgil's Georgicks Englished*, trans. Thomas May (London, 1628), 30.

11. Kevin Sharpe, *The Personal Rule of Charles I* (New Haven, CT: Yale University Press, 1992), 8.

12. Ibid., 66.

13. See Magurn, *The Letters of Peter Paul Rubens*, 8; and Fiona Donovan, *Rubens and England* (New Haven, CT: Yale University Press, 2004).

14. Historians of art have long cited the portrait of Gerbier's wife, Deborah Kip, accompanied by her children, to support this identification.

15. Lisa Rosenthal, "The Parens Patriae: Familial Imagery in Rubens's *Minerva Protects Pax from Mars*," *Art History* 12, no.1 (1989): 35n2. See also the catalogue entry in Gregory Martin, *The Flemish School circa 1600–circa 1900* (London: National Gallery, 1970), as

well as Kerry Downes, "Rubens's 'Peace and War' at the National Gallery," *Burlington Magazine* 121, no. 915 (1979): 397–398.

16. Donovan, quoting Reinhold Baumstark, notes that the work may be drawing upon a line in the *Works and Days* of Hesiod: "Peace nourishes the youth of the land" (*Rubens and England*, 169n65). Additionally, Hesiod writes of a carpenter, who constructs the plow, as a "slave of Athena" (*Works and Days*, line 430; trans. David W. Tandy and Walter C. Neale [Berkeley: University of California Press, 1996]). Alistair Fowler connects this image to "mynerves men" working with scythes and sickles in an anonymous poem in the Arundel Harington manuscript ("The Beginnings of English Georgic," in *Renaissance Genres: Essays on Theory, History, and Interpretation*, ed. Barbara K. Lewalski [Cambridge, MA: Harvard University Press, 1986], 112–113).

17. Rosenthal notes the associations among satyrs, Bacchus, fruits, and vines ("The Parens Patriae," 28).

18. Citing this timing, Martin reads the painting's allegory as "a moving rather than a static one" (*Flemish School*, 120). Thomas K. Rabb, thinking similarly, finds in the painting "a poignant expression of [Rubens's] unease" with the state of contemporary international negotiations (*The Struggle for Stability in Early Modern Europe* [Oxford: Oxford University Press, 1975], 129). Donovan suggests that the painting points to the future, noting especially the children, whose pending maturity suggests a coming peace (*Rubens and England*, 73).

19. An art historical debate persists regarding the body of the woman sitting above the satyr. Suggestions have included the goddesses Ceres, Venus, and others. For a more complete summary of the debate, see Martin, *Flemish School*, 118; Anthony Hughes, "Naming the Unnameable: An Iconographical Problem in Rubens' 'Peace and War,'" *Burlington Magazine* 122, no. 924 (1980): 157–163, 165; and Donovan, *Rubens and England*, 73.

20. Rubens, an apt student of the classics, turned to the figure of Minerva resisting Mars in earlier works as well to signify the contrast between intelligent strategy and violent rage. See Donovan, *Rubens and England*, 101–102, and Wolfgang Stechow, *Rubens and the Classical Tradition* (Cambridge, MA: Harvard University Press, 1968), for a broader discussion of Greco-Roman mythology in Rubens.

21. In *The Life of John Milton: A Critical Biography* (Oxford: Blackwell, 2000), Barbara Lewalski dates the sonnet to July or August 1648. Nigel Smith, David Norbrook, and Blair Worden, among many others, have reconstructed the complex print culture of the civil war and Interregnum periods. Nigel Smith finds this particular sonnet "unusually unknowing for Milton," in that the poet urges a future peace that looks nothing like the events as they actually unfolded (*Literature and Revolution in England*, 1, 280).

22. In John Milton, *Complete Poems and Major Prose*, ed. Merritt Y. Hughes (New York: Macmillan, 1957), the editor addresses these connections in his commentary appended to the sonnet. In addition, Roy Flannagan connects this poem to Milton's sonnet to Cromwell, observing the encouragements toward peacemaking in both poems (*The Riverside Milton* [Boston: Houghton Mifflin, 1998], 290).

23. Michael C. J. Putnam, "Vergil's *Aeneid*: The Final Lines," in *Poets and Critics Read Vergil*, ed. Sarah Spence (New Haven, CT: Yale University Press, 2001), 104. R.O.A.M. Lyne's earlier reading (1990), which explores an imbalance in Roman expectations for war, makes a different yet equally compelling case for the significance of cyclical motion ("Vergil and the Politics of War," in *Oxford Readings in Vergil's "Aeneid,"* ed. S. J. Harrison [Oxford: Oxford University Press]).

24. As Katherine O. Acheson observes, Milton would eventually conceive of peace in stronger relation to war; "Military Illustration, Garden Design, and Marvell's 'Upon Appleton House,'" *English Literary Renaissance* 41, no. 1 (2011): 146–188.

25. Marvell's attitudes toward the general's resignation and the subsequent ascent of Cromwell are exceptionally difficult to parse and have long occupied scholars. Nigel Smith, who argues that the *Ode* demonstrates Marvell's growing allegiance with republicanism, points out that the political inscrutability of the poem has "made it a major example in critical debates concerned with the relative merits of internal and 'aesthetic' interpretation, and contextual or 'historical' interpretation" (*Andrew Marvell*, 81).

26. See Annabel Patterson, *Marvell: The Writer in Public Life* (Harlow, UK: Longman, 2000), 32–33.

27. Julianne Werlin builds upon Hirst and Zwicker to explore the broader discourse of war, or a "martial consciousness" operating in the poem. "Marvell and the Strategic Imagination: Fortification in *Upon Appleton House*," *Review of English Studies* 63 (2012): 371.

28. Marvell, *Poems*, 215.

29. Acheson has read the "militarized garden" as evidence for a conception of peace in which "there is no state prior to, or better than, armed but peaceful vigilance" ("Military Illustration," 147). This language of invasion, vigilance, and protection is common in scholarship on the poem; see also Susan Snyder, *Pastoral Process: Spenser, Marvell, Milton* (Stanford: Stanford University Press, 1998), 52.

30. Patterson locates the dialectical relationship between the two figures in the "deliberate echo" in the cease/peace rhymes that appear in the *Horation Ode* and *Upon Appleton House* (*Marvell*, 49).

31. William Shakespeare, *King Lear*, 3.4.171, The Arden Shakespeare, ed. R. A. Foakes (London: Cengage Learning, 1997).

IN 1660, JOHN DRYDEN COMMEMORATED the return of Charles II
with a grand poem of praise. Famous for its promise of a renewed golden age to
follow on the heels of the Restoration, *Astraea Redux* has long been considered an
exemplum of courtly panegyric: rife with classical imagery and epic elevation, it
celebrates the Stuart dynasty with all the glittering artifice of a royal masque. Yet
for all its grandeur, the poem begins with a scene of ominous uncertainty:

> Now with a general Peace the World was blest,
> While Ours, a World divided from the rest,
> A dreadful Quiet felt and, worser far
> Than Armes, a sullen Intervall of Warre[.]
>
> (1–4)[1]

The deceptively hopeful declaration of stability in the first line swiftly dis-
solves into troubling isolation and uncertainty; the phrase "divided from the
rest" points to the geographical separation between England and other countries beyond the Channel. With their distinct lack of concrete imagery, these
lines contradict the carefully crafted structure of the heroic couplets; although
free from battle, the scene described here is nevertheless marked by "dreadful
Quiet." In this opening passage, Dryden is recalling the end of the Thirty Years'
War, which concluded at Westphalia in 1648. The English had managed not to
become directly involved with what had turned out to be the most brutal European conflict to date, but they had fallen into their own civil wars. The declarations of peace in other lands contrasted starkly with the difficult events they
faced at home. With a single sentence, Dryden paints a striking portrait of the
uncertain time after war but before peace, suggesting that the end of conflict

means little if the conditions for social and political stability are not created and sustained.

A degree of relief arrives in the next four lines of the poem; they heighten the foreboding of the opening section, but begin to impose some definition upon the amorphous "dreadful Quiet" by proposing a metaphor:

> Thus when black Clouds draw down the lab'ring Skies,
> E're yet abroad the winged Thunder flyes
> An horrid Stillness first invades the ear,
> And in that silence Wee the Tempest fear.
>
> (5–8)

Now the "sullen Intervall" resembles the moments before a storm—marked by the darkening sky, stagnating air, and diminishing motion among people and animals alike. Incapable of action, the English suffer the subtle attacks of "horrid Stillness," which fills their ears with oppressive nothingness.[2] Everything and everyone stands frozen, impotent and waiting for more powerful forces to alter the scene. Of course, within the world of *Astraea Redux*, Charles II represents precisely such a force: Dryden presents the king as a symbol of benevolent potency, poised to rescue the aimless English and restore them to peaceable order. This dark opening scene thus provides a useful contrast to the light and warmth that will radiate from the new monarch later in the poem. But these first eight lines also expose a question of great urgency for the decades that followed the English civil wars, a question that persisted into the early decades of the eighteenth century, and a question that we have not yet answered in our own period: When the engines of battle cease to grind, what should replace them?

Dryden's complete *Works of Virgil*, published near the end of his life, offers an especially urgent engagement with questions of lasting peace. The years that followed the spectacular revelry of the Restoration had rapidly given way to harder realities: plague and fire in London, the defeat of the British navy by the Dutch in two wars, the Exclusion Crisis, and perhaps most dramatic of all, the Revolution of 1688, in which the Catholic King James II lost his throne to the Dutch William of Orange and his wife, James's daughter Mary. It is no surprise, then, that in the dedication to the *Pastorals* of Virgil, Dryden locates his translation at the end of a long century of conflict. He hopes, however, that England might also be on the verge of a more peaceful future.[3] Addressing Hugh Lord Clifford, Baron of Chudleigh—whose late father had suffered politically and personally as a result of the Test Act—Dryden suggests that his young addressee may very well live to see the realization of lasting peace, should the Nine Years' War come to its hoped-for end:

> What I now offer to your Lordship, is the wretched remainder of a sickly Age, worn out with Study, and oppress'd by Fortune: without other support than the Constancy and Patience of a Christian. You, my lord, are yet in the flower of your Youth, and may live to enjoy the benefits of the Peace which is promised *Europe*: I can only hear of that Blessing: for years, and, above all things, want of health, have shut me out from sharing in the happiness. The Poets, who condemned their *Tantalus* to Hell, had added to his Torments, if they had plac'd him in *Elysium*, which is the proper Emblem of my Condition. The Fruit and the Water may reach my Lips, but cannot enter: and, if they could, yet I want a Palate as well as a Digestion. But it is some kind of Pleasure to me, to please those whom I respect.[4]

This passage includes many familiar gestures of humility: apologizing for his work by invoking old age and humble intentions, the poet deems his translation a "wretched remainder," not the work of a poet writing in the prime of life. Dryden did of course suffer ill health in the years preceding his death in 1700; mounting physical problems combined with the loss of his public and political standing after 1688 had certainly rendered him "worn out" and "oppress'd" by the time the *Virgil* appeared. These gestures of humility, however, also suggest a declaration of political belatedness.[5] Contrasting his own advanced age with the relative youth of Clifford, Dryden admits that even if the seventeenth century manages to come to a peaceful conclusion, such stability will arrive too late to offer any real solace for him.

The 1690s had been the "remainder of a sickly Age" for Dryden: despite attempts by James I to make peace early in the century, vicious political factionalism and frequent diplomatic crises had created decades of warfare on the Continent, in England itself, and on the high seas. Dryden's translation was published shortly before the ratification of the Treaty of Ryswick in September 1697, nearly half a year after negotiations had begun among William III, Louis XIV, and other European monarchs. The treaty, which ended the Nine Years' War, seemed to offer lasting peace, and many, including Dryden himself, expressed hope in this burgeoning peace at the same time that they fostered doubts about whether the settlement would last.[6] They were right to do so: by 1702 England would return to war with the French, after violations of the Ryswick agreement by Louis XIV. Looking back upon the preceding decades, as well as upon the social and political turmoil of his own life, Dryden now suggests that to see political peace realized would itself be a form of hell: better to suffer aged exile in a place of darkness, he laments, than to live surrounded by happiness but unable to taste its effects.

With the ratification of the treaty, the French king had acknowledged William as the legitimate king of England, and James II remained in exile in France. The anti-Williamite strains running through Dryden's late poetry, and especially the *Virgil*, are by now well known.[7] But Dryden, always an apt reader of Virgil, was especially sensitive to the complexity with which the Latin poet contemplated peace. Questions of peace certainly attend all of Virgil's poems; Dryden's translations reveal his awareness of these questions, and add further uncertainties. The *Georgics*, however, present a particularly rich environment for sorting out various kinds of peace and for distinguishing the peace of the warrior-politician from that of the poet. Like their Latin counterparts, and perhaps even more so, Dryden's four *Georgics* offer no promise of total unity or stability. Despite his disillusionment with political peace, Dryden attempts to construct peace on the page: for the aging poet, the act of translating Virgil is itself an art of peace. Again and again, he adds to and alters the Latin, amplifying the successes of rural peace and condemning loudly the proponents of false political calm. Of the fifteen occurrences of the words "peace" or "peaceful" in Dryden's translation of the *Georgics*, only one is a direct rendering of the Latin noun *pax*. The other fourteen appear in lines the poet has manipulated to convey lasting peace as inextricably linked with nature and agriculture. In other words, Dryden frequently uses this term to intensify the Virgilian notion that the farmer, a practitioner of benign agricultural arts, derives his peaceful existence from his alliance with nature, rather than from success in war or public life.[8] These manipulations, however, also put special pressure on the very word "peace" itself, stretching it in so many semantic directions that it begins to appear that the English term cannot adequately demarcate the difference between the forced stability imposed by a strongman and the hard-won tranquility achieved by a farmer. By exposing this linguistic inadequacy, Dryden indicts the English state for failing to take seriously the project of making lasting peace.

THE ENGLISH *VIRGIL*

Dryden, of course, was one of many seventeenth-century Virgilian translators. His *Virgil*, printed in ten editions between its publication year and 1790, often reproduces the language of earlier English versions, with the result that one scholar has described it as "a kind of summation of English versions."[9] Nonetheless, this particular *Virgil* has long been singled out for its exceptional success as a publication by subscription, as well as for the contemporary conception of it as a definitively English translation, attractive to patrons on both the Tory and Whig ends of the political spectrum.[10] Yet despite the admittedly aggregate quality of this translation, no earlier version turns as frequently to the English word "peace." Neither Thomas May nor John Ogilby uses the term more than a few times when translating the *Georgics*. Dryden, on the other hand, collapses a whole range of concepts—leisure, tranquility, quiet, security, stability—into "peace." In returning so often to this word, he confronts the problem of peace at the end of a very long century of battle, during which the term had tended to signify little more than, as Dryden himself had put it in 1660, a "sullen Intervall of Warre."[11]

In Virgil, Dryden found a poet deeply concerned with questions of peace and stability, particularly in relation to the strength of the central powers at Rome. Who benefits under the protection of such powers? Who might be left behind? To what extent can those not seated at the center of power exercise control over their own lives? Virgil asks these questions from the very first lines of his *Eclogues* forward, and Dryden, whose own attitudes about translation led him always in pursuit of the nebulous "sense" of a text, was well suited to detect Virgil's concerns.

Dryden had made his print debut as a translator in 1680, with his contributions to *Ovid's Epistles*, published by Jacob Tonson, who would eventually manage the publication of the *Virgil*. Some have suggested that the poet's interest in Ovid at this point in his career indicates his commitment to experimenting in preparation for writing an original epic;[12] with that hypothesis in mind, we might understand that Dryden's meditation on what it means to bring the work of an ancient writer into modern English marks a quite serious interest in preparing himself, not unlike Milton, as next in line to inherit the capacity for epic poetry.

Dryden's preface to the volume is widely cited for its interest in the special opportunities and responsibilities that attend the task of translation. Best known for advancing a model of translation consisting of three kinds—metaphrase, paraphrase, and imitation—running along a spectrum from most to least literal, the preface also makes a special point of exploring the notion that a text has a fundamental "sense." In defining the middle way of translating, or paraphrase, Dryden writes that "the Authour is kept in view by the Translator, so as never to be lost, but his words are not so strictly follow'd as his sense, and that too is admitted to be amplyfied, but not alter'd."[13] This notion of maintaining the sense has a long history, rooted at least as far back as debates in late antiquity about how best to preserve the word of God in translations of the Bible. Like Jerome defending verbal deviations between Greek and Latin, Dryden believes in a nebulous, core meaning that can be transferred from language to language—this "sense" persists where the word does not. In translation, writes Dryden, the sense of a text can be "amplyfied"; according to this vision of translation, the movement from one language to another does not risk loss but actually offers the opportunity for louder, perhaps even clearer, meanings to resound.

As he translated Virgil, Dryden made shrewd choices about which aspects to amplify. At issue in this chapter is the word "peace," which echoes through Dryden's English *Georgics* far more than in other translations or even in the Latin poem. Dryden also demonstrates heightened sensitivity to the sustained exploration of what it means truly to be at peace, an issue that haunts the *Eclogues*, *Georgics*, and *Aeneid*. By virtue of their formal distinctions, the various genres that make up Virgil's body of work approach similar questions but produce discrete—though complementary—results. Taken together, these poems accomplish a more complete negotiation of questions of peace than would a single work or a single genre. The richness of their interconnections guarantees that each new poem bears the traces of the poet's earlier efforts; the twin senses of regression and circularity that result are as much a comment on the making of poetry as they are on the making of empire.

The *Eclogues*, for instance, written before Octavian's definitive ascension to power, famously begin with an unfair and unequal eviction. The first poem establishes the stark contrasts by which rural tranquility is both defined and undermined throughout the rest of Virgil's oeuvre, particularly in his middle work:

> Tityre, tu patulae recubans sub tegmine fagi
> silvestrem tenui musam meditaris avena:
> nos patriae finis et dulcia linquimus arva;
> nos patriam fugimus: tu, Tityre, lentus in umbra
> formosam resonare doces Amaryllida silvas.
> $(1.1–5)^{14}$

> (Tityrus, you lying under the shade of the beech tree meditate the woodland muse on your delicate pipe; we forsake the borders of our land and the charming fields; we flee the fatherland: you, Tityrus, lazy in the shade, teach the forests to resonate lovely Amaryllis.)

Dryden expands Virgil by a line in his version:

> Beneath the Shade which Beechen Boughs diffuse,
> You *Tity'rus* entertain your Silvan Muse:
> Round the wide World in Banishment we rome,
> Forc'd from our pleasing Fields and Native Home:
> While stretch'd at Ease you sing your happy loves:
> And *Amarillis* fills the shady Groves.
> (*Pastorals* 1.1–6)

Several small adjustments appear here: instead of beginning with Tityrus, Dryden emphasizes the shepherd's position under the shade of the beech tree; he also creates a pun with the word "rome," by which of course he means "roam," but making good use of the flexibility of English spelling in this period, also gestures toward the power at Rome distinguishing favorites from exiles. Although he takes these and other liberties with the syntax, he preserves Virgil's choice to frame the opening stanza of the poem with images of shade, which appear in the first and last lines of both versions here. As careful readers of the Roman poet have long noted, *umbras* link the *Eclogues*, *Georgics*, and *Aeneid* to one another; although Virgil makes many words echo to one another across his oeuvre, shade—which can suggest many things, from simple shadows to political threats to hellish gloom—is one of his most powerful recurring images.

The first line of the *Eclogues* creates an unforgettable loop between the beginning of the *Eclogues* and the end of the *Georgics*:[15] concluding his song, the georgic poet addresses Tityrus *sub tegmine fagi* as well. Dryden alters Virgil's line somewhat at the end of his own version, omitting Tityrus's name. Yet he does conclude the poem by amplifying the sound of the word "Shade," placing it at the end of the penultimate line: "And bold, through Youth, beneath the Beechen Shade, / The Lays of Shepherds, and their Loves have plaid" (4.818–819). All rhyme creates backward motion, reminding us of the sound we heard at the end of the first line. Here, the zeugma of the second line heightens this backward movement, as though pointing back into the couplet, leading us back to "Shade." As the final lines of the *Georgics* return us to the commencement of the *Eclogues*, they point to the possibility that the entire agricultural project is always fundamentally under threat, since it depends on the fundamental fact of being granted access to land. By making the shades ring in our ears, Dryden lays bare Virgil's contingent visions of peace.

In addition to framing the first stanza of the *Eclogues*, images of shade also frame the larger collection. The word *umbra* appears three times in the concluding lines of the final eclogue, as the poet warns of the coming night:

> surgamus: solet esse gravis cantantibus umbra,
> iuniperi gravis umbra, nocent et frugibus umbrae.
> ite domum saturae, venit Hesperus, ite capellae.
> (10.75–77)

> (We should rise; the shade is often burdensome to singers, the shade of the juniper burdens [us], and the shade harms the crops. Go home full, Hesperus comes, go home, goats.)

By suggesting that these shades menace the corn crop, Virgil points to another threat to the agricultural work of the *Georgics*.[16] Dryden concludes his own *Pastorals* with an ominous triplet:

> Now let us rise, for hoarseness oft invades
> The Singer's Voice, who sings beneath the Shades.
> From Juniper, unwholsom Dews distill,
> That blast the sooty Corn; the with'ring Herbage kill;
> Away, my Goats, away: for you have browz'd your fill.
> (10.110–114)

The phrase "beneath the Shades" recalls Tityrus reclining in conversation with Meliboeus even more explicitly than do Virgil's own lines. Dryden does not translate each instance of *umbra*, but he creates a triple structure of his own, casting a similarly ominous shadow over the English version. The harshness of "kill" echoes through "distill" and "fill," and even more threateningly, the rhyme depends on the repetition of "ill."

As these examples show, Dryden takes seriously the task of "amplyfying" the sense of threat he detects in Virgil. When he comes to the end of his *Aeneis*, however, he makes a sharp turn away from the Latin. Surely the most powerful example of Virgil's dark vision, the death of Turnus at the hands of Aeneas exposes the epic hero's failure to act mercifully. In the final lines of the poem, Aeneas runs his sword through the body of Turnus, whose soul *cum gemitu fugit indignata sub umbras* (12.952), "with a groan fled, indignant, beneath the shades." At the end of his *Aeneis*, however, Dryden veers dramatically away from the Latin:

> He rais'd his Arm aloft; and at the Word,
> Deep in his Bosom drove the shining Sword.
> The streaming Blood distain'd his Arms around:
> And the disdainful Soul came rushing thro' the Wound.
> (12.1374–1377)

Making no mention of the shady underworld in these lines, Dryden trains his focus squarely on Aeneas's bloody arms—suggesting both weapons and limbs—creating a terrible echo of the epic's opening phrase, *arma virumque cano*, and concluding the entire translation with the somewhat awkward rhyme "around"/"Wound."[17] Nothing settles, nothing rings triumphant, and Dryden leaves us only with the image of Turnus's spirit in the midst of its flight from his mangled body. The wound left gaping here at the end of the English *Virgil* encourages several simultaneous readings: in the simplest sense, this final image heightens the drama of the Latin poem; yet it also suggests an active resistance to the sense of completion that Virgil created with his *umbras*. The verbal continuities of the Latin poems frequently link poetics and politics—the long shadow of Rome, for instance, suggests both the possibility of patronage and the potential arbitrariness of strong centralized power. In his translation, however, Dryden rejects these links, choosing instead to strengthen Virgil's criticism of the violent origins from which imperial authority proceeds. At the same time that this choice suggests a dark interpretation of the *Aeneid*, it also marks a refusal of poetic continuity; in stepping distinctly away from the Latin text, Dryden leaves a gaping wound where the poem should have closed itself off—at least at the level of the word, if not in the larger narrative. This jagged edge might perhaps point to Dryden's own disappointment at not bringing his own career to a culmination with an original epic; the *Aeneis* represents a magnificent literary triumph, but perhaps not a wholly satisfying one. Most importantly, though, it would have been impossible to read these lines in the summer of 1697 without thinking of the warrior king who had spent nearly a decade pursuing battle.

In the *Dedication of the Aeneis*—addressed to the Earl of Mulgrave, a self-taught Latinist and an opponent of William III—Dryden had used the image of a wound to explain the political ramifications of civil war, writing, "The Commonwealth had receiv'd a deadly Wound in the former Civil Wars betwixt *Marius* and *Sylla*."[18] In concluding his *Aeneis* with the image of a gaping wound, rather than the nebulous respite of shadow, Dryden leaves the poem, along with Turnus, exposed and bleeding on the battlefield. Although he ruptures the continuity of the Latin poet's work, he creates a new point of connection between the epic itself and his own retelling of Roman history, one infused with deep criticisms of an English state he understood to be still wounded by the factionalism of the middle and later seventeenth century.

These brief examples demonstrate how urgently some of the interconnected moments in Virgil's oeuvre confront the problem of stability, and the extent to which Dryden was acutely aware of how he might exploit those moments as he contemplated the likelihood that England would ever achieve lasting peace. The central figures of these poems participate in a perpetual struggle to achieve or maintain peace: if one shepherd has been granted leave to remain in his fields, another finds himself evicted; if one farmer enjoys a life tending vines, another is compelled to retool his scythe as an implement of war; if one soldier will rise to power in Latium, another must die at his feet. Yet despite Dryden's interest in strengthening the darkest strains of the Latin poems, he offers glimpses of what sustained peace might look like in his *Georgics*.

DRYDEN'S *GEORGICS*: "NOR WHEN THE WAR IS OVER, IS IT PEACE"

Elsewhere in the *Dedication of the Aeneis,* Dryden describes Virgil's acute awareness of the political machinations that marked the world around him:

> I say that *Virgil* having maturely weigh'd the Condition of the Times in which he liv'd: that an entire Liberty was not to be retriev'd: that the present Settlement had the prospect of a long continuance in the same Family, or those adopted into it: that he held his Paternal Estate from the Bounty of the Conqueror, by whom he was likewise enrich'd, esteem'd and cherish'd: that this Conquerour, though of a bad kind, was the very best of it: that the Arts of Peace flourish'd under him: that all Men might be happy if they would be quiet. . . . These things, I say, being consider'd by the Poet, he concluded it to be the Interest of his Country to be so Govern'd: To infuse an awful Respect into the People, towards such a Prince: By that respect to confirm their Obedience to him; and by that Obedience to make them Happy.[19]

Here Dryden treats both Augustus and Virgil carefully. He recognizes Virgil's shrewd understanding of an imperial government that sought to impose unity and stability on its people. A key phrase in this incisive passage, "Arts of Peace," arrives tinged with irony; for Dryden, "art" can mean artistic production—poetry, music, painting—or it can connote superficial, heavily calculated social and political behavior. In many of his poetic and prose writings, he blames the latter for occluding the true expression of "nature," either in poetry or in life. To say, therefore, that the "Arts of Peace" flourished under Augustus is to say, on one hand, that poetry found support from the emperor, and that such poetry was charged with the representation of peace; yet on the other hand, it is also to say that peace and stability were the results of deliberate—and at times coercive—political design, and that perhaps their effects were merely superficial.

In many senses, then, Virgil's was an age marked by peace achieved through art. According to Dryden, the Roman poet understood that although "an entire Liberty was not to be retriev'd," he could still attempt a "Divine Poem" that might please—though not blindly celebrate—all interested parties. Dryden, of course, continues to conjure up his own literary and political age at the same time that he illustrates Virgil's. When he writes that "all Men might be happy if they would be quiet," he recalls his own much earlier poem *Religio Laici,* which approaches its conclusion by suggesting

> That private Reason 'tis more Just to curb,
> Than by Disputes the publick Peace disturb.
> For points obscure are of small use to learn:
> But *Common quiet* is *Mankind's concern*.
> (447–450)

This poem, like *Astraea Redux, Absalom and Achitophel,* and several others written before the Revolution, blames clerics, fanatics, and mob rioters for interrupting the "publick Peace." Yet the emphasis shifts in the dedication; "Common quiet" may still be mankind's primary "concern," but such quiet derives from submission to newly strengthened political power. Dryden writes that the epic honors the "Conqueror"—likely referring to both Augustus and William of Orange—even though true peace and freedom have not yet been realized under him, and perhaps may never be.[20]

Although Dryden attaches the phrase "Arts of Peace" to his *Aeneis,* the *Georgics* provide a better path to understanding what, exactly, he means by it. When read together and alongside the dedication, the fourteen new insertions of the word "peace" in this poem bring to light at least one dimension of the conversation that was taking place, through vast ranges of space and time, between two poets interested in the vicissitudes of political power. This conversation explores the relationship shared by a ruler and his people, the meaning of true peace, and the value of looking to agriculture as a model for that peace. Reading Virgil in Dryden's English shows us how useful a tool Dryden found the Roman poet for addressing the problems of his own historical moment. This reading also grants us access to the ways in which Dryden interpreted, and chose to represent, his literary ancestor. In translating the *Georgics,* Dryden had an opportunity to expand upon his frustrations with William's incessant need to make war; as Dryden's biographer notes, by the mid-1690s, a "vocal 'country' opposition" had formed, primarily made up of landowners who lost agricultural workers to military conscription, and paid heavy taxes to support the war.[21] In this way, conversations about political peace were inextricable from conversations about agricultural productivity, and the English *Georgics* often reflect these tensions.

Significantly, however, Dryden's Virgilian georgic peace also transcends topical concerns. His translation presents several broad conceptions of peace that stand in hierarchical relation to one another. In the English translation, the single word "peace" functions variously to draw out the complexities of Virgil's own visions of the stability that might follow the civil wars. The highest form of peace in the poem is an idealized one: the land was at peace before agricultural labor was imposed on humanity during the transition from the golden age under Saturn to the iron age under Jupiter—or, more often in Dryden's English, Jove. In this world, cultivated land and its fruits and crops enjoy a natural peace separate from human affairs—though such peace is at times anthropomorphized and militarized, perhaps to heighten the disparity between it and the unattainable, perfect peace of a lost age, or, as in the case of Marvell's *Upon Appleton House*, to reinforce the fallenness of those who would read and write about an ideal state. Less perfect, though still admirable, is the farmer's peaceful life, which demands that he study and care for the land so that he may produce crops. Dryden, who had developed this idea memorably in the scene featuring Kentish shepherds—who live and love far from the noise of war—in *King Arthur* (1691), returns to it in several passages in the *Georgics*. To emphasize the tenuousness of this peace, he frequently contrasts the farmer's tranquility with political unrest, which often threatens to interrupt life on the farm. Peace derived from political maneuvering or conquest—for Dryden, the least natural and most fragile kind of peace—lies at the bottom of the hierarchy. The translation presents natural peace as a pure standard; despite human manipulation or mismanagement, the land embodies an enduring, renewable peacefulness. All human peace, on the other hand, whether pastoral or political, suffers the constant threat of mutability and destruction.

In a didactic passage comparing grape and olive cultivation, Dryden uses the word "peace" first to emphasize the naturalness of the plants, and then again to translate its direct Latin counterpart. First, Dryden's addition:

> Besides, in Woods the Shrubs of prickly Thorn,
> Sallows and Reeds, on Banks of Rivers born,
> Remain to cut; for Vineyards useful found,
> To stay thy Vines, and fence thy fruitful Ground.
> Nor when thy tender Trees at length are bound;
> When peaceful Vines from Pruning Hooks are free,
> When Husbands have survey'd the last degree,
> And utmost Files of Plants, and order'd ev'ry Tree;
> Ev'n when they sing at ease in full Content,
> Insulting o're the Toils they underwent;
> Yet still they find a future Task remain

(2.572–582)

No linguistic equivalent for "*peaceful* Vines" appears in the Latin text. Dryden's two lines—"Nor when thy tender Trees at length are bound; / When peaceful Vines from Pruning Hooks are free"—render the single Latin line, *iam uinctae uites, iam falcem arbusta reponunt* (2.416); generally, Dryden requires about a line and a half of English pentameter for every Latin hexameter. In the Latin text, the pruning hooks are no longer in use and the grape plants have been bound, implying that the vines have settled into a state of peace after having been provoked and then constrained—*uinctae*—by farm tools. Yet Dryden heightens the contrasts here: like the farmer's peace, which stands in opposition to political turmoil, the vines' peace becomes quite visible when juxtaposed with the edged implements of agriculture from which they have been liberated.

Virgil then moves on to celebrate the humble olive, which demands only a fraction of the upkeep required by the tender vines. Here Dryden translates "peace" directly from *pax*, which appears in its dative form in the corresponding Latin passage:

> Contra non ulla est oleis cultura, neque illae
> procuruam exspectant falcem rastrosque tenacis,
> cum semel haeserunt aruis aurasque tulerunt;
> ipsa satis tellus, cum dente recluditur unco,
> sufficit umorem et grauidas, cum uomere, fruges.
> hoc pinguem et placitam Paci nutritor oliuam.
> (2.420–425)

> Quite opposite to these are Olives found,
> No dressing they require, and dread no wound;
> Nor Rakes nor Harrows need, but fix'd below,
> Rejoyce in open Air, and unconcernedly grow.
> The Soil it self due Nourishment supplies:
> Plough but the Furrows, and the Fruits arise:
> Content with small Endeavours, 'till they spring,
> Soft Peace they figure, and sweet Plenty bring:
> Then Olives plant, and Hymns to *Pallas* sing.
> (2.586–594)

Both poets note that tools need not be used very much to raise this crop, which mostly requires natural resources. Significant additions by Dryden include two imperatives: "Then Olives plant," and "Hymns to *Pallas* sing." Because Pallas, or Minerva, had by this time long been associated with the iconography of peace, Dryden has chosen here to articulate Virgil's *placitam Paci* (2.425)—"pleasing to Peace"—by making explicit mention of the goddess herself. Although the olive itself receives roughly equal treatment in both texts, Dryden's "peace" comes at the beginning of the penultimate line quoted here, rather than in the middle of a line, as *Paci* appears in Virgil's final hexameter. Moreover, this passage, when read in the context of the vine episode before it, becomes a part of the larger contrast between nature's peaceful objects and the intrusive ones wielded by farmers for the raising and collecting of crops. Olives "figure" "Soft Peace" because they grow without the sharp discipline of pruning.

This independence also marks the land before human intervention, a point emphasized by Dryden's first addition of "peace" to Virgil's poem. Early in book 1, the poetic persona explains the farmer's particular difficulties, followed by a description of the age before labor and landowning:

> Nec tamen, haec cum sint hominumque boumque labores
> uersando terram experti, nihil improbus anser
> Strymoniaeque grues et amaris intiba fibris
> officiunt aut umbra nocet. pater ipse colendi
> haud facilem esse uiam uoluit, primusque per artem
> mouit agros, curis acuens mortalia corda
> nec torpere graui passus sua regna ueterno.
> ante Iouem nulli subigebant arua coloni;
> nec signare quidem aut partiri limite campum
> fas erat; in medium quaerebant ipsaque tellus
> omnia liberius nullo poscente ferebat.
>
> (1.118–128)

(Nor however, even though the work of men and oxen would be proven in turning the ground, do the shameless goose and the Strymonian crane do nothing [harmful], and the chicory plants, with bitter fibers, block the way, or else the shadow harms [the field]. The father himself did not wish the way of cultivating to be easy, and first through art moved the fields, by care sharpening mortal intellects, and did not suffer his reign to be lethargic in heavy sloth. Before Jove no farmers subjugated the fields, nor even to mark or divide the field with a boundary was allowed; they sought common space, and the land itself brought forth all things more freely, demanding nothing.)

Although both poets point to Jove as the figure responsible for humanity's toils, Dryden's text takes on a particularly postlapsarian cast with its "hard Decrees," "toil," and "grudging Soil":

> Nor yet the Ploughman, nor the lab'ring Steer,
> Sustain alone the hazards of the Year:
> But glutton Geese, and the *Strymonian* Crane,
> With foreign Troops, invade the tender Grain:
> And tow'ring Weeds malignant Shadows yield;
> And spreading Succ'ry choaks the rising Field.
> The Sire of Gods and Men, with hard Decrees,
> Forbids our Plenty to be bought with Ease:
> And wills that Mortal men, inur'd to toil,
> Shou'd exercise, with pains, the grudging Soil:

Himself invented first the shining Share,
And whetted Humane Industry by Care:
Himself did Handy-Crafts and Arts ordain;
Nor suffer'd Sloath to rust his active Reign.
E're this, no Peasant vex'd the peaceful Ground;
Which only Turfs and Greens for Altars found:
No Fences parted Fields, nor marks nor Bounds
Distinguish'd Acres of litigious Grounds:
But all was common, and the fruitful Earth
Was free to give her unexacted Birth.

(1.177–196)

The two English passages I have been discussing here, when read together, indicate the kinds of amplifications and additions Dryden makes throughout his translation. Both poets relate Jove's role in making husbandry a difficult business, but Dryden expands the meaningful potential of Virgil's language as far as he can. Where Virgil describes fieldwork as a kind of skill or art—*primusque per artem mouit agros*—Dryden exploits the opportunity to emphasize the artificiality of all human labors by referring to three concepts—"Humane Industry," "Handy-Crafts," and "Arts"—in place of Virgil's single word *artem*. Dryden also takes his time explaining the god's "hard Decrees," ending a series of lines with vivid images of labor: "inur'd to toil," "the grudging Soil," "the shining Share."

Before he dramatizes the heavenly ordinances of Jove, however, Dryden recasts the animal imagery of this passage into an explicitly military scene. Virgil's birds impede—*officiunt*—the growth of the wheat, but Dryden's "glutton Geese and Strymonian crane," aided by "foreign Troops," commit an invasion upon the defenseless crop. In the same way that Dryden probably included both William of Orange and Augustus Caesar when he made mention of a "Conqueror" in his *Dedication*, the specific addition of a "foreign" avian troop, eager to steal the farm's carefully tended resources without penalty, surely suggests, if only briefly, William's invasion of James II's realm. When represented in this way, the greedy incursions of the birds and the weeds—and the usurping William—appear especially heinous because they offend the "tender Grain," the product of the "peaceful ground" mentioned several lines later.

In Virgil's Latin, the verb *subigebant* suggests that the act of turning over the soil is especially invasive. Dryden's English line puts additional pressure on the idea that the farmer, in turning the soil, has troubled—or "vex'd"—it. Here Dryden recalls his own translation of the inevitable flaws that attend peace in Virgil's fourth eclogue:

> Yet, of old Fraud some footsteps shall remain,
> The Merchant still shall plough the deep for gain:
> Great Cities shall with Walls be compass'd round:
> And sharpen'd Shares shall vex the fruitful ground.
> (*Pastorals* 4.37–40)

The echo is Dryden's; Virgil's Latin—*telluri infindere sulcos*—primarily stresses the act of plowing the soil, and uses no adjectives that would warrant Dryden's "fruitful." When Dryden writes in his *Georgics* that Jove "swelled, with raging Storms, the peaceful Flood" (1.198), he expands the sense of the corresponding half-line: *iussit pontumque moueri* (1.130), "and he ordered the sea to stir." Virgil's rising sea shares space, as well as the verb *iussit*, with a pack of rapacious wolves in the first half of the same line, but Dryden allots a complete line to each and reverses their order. By positioning the phrase "peaceful Flood" at the end of a line, Dryden recalls the "peaceful Ground" mentioned earlier.

This echo reverberates in the poem's second book, in a didactic passage encouraging the farmer to plant his crops in a favorable location: "Be not seduced with Wisdom's empty Shows, / To stir the peaceful Ground where *Boreas* blows" (2.428–429). Virgil's lines figure the ground as "stiff" or "rigid"—*Nec tibi tam prudens quisquam persuadeat auctor / tellurem Borea rigidam spirante mouere* (2.315–316). Stiff soil does suggest a kind of spatial peace—as opposed to the chaos of wind-blown soil—but by repeating his phrase "peaceful ground," Dryden directly aligns this passage with the earlier one. With this realignment, the poem links the farmer with original, pre-agricultural peace, so long as he subdues his own will and learns to read the land. In order to raise successful crops, he must understand the earth's cycles and patterns, know the paths the wind takes, and resist the temptation to rely on human "Wisdom" and its "empty Shows."

In addition to undertaking this learning, the farmer must also commit to carrying out labor in perpetuity; he is destined for failure "unless the Land with daily Care / Is exercis'd, and with an Iron War, / Of Rakes and Harrows, the proud Foes expell'd" (1.231–233). Ensuing lines observe the various "Arms" laborers "wield" (1.239) as they take up these daily battles; here Dryden renders Virgil's word *arma* (1.160) directly, but the earlier image of "Iron War" is his own; it is perhaps a dramatic extension of the Latin verb *insectabere* (1.155), which suggests an aggressive or hostile pursuit of something. By making this change, Dryden heightens the sense of material mutability between the states of peace and war that Virgil has already begun to convey; at the same time, however, Dryden's version gestures more dramatically toward the closing scene of this book, in which the scythe will be modified for use as a sword. His translation also shifts the way we read the facing illustration, which displays an array of laborers' tools (Fig. 5). The plate appeared at roughly the same location when it was used to adorn Ogilby's translation of the poem, but that version does not render the farmer's implements in military terms, nor does it provide any precedent for Dryden's vision of "Iron War." In the later translation, the image yields greater significance: when considered next to Dryden's military language, the scene cannot be read only as an idealized vision of rural work. Instead, it invites comparison with soldiers' preparations for battle, fusing the material link between the worlds of peace and war.

When Dryden first introduces the image of the "peaceful ground," no crops have yet been planted, no farmers have begun to rake or plough. In those early moments, his *Georgics* have not yet united the "peasant" with "peace." Instead, the poem characterizes the farmer as an intruder. Later, however, the farmer works in concert with nature's inherent peacefulness, and stands in contrast to the manipulations of social and political striving. In this way, Dryden's reading and rendering of Virgil's poem ultimately model country life as the primary mode of access to nature's peace in a world divided into "Marks" and "Bounds" and "litigious Grounds." The farmer's life keeps alive the hope that a state of true peace—not simply a paused cycle of war and conquest—may be possible.

In this way, despite the farmer's early, somewhat unfavorable status, and despite the inescapable connections between his tools and those of a soldier, he and his way of life come to represent, for both Dryden and Virgil, a welcome alternative to political intrigue and the pursuit of wealth or renown. The following passage, perhaps the best known and most frequently translated from the Latin *Georgics*, enacts a dramatic shift away from Jove's "hard Decrees" and toward an ecstatic celebration of the farmer's life:

> Oh happy, if he knew his happy State!
> The Swain, who, free from Business and Debate,
> Receives his easy Food from Nature's Hand,
> And Just returns of cultivated Land!
> No Palace, with a lofty Gate, he wants,
> To pour out Tydes of early Visitants:
> With eager Eyes devouring, as they pass,
> The breathing Figures of *Corinthian* Brass.
> No Statues threaten, from high Pedestals;
> No *Persian* Arras hides his homely Walls,
> With Antick Vests; which thro' their shady fold,
> Betray the Streaks of ill dissembl'd Gold.
> He boasts no Wool, whose native white is dy'd

Figure 5 Dryden, *Georgics* plate 2, Rare Book Collection, Howard Gotlieb
Archival Research Center

> With Purple Poyson of *Assyrian* Pride.
> No costly Drugs of *Araby* defile,
> With foreign Scents, the Sweetness of his Oyl.
> (2.639–654)

With his translation, Dryden redirects the Latin poem, adding social and political corruption to war as powerful antagonists to peace. This redirection emphasizes the differences between natural arts—arts close to nature—and those arts
meant for war, for politics, and for courtly maneuvering.[22] When considered next
to the "homebred Plenty" cultivated on the farm, the material conditions of courtly
artists and artisans become sinister: "eager Eyes" devour "breathing Figures of
Corinthian Brass," "Statues threaten," and "Antick Vests . . . Betray the Streaks of
ill dissembl'd Gold."

Dryden expressed a similar, though more overt, disdain for the court in his
Dedication to the Georgics, addressed to Philip Stanhope, Earl of Chesterfield. The
poet figures Stanhope, who had roundly refused to support William III, as a kind
of courtly Cincinnatus:

> You saw betimes that Ingratitude is not confin'd to Commonwealths; and
> therefore though you were form'd alike, for the greatest of Civil Employ-
> ments, and Military Commands, yet you push'd not your Fortune to rise
> in either; but contented yourself with being capable, as much as any who-
> soever, of defending your Country with your Sword, or assisting it with
> your Counsel, when you were call'd. . . . I commend not him who never
> knew a Court, but him who forsakes it because he knows it. (142)

Dryden praises Chesterfield for having refused the courtly life after he "contented"
himself "with being capable" of serving as a soldier and a public official: war will
always keep grinding away, and politics will always offer "false Dice" (142), but
the wise know when to withdraw. A few years later, Dryden would echo these sentiments in the opening lines of "To My Honour'd Kinsman, John Driden" (1700):

> How Bless'd is He, who leads a Country Life,
> Unvex'd with anxious Cares, and void of Strife!
> Who studying Peace, and shunning Civil Rage,
> Enjoy'd his Youth, and now enjoys his Age:
> (1–4)

Though perhaps a rather conventional enactment of the *beatus ille* trope when read
in isolation, this passage gains special resonance when considered in light of the
poem's nine other uses of the word "peace." Six of these appear within a span of

twenty-nine lines, in which Dryden considers the difficulty of crafting peace from war. He criticizes peace achieved corruptly: "*Munster* was bought, we boast not the Success;/Who fights for Gain, for greater, makes his Peace" (140–141). Immediately afterward, the poem approaches the possibility of lasting peace, which Dryden considers in deeply negative terms: "Enough for *Europe* has our *Albion* fought:/Let us enjoy the Peace our Blood has bought" (157–158). Here, peace is inextricably connected to the bloodshed of war; it becomes something "bought," recalling the earlier lines, with exhaustive military labor. When put this way, peace hardly seems like something that can ever be fully "enjoy[ed]."

In contrast to the emphasis on retirement that marks "To My Honour'd Kinsman," Dryden's *Georgics* translate government itself into rustic terms, extolling the "Country King" as a benevolent ruler:

> But easie Quiet, a secure Retreat,
> A harmless Life that knows not how to cheat,
> With homebred Plenty the rich Owner bless,
> And rural Pleasures crown his Happiness.
> Unvex'd with Quarrels, undisturbed with Noise,
> The Country King his peaceful Realm enjoys:
> Cool Grots, and living Lakes, the Flow'ry Pride
> Of Meads, and Streams that thro' the Valley glide;
> And shady Groves that easie Sleep invite,
> And after toilsome Days, a soft repose at Night.
> Wild Beasts of Nature in his Woods abound;
> And Youth, of Labour patient, plow the Ground,
> Inur'd to Hardship, and to homely Fare.
> (2.655–667)

The figure of the "Country King" is Dryden's; he also expands Virgil's *secura quies* (467) into the complete line, "Unvex'd with Quarrels, undisturbed with Noise." Another significant echo sounds here: "Unvex'd" recalls the description of life before agriculture when "no Peasant vex'd the peaceful Ground," Dryden's translation of the fourth *Pastoral*, and his use of the word in an initial position in the opening lines of "To My Hounour'd Kinsman," quoted above. The peace depicted in this passage, however, belongs to the farmer-king who rules a realm of "patient" labor. Dryden achieves such an effectively idealized representation of the peasant in this moment because he makes him not only the ruler of the natural realm, but also an inextricable part of it. His dominion extends to both the "Beasts of Nature" and the "Youth, of Labour patient"—two entities that each occupy a full line of their shared couplet. The semicolon separating them, as well as Dryden's decision to end both lines with phrases describing the two groups' primary activities—"in his Woods abound" and "plow the Ground"—suggests that the animals and the farmers, as creatures living by nature's laws, enjoy roughly equal status in the "peaceful Realm."

One scholar has suggested that the farmer-king inhabits a "kingdom of the mind"[23] not meant to represent any specific location or reject any single public problem. Elsewhere in the poem, however, Dryden does invoke the peaceful peasant as a distinct antithesis to war and corruption. One particularly memorable passage, significantly expanded from the Latin poem, casts the "peaceful Peasant" as a forced participant in a war instigated by imperial and urban forces:

> Heav'n wants thee there, and long the Gods, we know,
> Have grudg'd thee, *Caesar*, to the World below:
> Where Fraud and Rapine, Right and Wrong confound; ⎫
> Where impious Arms from ev'ry part resound, ⎬
> And monstrous Crimes in ev'ry Shape are crown'd. ⎭
> The peaceful Peasant to the Wars is prest;
> The Fields lye fallow in inglorious Rest.
> The Plain no Pasture to the Flock affords,
> The crooked Scythes are streightned into Swords:
> And there *Euphrates* her soft Off-spring Arms,
> And here the *Rhine* rebellows with Alarms:
> The neighb'ring Cities range on sev'ral sides,
> Perfidious *Mars* long plighted Leagues divides, ⎫
> And o're the wasted World in Triumph rides. ⎬
> So four fierce Coursers starting to the Race, ⎭
> Scow'r thro' the Plain, and lengthen ev'ry Pace:
> Nor Reins, nor Curbs, nor threat'ning Cries they fear,
> But force along the trembling Charioteer.
>   (1.676–693)

Dryden makes several important additions to Virgil's markedly shorter passage. Both triplets, for instance, include interventions blaming the world's ills on royal corruption and overzealous warmongering. Dryden inserts "crown'd" as the concluding rhyme of the first triplet, connecting "Crimes" to monarchy. In the second, he transforms Virgil's *saeuit toto Mars impius orbe* (1.511)—"impious Mars rages over the whole world"—into two lines that describe the god of war as "perfidious" and the earth as "wasted," an adjective that sounds especially ominous as its initial consonant repeats in the sound of "world."

The most significant intervention in this passage, however, occurs at line 681, where Dryden invents and inserts the specific image of the "peaceful Peasant . . . prest."[24] Earlier English translators of the *Georgics* recreate Virgil's emphasis; the verb *squalent*—meaning "overgrown"—in the phrase *squalent abductis arua colonis* (1.507), calls more attention to the neglected fields than to the conscripted farmhands. Thomas May, nearly erasing the presence of the farmers, writes: "The plowes neglected lay, the fruitlesse ground / Ore-grown with weeds, for want of tillers mournd."[25] John Ogilby's lines of 1654, altered from his initial translation of 1649, look somewhat more like Dryden's, but do not render the fieldworkers as explicitly "peaceful" figures: "None to the scorned Plough due honor yeelds, / Swains, prest for Souldiers, leave neglected fields."[26]

In addition to this change, Dryden makes a significant choice in his description of the moment when "The crooked Scythes are streightned into Swords." Nearly all the line's words hew closely to the Latin, with the exception of its verb. Whereas Dryden chooses the construction "are streightned," Virgil's verb, *conflantur* (508), calls to mind the specific act of forging, with heat, one metal shape from another. This is all the more surprising given Dryden's lines late in book 2, which employ the verb "forge" while adding another version of "peace." For Virgil's *necdum etiam audierant inflari classica, necdum / impositos duris crepitare incudibus enses* (2.539–540), Dryden writes, "While peaceful *Crete* enjoy'd her ancient Lord, / E're sounding Hammers forg'd th' inhumane Sword" (2.787–788). Here Dryden follows Virgil relatively closely, as both poets depict an idealized time before humanity knew of war or weaponry. In their translations of the conclusion of book 1, May and Ogilby write, respectively, "crooked sickles into swords were turn'd,"[27] and "crooked Sithes to Swords transformed are."[28] All three poets replicate Virgil's passive construction, but Dryden's remains the most specific, pointing to the change in the shape of the metal shaft, from curved to straight. The difference is small, but significant: the translation by Dryden more immediately emphasizes the objects' common material foundation. The farmer always holds in his hand a potential implement of war, and the soldier an implement of peace.

Dryden exploits other moments, too, that are especially fit for communicating his distrust for the end of war. In book 3, Virgil describes a confrontation between two bulls competing for the attentions of a heifer (219–228). As the passage progresses, the natural competition between two male animals for the right to mate with a single female transforms into a violent battle with an outcome couched in the language of exile and monarchy. After a bloody defeat, the losing bull, now an exile, grieves far from both his foe and his homeland—*longeque ignotis exulat oris* (3.225)—gazing back on the long-held kingdom he has lost—*aspectans regnis excessit auitis* (3.228). Dryden's rendition accentuates Virgil's emphases:

A beauteous Heifer in the Woods is bred;
The stooping Warriours, aiming Head to Head,
Engage their clashing Horns; with dreadful Sound
The Forest rattles, and the Rocks rebound.
They fence, they push, and pushing loudly roar;
Their Dewlaps and their Sides are bath'd in Gore.
Nor when the War is over, is it Peace;
Nor will the vanquished Bull his Claim release:
But feeding in his Breast his ancient Fires,
And cursing Fate, from his proud Foe retires.
Driv'n from his Native Land, to foreign Grounds,
He with a gen'rous Rage resents his Wounds;
His ignominious Flight, the Victor's boast,
And more than both, the Loves, which unreveng'd he lost.
Often he turns his Eyes, and, with a Groan,
Surveys the pleasing Kingdoms, once his own.

(3.339–354)

Such lines as "Surveys the pleasing Kingdoms, once his own" and "Driv'n from his Native Land, to foreign Grounds" represent their Latin counterparts in a more or less straightforward way, although given the moment in which the translation appears, they also evoke James II in exile. In addition, Dryden expands Virgil's imagery of the bulls' mutual struggle. This subtle expansion adds strength to the most significant alteration in the passage, which arrives as a line inserted between Virgil's description of the conflict and the moment in which the vanquished bull retreats. Here Dryden adds, "Nor when the War is over, is it Peace." This line of course anticipates the vanquished bull's preparations to fight again—an event that occurs in both poems—but it also speaks to events contemporary with the publication of the *Virgil*, including the still uncertain peace ratified at Ryswick. By shifting the passage toward a criticism of war, Dryden conjures up the ousted James II, imagined here as gazing mournfully upon his conquered England in the years after the Revolution. These connections become all the more meaningful when we remember that Dryden originally published a translation of the poem's third book in Jacob Tonson's *Annual Miscellany* for 1694, and did not revise it for the full *Virgil* published three years later. Read in this light, Dryden's suggestion that peace does not necessarily follow naturally after war becomes all the more gloomy: even if the yearly cycle of battles does cease, he suggests, the English ought not to hope too fervently for a miraculous time of peace.

At no point in Dryden's translation of the *Georgics* do "war" and "peace" appear as close to one another as they do here. Yet the poem flatly refuses to depict peace arising from war. Human conflicts stand too far removed from the simple olive, or the untilled ground, to produce any kind of permanent peace. Moreover, although Dryden almost always adds "peace" where Virgil provides no literal *pax*, his alterations—even those that simultaneously invoke contemporary events—should be considered not merely acts of creativity but also interpretations of Virgil's complex attitudes about war and the state. Dryden does, in book 2, add a line beseeching Caesar to "Triumph abroad, secure our Peace at home" (2.240), but he never refers explicitly to "peace" to mean the realized outcome of war. The kind of peace endorsed by Dryden's translation of the *Georgics* has nothing to do with treaties or battlefield heroics. The translation rejects war as a source of social, artistic, or political peace.

Where, then, do Dryden and Virgil locate peace? What kind of peace is possible in the time after Jove has ordered humanity to toil, after humanity has learned to make weapons, and after kings have learned to conquer? The *Georgics*, in both English and Latin, offer life on the farm as an accessible alternative to war, although such a life is always marked by the memories of battle. It provides a refuge for the war- and world-weary:

> But worn with Years, when dire Diseases come,
> Then hide his not Ignoble Age, at Home:
> In Peace t' enjoy his former Palms and Pains;
> And gratefully be kind to his Remains.[29]
> (3.151–154)

Here, Dryden translates the poem's encouragement of quiet retirement for Cyllarus, a "fiery Courser" (130) who, "trembling with Delight" (132) at the sounds of war, spent his life "bear[ing] his Rider headlong on the Foe" (140). Dryden adds "peace" to Virgil's *abde domo, nec turpi ignosce senectae* (3.96), augmenting the image of graceful aging already present in the Latin. Although Cyllarus has long loved the thrill and gore of the battlefield, the *Georgics* nevertheless allow him an opportunity to retire in peace, "at Home." The poem, like its dedication, does not condemn those who have been to war or participated in public life, but it does insist that they can only live peacefully in a place where knowledge of the wheatfield trounces knowledge of the battlefield.

The English poet's final two additions of "peace" occur in close proximity to one another; in fact, before their appearance, the two closest instances of "peace" belonged to the description of the "peaceful Ground" and the "peaceful Flood." There, seven lines separated the two images. In the following example, "peaceful" follows a mere three lines after "peace," perhaps implying that the original peace may not be as inaccessible as suggested previously:

Thus have I sung of Fields, and Flocks, and Trees,
And of the waxen Work of lab'ring Bees;
While mighty *Caesar*, thund'ring from afar,
Seeks on *Euphrates* Banks the Spoils of War:
With conq'ring Arms asserts his Country's Cause,
With Arts of Peace the willing People draws:
On the glad Earth the Golden Age renews,
And his great Father's Path to Heav'n pursues:
While I at *Naples* pass my peaceful Days,
Affecting Studies of less noisy Praise;
And bold, through Youth, beneath the Beechen Shade,
The Lays of Shepherds, and their Loves have plaid.

(4.807–818)

The poem concludes with a scene of simultaneous activity. The poet was singing—*canebam* (559)—"While"—*dum* (560)—Caesar was waging war. Although these activities happen at the same time, they are carried out by different agents, and to different ends. In Dryden's translation, however, the word "peace" adheres to the work of the poet and to that of the conqueror, despite the distinction between the two that appears in the Latin and persists in the English.

The "Arts of Peace" are Dryden's invention. When placed so near to the poet's "peaceful Days," the contrast between a conqueror's peace and a farmer's peace becomes remarkably clear. Virgil's poet enjoys days *oti* (564)—at leisure or rest—which of course must imply peacefulness. Yet given the frequency with which Dryden chooses "peace" when the Latin referent might have been translated by any number of other words, this final instance cannot have been a careless choice. L. P. Wilkinson explains Augustus's presence at the end of Virgil's poem in this way: "Here for the first time we hear proclaimed the Augustan ideal of empire, *paci imponere morem*."[30] When Dryden makes use of the phrase "Arts of Peace," he subtly acknowledges the coerciveness of imperial peace, despite having described the conquered peoples as "willing"—an adjective I take to be tinged with irony. Dryden's *Georgics* insist on a difference between the conqueror's and the poet's capacities for making peace, and offer representations of stability detached from success on the battlefield.

Whereas scholars of the classics continue to debate the nature of the relationship between the poet and the warrior at the end of the Latin *Georgics*, Dryden has driven a decisive wedge between the two. In the final moments of the fourth book, the "Arts of Peace" signify Octavian's political attempts to end the civil wars. When Dryden repeats the phrase in his *Dedication of the Aeneis*, it gains further signification: the "Arts of Peace" become more than the art of ending war; they come to mean poetry produced by a writer who understands the imperial expectation that artistic productions will foster obedience rather than dissent.

Understanding, however, does not necessarily beget complicity. As scholars of both Latin and English literature have shown, Virgil's poems tend not to endorse or reject outright the idea of empire. They do, however, ask difficult questions about how centralized power can create peace, at what price, and with what degree of success. Dryden senses these questions in Virgil's *Georgics* and brings them to the fore in his own translation, but that translation also reflects a conversation of profound importance in seventeenth- and eighteenth-century England. Decade after decade, wars recurred at home and abroad, but decade after decade, its poets contemplated peace.

FROM PEACE TO WAR: THE *AENEIS*

Read alone, Dryden's *Georgics* suggest some degree of hope about the kind of peace that might be made and maintained. Yet of course, Virgil's body of work does not end here, and as we turn from the fourth georgic to the first book of the *Aeneis*, we find a dramatic indictment of the whole political state. In his translation of the epic, Dryden indicates disappointment not only with the ruling classes, but also with the people subject to those rulers. In his translated epic, Dryden asks us to consider the origins of war and the forces that prevent peace from being fully achieved. Whereas his *Georgics* offer a certain degree of hope, his *Aeneis* largely turns away from such sentiments.

As is well known, the *Aeneid* was made public only after Virgil's death, and against his wishes. The poem considers the crystallization of imperial power under Augustus: it looks backward, at the ancient adventures of Aeneas, in order to laud and to advise the emperor as he takes control of Rome. In contemplating the poet's attitudes about this nascent power, one scholar urges us to acknowledge "the fervor of Vergil's hope in the Augustan empire. To one whose boyhood and early manhood had been ravaged by the seemingly endless violence of the civil wars, the promise of peace and order was among the intensest of wishes."[31] Although many of his subsequent readers, from the medieval to postmodern eras, assumed the poet's complicity with the Augustan regime, others as distinct in time from Dryden himself to classicists writing concurrently with the brutalities of twentieth-century wars have exposed many passages where the epic communicates apprehensions about the burgeoning political stability under Augustus.[32]

The opening scene of the *Aeneid*, of course, is anything but peaceful. The sea, having been whipped into a frenzy at Juno's behest, tosses the Trojan fleet so fiercely that it might have been swallowed up by waves had Neptune not noticed their peril. In Dryden's English, Neptune pacifies the raging waters as though he were calming a riotous mob:

> As when in Tumults rise th' ignoble Crowd,
> Mad are their Motions, and their Tongues are loud;
> And Stones and Brands in ratling Vollies fly,
> And all the Rustick Arms that Fury can supply:
> If then some grave and Pious Man appear,
> They hush their Noise, and lend a list'ning Ear;
> He sooths with sober Words their angry Mood,
> And quenches their innate Desire of Blood:
> So when the Father of the Flood appears,
> And o're the Seas his Sov'raign Trident rears,
> Their Fury falls: He skims the liquid Plains,
> High on his Chariot, and with loosen'd Reins,
> Majestick moves along, and awful Peace maintains.
>   (1.213–225)

The images of the violent mob and the sober man come directly from Virgil's poem, where the *gravem virum*—or dignified man—mollifies the *animos* and *pectora*, the minds and the hearts, of the crowd, which *saevit*, or rages, as a wild mass (1.151, 153, 149).[33] The comparison in both poems between turbulent seas and frenzied rioters lends concrete definition to the stormy waters, of course, but it also works in the opposite direction: this image suggests that social unrest and peace arise from the same changeable material. The mob transforms into states of agitation or calm by the influence of such external forces as Juno's wrath or Neptune's tranquility.

Dryden, however, accuses the mob of harboring an "innate Desire of Blood," and therefore of bearing some responsibility for social disorder and destruction. This phrase is perhaps a slight extension of *saevit*, but no words for "blood," "bloody," or "bloodthirsty" appear in the Latin. Moreover, his special attention to "Rustick Arms" perhaps also suggests such midcentury factions as the Levellers or club-men, or the rural laborers who had supported the rebellion raised by the Duke of Monmouth in 1685. But at the very least this image captures the sudden, changeable whims of a mob willing to attack with whatever implements they might have nearby. By ascribing to the mob a natural tendency toward violent rage, Dryden's text conflicts somewhat with the Latin poem. There, the interloping Juno requests that Aeolus stir the seas into a violent storm—the ocean does not incite itself into a tempest—but Neptune, the divine embodiment of watery nature, prefers a calm realm. Virgil accuses the mob of being *ignobile*, or base, but he does not charge it with an inborn taste for blood. For Virgil, the gods themselves manifest tendencies against or toward order.[34] In Dryden's hands the verb *saevit*, used in the *Georgics* for the impious Mars himself, becomes an explicitly human manifestation of the abstract qualities that the gods, from their positions on high, represent.[35] Therefore, although it may be tempting to read Dryden's phrase as a rather typical example of his career-long tendency to disparage the rabble, I understand it as a redirection of Virgil's epic for the purpose of exploring with greater scrutiny the origins of war. The mob's "innate Desire for Blood" betrays its penchant for violence, and as a result its culpability for the problems of history. In both the Latin and the English poems, the origins and vicissitudes of battle belong to larger conflicts waged among the gods, but Dryden's translation makes careful adjustments that suggest human forces bear much—or even most—of the blame for the horrors of war.

As he sharpens this sense of repulsion from the disorderly mob, Dryden also heightens the representation of Neptune as a benevolent king. The sea god restores the calmness of the ocean with a wave of his trident, the image of which Dryden places just before a triplet, underscoring its three-pronged power to spread peace. Virgil refers to Neptune as a *genitor*, connoting a father or begetter, so Dryden makes him the "Father of the Flood." But in the English poem the trident is "Sov'raign," and the god himself receives such regal adjectives as "Majestick" and "awful." Both Virgil and Dryden load their poems with gestures meant subtly to advise or criticize real men in power, but here Dryden makes the passage more immediately political than it may be in the Latin.

With the ocean pacified, Aeneas and his men arrive safely onshore in Libya, where they begin to feast on *Cererem corruptam undis* (1.177)—corn corrupted by waves—or, for Dryden, "Corn infected with the Brine" (1.253). During this moment of relative tranquility, Aeneas comforts his men by reminding them that despite the travails they have suffered, stability awaits them. He concludes with an abbreviated version of the prophecy that Jove will relate to Venus later in the same book:

> per varios casus, per tot discrimina rerum
> tendimus in Latium, sedes ubi fata quietas
> ostendunt; illic fas regna resurgere Troiae.
> durate, et vosmet rebus servate secundis.
> (1.204–207)

> (Through various calamities, through so many crises, we press on towards Latium, where the fates show a restful place; there the divine reign of the Trojans will be restored. Endure, and protect yourselves for favorable things.)

Yet at the same time that Aeneas promises a new Troy, Virgil's narrator notes that the ostensibly confident and hopeful leader is *curisque ingentibus aeger*, or made ill by profound apprehensions. From his position atop a hill, Aeneas can assert himself as a leader of men, but he cannot see confidently into the future; even worse, his memories of the violent challenges only recently surpassed invade his faith in the prosperity and renewal that the gods have promised. Neither the epic nor Virgil's other poems can offer peace for human beings unmarred by the violence that has preceded it or that threatens to dismantle it; the mythological golden age, a time of truly innocent peace, remains always out of reach.

In contrast to the beleaguered Aeneas, Jove can indeed foresee and foretell the future prosperity of the Trojans and the victories of Augustus. Although in the Latin text Aeneas simply credits the *fata*—fates—with having directed the Trojans toward *quietas*, or peaceful rest, Dryden also mentions Jove by name, as if gesturing toward the coming prophecy. Moreover, by making explicit mention of the god, the English translation reinforces the relative impotence of Aeneas—and by extension, of human beings more generally. In this version of the speech, the god can "foredoom," but the man can only hope:

> An Hour will come, with Pleasure to relate
> Your Sorrows past, as Benefits of Fate.
> Through various Hazards, and Events we move
> To *Latium*, and the Realms foredoom'd by *Jove*:
> Call'd to the Seat, (the Promise of the Skies,)
> Where *Trojan* Kingdoms once again may rise.
> Endure the Hardships of your present State,
> Live, and reserve yourselves for better Fate.
> (1.283–290)

Whereas Virgil's Aeneas reassures his men with promises of peaceful possessions (*sedes . . . quietas*) and happier times to follow (*rebus . . . secundis*), Dryden's offers no explicit guarantee of rest or happiness, only the implied prosperity of a kingdom rebuilt—a vision troubled by the uncertainty of the auxiliary verb "may." The "better Fate" to come rhymes with the "present State" in the previous line; this rhyme is one of the most common in Dryden's translation of the epic, along with "cease"/"peace." These rhyming pairs often work against one another; here, for instance, despite the fact that the couplet resolves with a "better Fate," its pairing with "present State" reminds the men that the only thing they know for sure is their present suffering, derived from the recent war and dangerous sea voyage. True restfulness resides somewhere in the very uncertain future; Dryden's line, imitating a pattern of movement that dominates much of Virgil, sends us backward.

As Aeneas and the Trojans prepare to rest on the Lybian shore, Jove happens to notice them:

> Et iam finis erat, cum Iuppiter aethere summo
> despiciens mare velivolum terrasque iacentis
> litoraque et latos populos, sic vertice caeli
> constitit et Libyae defixit lumina regnis.
> atque illum talis iactantem pectore curas
> tristior et lacrimis oculos suffusa nitentis
> adloquitur Venus:
>
> (1.223–229)

Here Dryden rather uncharacteristically matches the Latin nearly line for line, answering Virgil's six and a half hexameters with seven pentameters:

> The Day, but not their Sorrows, ended thus.
> When, from aloft, Almighty *Jove* surveys
> Earth, Air, and Shoars, and navigable Seas,
> At length on *Lybian* Realms he fix'd his Eyes:
> Whom, pond'ring thus on Human Miseries,
> When *Venus* saw, she with a lowly Look,
> Not free from Tears, her Heav'nly Sire bespoke.
>
> (1.307–313)

In this passage, Dryden makes explicit the contrast between the human and divine realms established by Virgil. The heightening of this distinction extends the earlier contrast between the peace-granting Neptune—whom Dryden takes care to describe as "High in his Chariot"—and the ocean, represented in both the Latin and English poems as an unruly crowd of people. Here, Dryden also amplifies Virgil's simpler *iam finis erat*—"now all was ended"—with "The Day, but not their Sorrows, ended thus"; in Dryden's phrase, the losses mourned by Aeneas in the preceding lines reverberate into the present passage. A few lines later, Dryden extrapolates "Human Miseries" from Virgil's *curas*; by specifying "Human" suffering, Dryden both emphasizes the persistence of pain caused by war and sharpens the contrast between Aeneas and the god already heightened by his rendering of the soldier's speech to his men. The cares of Aeneas make up only a part of Jove's total survey, which spans oceans and civilizations, encompassing the entire world in all times and places. Although depicted only briefly, the god's vast purview, which comes at last to settle upon Aeneas, partially undermines the drama of the prophecy he later imparts to Venus.

Sensing the weight of her human son's cares, the goddess beseeches Jove to grant her a vision of the future. He acquiesces, describing the victories that Aeneas and his long line of descendants will achieve in war, and promising that even Juno will someday make peace with the new Troy. The Latin construction *mecumque*—"and with me"—intensifies the future alliance between Juno and Jove as they smile upon the Roman Empire. Under the unified aegis of the gods, the prophecy claims, Augustus will rule an expansive state bounded only by the limits of the earth itself. This vision grants the Romans under Augustus a purview approaching the magnitude of Jove's, which the poet takes care to emphasize as the eyes of the god come to rest upon Aeneas and his men. In this moment, Jove's vision foretells an age when Augustus will see the world with the eyes of a god, and will preside almost as powerfully.

Finally, the prophecy models peace as a state in which the forces of war have been restrained within the Temple of Janus:

> aspera tum positis mitescent saecula bellis;
> cana Fides et Vesta, Remo cum fratre Quirinus
> iura dabunt; dirae ferro et compagibus artis
> claudentur Belli portae; Furor impius intus
> saeva sedens super arma et centum vinctus aënis
> post tergum nodis fremet horridus ore cruento.
> (1.291–296)

> (Then the harsh times will grow mild, with wars having been set down; wise Faith and Vesta, and Quirinus with his brother Remus will impart the laws; awful with iron and narrow structures, the gates of war will be closed; inside, Furor, sitting upon fierce weapons, and bound behind his back by one hundred bronze knots, will rage, frightful, with a bloody mouth.)

Here, the prophecy does not quite suggest that the age of peace under Augustus will be a golden one. Virgil makes no mention of *pax, otium, quietas, concordia*, or any other word with a positive meaning. Even at his most hopeful, he avoids depicting the end of war with any real specificity. Yet although the line *aspera tum positis mitescent saecula bellis* guarantees nothing but the cessation of war, it does harbor the subtlest hint of an alternative, georgic peace: the verb *mitescere* communicates the idea of making harshness mild, but it can also mean the bringing of fruit into ripened maturity. Perhaps this sense of the verb motivates Dryden's decision to heighten the idea of peace arising as the result of a softening process in his translation of the passage:

> Then dire Debate, and impious War shall cease,
> And the stern Age be softened into Peace:
> Then banish'd Faith shall once again return,

And Vestal Fires in hallow'd Temples burn;
And *Remus* with *Quirinus* shall sustain
The righteous Laws, and Fraud and Force restrain.
Janus himself before his Fane shall wait,
And keep the dreadful issues of his Gate,
With Bolts and Iron Bars: within remains
Imprison'd Fury, bound in brazen Chains:
High on a Trophie rais'd, of useless Arms,
He sits, and threats the World with vain Alarms.

(1.380–407)[36]

The first two lines, which render Virgil's *aspera tum positis mitescent saecula bellis*, are of particular relevance here: words signifying harshness and war occupy the beginning and end of the Latin line, which holds near its center the verb that promises the milder age to come. As the line proceeds from left to right, it offers a respite only in its middle; by the time it reaches its end, it has turned its focus once again to war, even if that war has ended. The "cease"/"Peace" rhyme in Dryden's corresponding couplet, "Then dire Debate, and impious War shall cease, / And the stern Age be softened into Peace," enacts a similar trajectory. By adding the phrase "dire Debate," Dryden redirects the Latin line, which describes a more general age of bitterness, in such a way that it may in English be gesturing toward the factional discord of the later seventeenth century. Dryden also adds the word "Peace" here; rooted in the verb *mitescere*, Dryden's phrase "softened into Peace" ostensibly offers a more explicit promise of a stable future than the Latin poem. But in the same way that the Latin line insists on ending with *bellis*, and therefore offers no complete respite from the memory of war, the echo of "cease" in the second line's "Peace" erodes the hope attempting to materialize at the end of the couplet. The couplet may be a neatly measured one, but its orderly surface envelops discord and counterpoint: as in *Upon Appleton House*, here peace arrives burdened with the knowledge of what has ceased.

In the same way that the Latin hexameter and English couplet offer formally complete containers for unstable, and even volatile, contents, the prophecy itself concludes with an image of discord contained, but not destroyed. Under Augustus, *Furor impius*—impious Rage, or, in Dryden's translation, Fury—will be imprisoned, impotent and seething, within the Temple of Janus. The Latin representation of *Furor impius*, perched atop *saeva arma*, recalls the image of active war loosed upon the earth in the *Georgics'* first book, when impious Mars rages over the whole world (*saeuit toto Mars impius orbe* [511]). Moreover, this image establishes another point of connection within Virgil's poetic corpus; these connections are not arbitrary, but rather signify a network of interrelated meditations on peace and the war. Although the *Georgics* present a model of viable, accessible peace, the same raging war continues to pose a threat.

In translating the prophecy's conclusion, Dryden transforms an image of bloody violence into one that more forcefully communicates the risk that peace may fail to hold. Dryden at first appears to lessen the gruesomeness of the prophecy's final image; in place of the *ore cruento*, or bloodstained mouth, Dryden's Fury "threats the World with vain Alarms." Whereas Virgil stresses the recent memory of bloodshed, the evidence of which limns the mouth of his *Furor*, Dryden depicts a seething being shouting threats to his captors. Although these "vain" words have no immediate effect, they nevertheless suggest a persistent will to do harm again.

Even the doors of the temple enclosing this furious figure reinforce the mutability and contingency of peace, since a closed door, no matter how heavy, can always be opened up again. Yet the prophecy of Jove intensifies the degree to which the door itself poses a threat to peace: the warlike impulses housed within it can only ever be contained and controlled; they remain, bound yet alive and enraged, within the very structures of peace. Dryden crafts his translation in such a way as to amplify the troubled peace that pervades the Latin epic, which offers no true respite from war. Although the *Georgics* inhabit a time after the narrative of the *Aeneid*, such a position can suggest peacefulness only because it has yet to be subjected to future events. In this way, the *Georgics* resemble the Temple of Janus: they contain war by constructing peace after battle has ceased, despite the fact that the remnants of war remain bound within the tools and processes of agricultural labor.

Dryden's translation of the *Georgics* is keenly attuned to the complex balance of conditions that Virgil proposes as the makings of a peaceful life: deep awareness of natural cycles, arduous yet productive labor, and sheer distance from battle. The *Georgics* do not advise oblivion, nor do they place naïve hope in a future without conflict. Yet they do propose a form of positively defined peace, as opposed to the negative peace—or, even, the not-war—with which the *Aeneid* begins. Rather than simply impose his own concerns about the obstacles to peace plaguing seventeenth-century England, Dryden uses the various forms of Virgilian peace to draw out distinct problems and, particularly in the *Georgics*, to show potential solutions. Although often understood to have initiated the vogue for English georgic poetry, this translation also appeared in the middle of a period in which georgic imagery helped poets challenge the notion that the end of war necessarily signals the beginning of peace. Recall the ideas that adhere to the phrase "Arts of Peace" in Dryden's *Virgil*: those in power take great pains to represent their reigns as the foundations of lasting stability, and art made under such conditions both reflects those aims and tends to find in them the ever-present threat of conflict.

Near the end of his life, Dryden produced his own art of peace: the *Virgil*, produced as a bound book only through the support of subscribers whose politics often disagreed with one another, offers to its English readership a symbol of the meaningful results that can derive from engagements with the past. In Virgil, Dryden found a creative mind neither lulled by peace nor soured by failures to uphold it; he learned from the Roman poet to see peace as labor, a process as simple as it is arduous.

As an alternative art of peace, the georgic offers stability, creativity, and productivity as constant negotiations of violent or destructive impulses. In the next chapter, we will consider a poet who knew Dryden's Virgil, and who also turned to the georgic to articulate a profound sense of having been marked forever by civil conflict. Like Dryden, she offers a qualified form of hope, constructing peace from the remnants of literary and political history.

NOTES

1. Dryden, *Works*, vol. 1.
2. The editors of the University of California edition of Dryden's works note the vituperations leveled against the poet by his enemies—among them Martin Clifford and Alexander Radcliffe—for his ostensibly impossible image of stillness that "invades" (ibid., 220).
3. This chapter includes a revised version of my "The Sword, the Scythe, and the 'Arts of Peace' in Dryden's *Georgics*," which appeared in *Translation and Literature* 23, no. 1 (2014): 23–41.
4. Dryden, *Works*, 5:3–4.
5. In *Dryden and the Traces of Classical Rome*, Paul Hammond suggests the deep sense of belatedness and distance from his own time that motivates much of Dryden's work as a translator; for Hammond, Dryden creates from classical materials a "macaronic space" in which exists "an imagined world composed from both English and Roman materials" (20–21).
6. In a letter to their sons written jointly by Dryden and his wife in the weeks before the treaty was signed, Elizabeth writes that the boys' father "expreses a great desire to see my deare Charlles: and trully I see noe reason why you should not both come together, to be a comfort to woon another. and to us both: if the king of france include Ingland in the peace" (3 September 1697, in *The Letters of John Dryden with Letters Addressed to him*, ed. Charles E. Ward [Durham, NC: Duke University Press, 1942], 95).
7. Most notably, Steven Zwicker has made the poet's political engagements clear by showing the pervasiveness of Jacobite language in his body of work; see *Politics and Language in Dryden's Poetry: The Arts of Disguise* (Princeton, NJ: Princeton University Press, 1984). See also Hammond, *Dryden and the Traces of Classical Rome*, especially chap. 4; Davis, *Translation and the Poet's Life*; Tanya Caldwell, "Honey and Venom: Dryden's Third *Georgic*," *Eighteenth-Century Life* 20, no. 3 (1996): 20–36, and *Time to Begin Anew: Dryden's "Georgics" and "Aeneis"* (Lewisburg: Bucknell University Press, 2000). The foundations of the Tory party itself, of course, rested upon land ownership. The *Georgics*, which offer the olive crop as a symbol of true peacefulness, accommodates the Tory position insofar as it offers a model of life far removed from urban mercantilism.
8. James A. Winn also comments on one of Dryden's insertions of "peace" into the *Georgics* (1, 681) in "'Thy Wars Brought Nothing About': Dryden's Critique of Military Heroism," *The Seventeenth Century* 21, no. 2 (2006): 364–382.

9. Stuart Gillespie, *English Translation and Classical Reception: Towards a New Literary History* (Oxford: Wiley-Blackwell, 2011), 11. See also Robin Sowerby, *The Augustan Art of Poetry: Augustan Translation of the Classics* (Oxford: Oxford University Press, 2006), passim, for sustained treatment of the aesthetic influence of classical translation on Dryden's writing more broadly.

10. The definitive work on the subscribers to the *Virgil* remains the essay by John Barnard, "Dryden, Tonson, and the Patrons of *The Works of Virgil* (1697)," in *John Dryden: Tercentenary Essays*, ed. Paul Hammond and David Hopkins (Oxford: Oxford University Press, 2000), 174–239.

11. Dryden, *Astraea Redux*, line 4, in *Works*, 1:22.

12. See commentary on the preface to *Ovid's Epistles* in Dryden, *Works*, 1:330.

13. Dryden, *Works*, 1:114. Tanya Caldwell has demonstrated the fundamental influence of John Denham on Dryden's notions of translation. See "John Denham and John Dryden," *Texas Studies in Literature and Language* 46, no. 1 (2004): 49–72.

14. The Latin text for all Virgilian poetry—with the *exception* of the *Georgics*, which is quoted from Thomas's edition—is taken from the Loeb Classical Library: *Virgil*, trans. H. T. Rushton Fairclough, rev. ed., ed. G.P. Goold, 2 vols (Cambridge, MA: Harvard University Press, 1986). In all cases in this chapter, quotations from modern editions have been checked against the edition Dryden would have used, *P. Virgilii Maronis Opera Interpretatione et Notis Illustravit Carolus Ruaeus, Soc. Jesu.* (London, 1687). There regularly occur small differences in orthography that do not affect grammatical interpretation, such as "Sylvestrem" in the Ruaeus, for "silvestrem" here (it is also of use to note that when quoting from Thomas, I follow his choice of "u" for "v"). There are also differences in punctuation between the seventeenth- and twentieth-century editions; a closer consideration of these differences may help to explain how Dryden lineated his translation, since he and all other English translators need more words in their own language than Virgil did in his to express a given idea. My primary focus here does not tend toward comparative lineation, so I shall remain largely silent on questions of punctuation between editions.

15. For more specific commentary, see Mario Geymonat, "Capellae at the End of the Eclogues," *Harvard Studies in Classical Philology* 102 (2004): 315–318.

16. For a broader discussion of shades and closure in the Virgilian oeuvre, see Elena Theodorakopoulos, "Closure: The Book of Virgil," in *The Cambridge Companion to Virgil*, ed. Charles Martindale (Cambridge: Cambridge University Press, 2006 [online ed.]. For the connection to the *Georgics* in the concluding moments of the *Eclogues*, see D. F. Kennedy, "Shades of Meaning: Virgil, *Ecl.* 10.75–77," *Liverpool Classical Monthly* 8 (1983): 124.

17. The final line of the *Aeneis* has attracted attention for elevating the violence of Virgil's already gruesome image. Taylor Corse, finding a source for the phrase "disdainful Soul" in the second book of Spenser's *Faerie Queene*, explains the deviation by pointing to a similar line written by Dryden for the death of Mezentius, suggesting that he was recreating the verbal mirroring of the deaths of Turnus and Camilla in the Latin *Aeneid* (*Dryden's Aeneid: The English Virgil* [Newark: University of Delaware Press, 1991]), 25–26. Tanya Caldwell reads the death of Camilla in Dryden more generously, positing verbal echoes there, too, but accounts for the major differences between the final lines of the English and Latin poems by reading them as another instance of Dryden's habit of inserting into his translations his own attitudes about the problems of late seventeenth-century England. For Caldwell, "it is perhaps possible to feel that along with Turnus's, the poet's own 'disdainful Soul' has come 'rushing thro' the Wound.'" *Time to Begin Anew*, 178.

18. Dryden, *Works*, 5:278. Like most of the longer essay from which it derives, this passage is shot through with terms meant to evoke English politics of the civil war and Restoration periods.

19. Ibid., 281.
20. For an alternative reading of Dryden's *Aeneid* and its connections to William of Orange, see Paul Hammond, "Dryden's Virgilian Kings," *The Seventeenth Century* 29, no. 2 (2014): especially 154–155.
21. James Winn, *John Dryden and His World* (New Haven, CT: Yale University Press, 1987), 479.
22. Such a redirection also reflects Dryden's ever-growing interest in Epicureanism and disillusionment with court politics. See Hammond, "The Integrity of Dryden's Lucretius," *Modern Language Review* 78 (1983): 1–23. In his biography of Dryden, Winn also points to instances of Epicurean language both in the *Dedication* discussed here and in earlier writings.
23. Hammond, *Dryden and the Traces of Classical Rome*, 200.
24. For a discussion of this passage in relation to Dryden's *Works of Virgil* and its subscribers' political leanings, see Winn, *John Dryden and His World*, 480, and Barnard, "Dryden, Tonson, and the Patrons of *The Works of Virgil.*"
25. Virgil, *Virgil's Georgicks Englished*, trans. May, 25.
26. Virgil, *The Works of Publius Virgilius Maro Translated, adorn'd with Sculpture, and illustrated with Annotations*, trans. John Ogilby (London, 1654), 85. In the first edition of 1649, the lines read, "To the scorn'd Plow, no man doth honour yield, / Swains prest to arms, waste lies th' uncultured field" (56).
27. Virgil, *Virgil's Georgicks Englished*, trans. May, 25.
28. Virgil, *Works of Publius Virgilius Maro Translated*, trans. Ogilby, 85. This line is unaltered from the first edition.
29. This passage also recalls Dryden's "To my Dear Friend Mr. Congreve," in which the older poet, having retired from "th' Ungrateful Stage," beseeches the younger to "Be kind to my Remains":

> Already I am worn with Cares and Age;
> And just abandoning th' Ungrateful Stage . . .
> But You, whom ev'ry Muse and Grace adorn,
> Whom I foresee to better Fortune born,
> Be kind to my Remains; and oh defend,
> Against Your Judgment Your departed Friend!
> (66–67, 70–33; *Works*, 4:434)

For additional discussion of these two passages, see Davis, *Translation and the Poet's Life*, 168–169n3.
30. Wilkinson, *The Georgics of Virgil: A Critical Survey* (Cambridge: Cambridge University Press, 1969), 173.
31. Charles P. Segal, "'Aeternum per Saecula Nomen,' the Golden Bough and the Tragedy of History: Part I," *Arion* 4, no. 4 (1965): 617.
32. For Segal, the epic expresses "a pessimism about the cost of history, an acute sensitivity to the suffering of the individuals who participate in it" (ibid., 618). More recently, Craig Kallendorf has proposed "another Virgil" inherited by early modern Europe, one less complicit with the hegemonic structures of empire and classical educational systems, and more amenable to writers who had reason to doubt such institutions. Whereas Kallendorf treats the *Aeneid* almost exclusively, his ideas are relevant to the *Georgics* as well (*The Other Virgil: "Pessimistic" Readings of the "Aeneid" in Early Modern Culture* [Oxford: Oxford University Press, 2007], 14). S. J. Harrison provides a useful overview of the shifting perceptions of the *Aeneid* across the twentieth century, noting the distinctive turn toward darker or more ambiguous readings at midcentury, in "Some Views of the *Aeneid* in the Twentieth Century," in *Oxford Readings in Vergil's "Aeneid,"* ed. S. J. Harrison (Oxford: Oxford University Press, 1990).

33. In the *Aeneid* only, the line numbers in modern editions and that of Ruaeus do not agree; the earlier text includes four additional lines at the beginning of the poem not generally accepted by modern scholars as truly Virgilian.
34. See Segal, "'Aeternum per Saecula Nomen,'" 626.
35. Virgil also uses the word *saevae* as he introduces Juno in the early lines of the epic: *saevae memorem Iunonis ob iram* (1.4).
36. In *Dryden and the Traces of Classical Rome*, Paul Hammond suggests a link between the image of Fury "High on a Trophie rais'd" and Satan in *Paradise Lost* perched "High on a throne of royal state"; see chap. 4, n125.

3

CONTINGENCY

The Georgic Poetry of Anne Finch

Among the readers of Dryden's *Virgil* was the poet Anne Kingsmill Finch, whose husband Heneage was a two-guinea subscriber to the translation. By 1697, when the volume was published, Finch was living in Kent at Eastwell, the home of Heneage's nephew Charles, fourth Earl of Winchilsea. The Finches had settled there after the Revolution of 1688, during which King James II was forced into exile while his daughter, Mary, and her husband, the Dutch William of Orange, gained the throne. Anne had served as a maid of honor to James's wife, and Heneage had been a groom of the bedchamber, but in the wake of the Revolution Settlement, they found themselves on the political periphery. The Finches remained loyal to the ousted Stuarts: as dedicated Jacobites and nonjurors, they refused to pledge allegiance to William III, a king who expressed little interest in the arts and preferred instead to wage expensive, yearly battles against France. Although Anne had begun to write poetry during her time at court, the political upheavals of the late 1680s spurred her to write much more prolifically and across a broader range of subjects and styles. Her biographer, Barbara McGovern, has made a strong case for the hypothesis that Finch received an unusually full education, including contact with classical literature.[1] It is possible that Finch could read Latin, and certainly true that she knew ancient writers in English translations.

Finch no doubt appreciated the Jacobite resonances of Dryden's *Virgil*, but she explicitly praised its broader literary value. In her poem "All is Vanity," she contrasts Virgil's illustrious English translator with hack writers unduly impressed by their own small achievements:

> Like *Maro*, coulds't thou justly claim,
>   Amongst th'inspired tuneful Race,
> The highest Room, the undisputed Place;

And after near Two Thousand Years of Fame,
Have thy proud Work to a new People shown;
    Th' unequal'd Poems made their own,
In such a Dress, in such a perfect Stile
As on his Labours *Dryden* now bestows,
As now from *Dryden*'s just Improvement flows,
    In every polish'd Verse throughout the *British* Isle;
                    (184–193)[2]

Having earlier in the poem leveled her attack in agricultural terms, deeming the writer who cultivates "Palms" and "Bays" in honor of himself a "Deluded Wretch! grasping at future Praise" (173–177), Finch rebukes him here for coveting a reputation as lasting as that of Virgil and as worthy of such a translator as the former laureate. Crucially, however, in turning to Dryden, Finch makes a broader statement about literature and language. Dryden's was of course not the first English translation of Virgil, but it was certainly the most widely celebrated, and Finch, like other contemporary readers, understood its deeper significances: if the paramount poems of antiquity could be rendered into English couplets, then perhaps English, too, could generate similarly enduring literature.[3]

By couching her praise for Virgil and Dryden—and her disregard for hollow ambition—in poetry, Finch suggests the strength of her commitment to promoting and shaping the conversation between ancient poetry and the literature of her own moment. In order to demonstrate more completely the implications of these commitments, I turn in this chapter to one of her best-known poems, *The Petition for an Absolute Retreat*, reading it in conversation with Virgil's *Georgics*. In this meditation on the making and keeping of a peaceful life, Finch draws from the language of agriculture to exert poetic control over the illogic and turbulence that Stuart sympathizers experienced during the reign of William III.

More specifically, *The Petition* engages in a subtle but significant way with the second book of the *Georgics*, which takes as its point of departure the care and keeping of plants: raising vines, selecting healthy soil, and grafting trees. In relating these practices, Virgil finds analogues for war, history, and his own creative potential. The second book establishes deep connections between poetic, political, and agricultural work, but at the heart of these connections lies the problem of contingency: Virgil imagines the destructive power of storms to undermine the diligent work of the farmer, but he also extends these terms to consider the forces that perpetually threaten both political peace and poetic achievement. The second book of the *Georgics* knits these contingencies together, insisting upon their fundamental connectedness. The same intertwined threats inform Finch's vision of peace in *The Petition for an Absolute Retreat*, which points to poetic creation as a conditional yet potentially powerful challenge to political failure. Articulating friendship and political solidarity in terms of viticulture, Finch invokes the lessons on both contingency and survival imparted by the second book of the *Georgics*.

When *The Petition for an Absolute Retreat* has been considered in relation to classical poetry, the connections have usually been Horatian rather than Virgilian, with much attention focused on reverberations of the *beatus ille* tradition known, as one scholar has put it, "for the tag line, 'Happy the Man,' or, in this case, 'Happy the Woman.'"[4] Of course, in the second book of the *Georgics*, after Virgil has treated the vine and other trees at length, he commences his own famous praise of the "happy husbandmen," who live *fortunatos nimium*, or "too happy." Although these blissful farmers were sometimes taken by later readers and imitators to be emblematic of the poem's ultimate attitudes, classicists have long warned against this reading. When read in relation to Virgil's account of the dawning Iron Age—along with most of the rest of the *Georgics*—this idyllic vision reveals itself as an anomaly, not a metonymy.[5] Even more significantly, Virgil distinguishes himself from the contented farmers, who live happily precisely because they lack comprehensive knowledge: in contrast, he declares that his greatest achievement would be to know—and then to communicate through art—the workings of the universe:

> Me uero primum dulces ante omnia Musae,
> quarum sacra fero ingenti percussus amore,
> accipiant caelique uias et sidera monstrent,
> defectus solis uarios lunaeque labores;
> unde tremor terris, qua ui maria alta tumescant
> obicibus ruptis rursusque in se ipsa residant,
> quid tantum Oceano properent se tinguere soles
> hiberni, uel quae tardis mora noctibus obstet.
> (2.475–482)

> (Truly may the sweet Muses, whose sacred vessels I bring, accept me, struck with great love, and show me the ways of the skies and the stars, the many eclipses of the sun and the labors of the moon; from where the earthquake, where the strength of the sea grows, and having ruptured obstacles settles down into itself, why suns in winter hurry so much to dip into the ocean, or what hindrance opposes long nights.)

The grammatical forms here recall the opening lines of book 1, when the poet uses a series of relative clauses to declare that he will begin by singing the "what," "when," and "how" of agricultural labor. Read alongside this passage, the verb *incipiam*—"I will begin"—becomes all the more resonant. The work of raising crops and tending cattle is only the point from which the *Georgics* proceeds; the larger project here is learning and knowing. There is a deeply ethical quality to this task—in seeking the causes of both good and ill effects, the poet can begin to make sense of thunderstorms, harvests, plague, power, war, or any other difficult aspect of life on earth.

Although Virgil declares the pursuit of knowledge as the most worthy of human efforts, he never promises total success, and even suggests that such an achievement may not be desirable.[6] Human beings ought constantly to expand their knowledge, but they must accept that many things will remain beyond their powers of comprehension. According to this view, a healthy dose of humility prevents hubristic failure:

> felix, qui potuit rerum cognoscere causas,
> atque metus omnis et inexorabile fatum
> subiecit pedibus strepitumque Acherontis auari.
> fortunatus et ille, deos qui nouit agrestis,
> Panaque Siluanumque senem Nymphasque sorores.
> illum non populi fasces, non purpura regum
> flexit et infidos agitans Discordia fratres,
> aut coniurato descendens Dacus ab Histro,
> non res Romanae peritura que regna; neque ille
> aut doluit miserans inopem aut inuidit habenti.
> quos rami fructus, quos ipsa uolentia rura
> sponte tulere sua, carpsit, nec ferrea iura
> insanumque forum aut populi tabularia uidit.
>
> (2.490–502)

(Happy is he who is able to know the causes of things, and casts all fear, and inexorable fate, and the noise of greedy Acheron underfoot. And fortunate is he, who knows the gods of the countryside, Pan and old Silvanus and the sisters, the nymphs. The fasces of the people, the regal purple do not bend him, nor does the discord agitating unfaithful brothers, nor the Dacian descending from the river Danube, not the matters of Rome and not the ruined reigns; nor does he feel pain for the poor or feel envy for the wealthy. What fruit of the branch, what the willing country itself spontaneously brings forth, he seizes; he does not see the iron law and the wild forum or the record-office of the people.)

Much of this passage resonates with Finch's *Petition*—the plucking of seasonal fruit, the distance from public life. Her speaker has much in common with Virgil's *felix*, or happy one, whose knowledge grants him the power to achieve victory over the seemingly unpredictable and powerful force of fate. Yet because the challenge of knowing the causes of things is a steep one, Virgil offers an alternative path to happiness: a deep sense of humility. The *Georgics* represent the farmer as one who attempts to align human behavior with the causes and effects of nature, as well as one who maintains the utmost reverence for the "woodland gods" whose favor supports agricultural success. Aside from the blissful laborer of the *fortunatos* passage, Virgil's farmers live happily not as a result of naïveté, but because their lives are not dictated by dramatic shifts in political power. By synchronizing the rhythms of his life with those of nature, the farmer can actively enter into this grander and more stable temporality.

Finch's poem depends on the same appreciation for the power of aligning human action with natural cycles, and like Virgil's *Georgics*, it also links the making of poetry to the process of reckoning with history. Invoking both British and ancient history in her *Petition*, Finch indicates the power with which the past both informs and intrudes upon the present. Although much of the poem revels in dreams of a life that resembles the golden age renewed, its fundamentally uncertain structures preclude a wholly earnest interpretation. Reading *The Petition*, we are urged to remember that although Finch does not permanently inhabit a pastoral idyll, she is capable of creating and maintaining one in her mind, and on the page.

A VIRGILIAN RETREAT

In *The Petition for an Absolute Retreat*, Finch envisions a peaceable space removed from the disappointments of public life. The poem reflects the uncertainties of the years following the Revolution, as Finch sought to recover peace and stability.[7] She inscribed the poem to Catherine, Countess of Thanet, a fellow Jacobite and close friend; both women appear in the poem, though in a manner typical of seventeenth-century women's friendship poetry, Finch calls herself "Ardelia," and refers to Catherine as "Arminda." This renaming has several effects: it links Finch's poem to the political friendship poetry of Katherine Philips,[8] but like the works of Philips, it also reaches back into classical pastoral, a mode that in its deepest origins explores the fundamental artificiality of poetry, as well as the contingent conditions that make poetic creation possible.[9] Recall that in his first eclogue, Virgil—rewriting Theocritus—envisions a conversation between two shepherds, one of whom has recently been evicted from his land, which will presumably be occupied soon by a Roman soldier who has been rewarded for his service. Tityrus, who has been allowed to retain his position in the countryside, offers the unfortunate Meliboeus food, shelter, and song, but both men know the protection can only last for a short time. From their very beginning, the *Eclogues*—which would come to shape the pastoral tradition in English poetry more than any other group of poems—make explicit the fragility of poems and poets, and admit the awesome power of Rome, which suggests political power more generally, to threaten, interrupt, or even render powerless a culture's creative minds. Nevertheless, in capturing this knowledge within the artificial world of poetry, Virgil reasserts a degree of control over the world's hostility, countering it first and foremost with a fictional act of hospitality. Evoking this world, Finch infuses her poem with a striking doubleness: the names "Ardelia" and "Arminda" refer both to the fictional inhabitants of the poem's idealized retreat and to the living, breathing women who remain outside the poem. In this way, Finch's difficult realities are eased by their link to the idyllic peace coming into being on the page.[10]

Composed in trochaic tetrameter—a form often associated with charms and spells—the poem begins with a pair of powerful imperatives that reinforce the distance between real and imagined peace. In these early lines, Finch reinforces the drama of unrealized peace by situating the entire poem in a pointedly artificial space:

> Give me O indulgent Fate!
> Give me yet, before I Dye,
> A sweet, but absolute Retreat,
> 'Mongst Paths so lost, and Trees so high,
> That the World may n'er invade,
> Through such Windings and such Shade,
> My unshaken Liberty.
>
> (1–7)

Imploring "Give me" twice, Finch locates the poem distinctly in the present, creating a sharp contrast with the ideal future she implores "indulgent Fate" to grant her.[11] With the imperative verbs here and the many subjunctive verbs to follow in the body of the poem, Finch emphasizes even at the level of grammatical mood the difference between the idea of tranquility, which can be created and enjoyed on the page, and its actual implementation in life, which is much less easily manipulated or maintained by a single human being. Unlike Marvell and his vision of qualified peace at Nun Appleton, Finch specifically calls for an Edenic, "absolute Retreat," hidden by overgrown foliage and permanently disconnected from public life.[12]

In ensuing verse paragraphs, Finch introduces various aspects of life in retreat that align with natural cycles. For instance, she writes first of her plans to eat according to the seasons, consuming food grown on local farms:

Courteous Fate! afford me there
A *Table* spread without my Care,
With what the neigh'bring Fields impart,
Whose cleanliness be all it's Art,
When, of old, the Calf was drest,
(tho' to make an Angel's Feast)
In the plain, unstudied Sauce
Nor *Treufle*, nor *Morillia* was;
Nor cou'd the mighty Patriarch's board
One far-fetch'd *Ortolane* afford.
Courteous Fate, then give me there
Only plain, and wholesome Fare.

(22–33)

Like many of her contemporaries, Finch dismisses the artificiality of fashionable and imported food; following this passage are fourteen lines listing various fruits growing "within my easie Reach" (43) that Finch may pluck and eat.[13] With every line, she broadens the scope of her retreat, so that by the end of this verse paragraph, she has constructed an entire landscape abounding with fruit trees and fertile fields. Repeating this same constructive progression several times in the poem, Finch stages the imaginative making of her peaceful world.

Together, the images that make up the retreat all quite obviously evoke prelapsarian ease: no images of labor appear, and Finch finds many ways to describe the "Unaffected Carelessness" (71) that would define her life in this ideal retreat. Although it may be tempting to read the absence of work as an eliding of the efforts that would support the mistress of an estate, labor is in many ways beside the point for most of the poem, which enacts instead a creative reimagining of the mythical golden age and the biblical Eden, both of which informed much seventeenth-century landscape poetry: in these states, human beings live in harmony with nature, which provides for them without provocation. Only after the transition from gold to iron, or the fall of Adam and Eve, does nature become hostile and demand the relentless labor of cultivation. In aligning her poem with these terms, Finch locates it outside of time, shifting the poem not only away from the urban centers of political power, but also away from human history more broadly considered.

As it dramatizes the imagined unfolding of this peaceful rural space, *The Petition* focuses on what *could* be, as a result of deliberate effort, rather than what *was* or what *is*. Crucially, Finch's paradise exists nowhere but in her mind and on the page. It is at once a vision and a supplication, and it draws heavily from the classical pastoral tradition, sometimes refracted through Milton and Marvell. Yet in occupying an imagined space, the poem also draws attention to the poetic work that generates and sustains its vision of peace. Even at its most vividly descriptive, the poem nevertheless implies its own contingency.

Strikingly, the poem depends on paradoxical premises: although it invokes a world outside of political history, political history itself motivated the writing of it. Had the Revolution of 1688 not occurred, Finch would not have been composing the same kind of peace-seeking poems in the 1690s; in its very title, the poem admits that its speaker can only "petition" for stability: she does not command, realize, or impose. Moreover, although the poem takes up natural, rural subjects, it keeps in view the political forces that wrought the rupture and loss that motivated the turn to those subjects, and by extension it perpetually acknowledges the overwhelming forces preventing a petition from transforming into something tangible.

In this way, Finch, like Dryden, demonstrates a Virgilian sensibility: the *Georgics*, also highly dependent on subjunctive constructions, urge rural laborers to accept the overwhelming force of nature, as well as to accept the cycle of work required for surviving in relation to it.[14] In setting these rules, the poem suggests broader application of the lessons of farming, encouraging the perpetual cultivation of a fruitful life despite the chaotic forces threatening that aim. In Virgil's body of work, images of overwhelming force often suggest the city of Rome and the long shadow it casts across the countryside. The contingencies generated by war and politics threaten to overturn the terms of daily life just as brutally as a storm threatens to uproot carefully tended crops. This point becomes most dramatically clear midway through the *Georgics'* first book, which establishes many of the links between natural and historical forces that will reach their full expression in the second:

> sic omnia fatis
> in peius ruere ac retro sublapsa referri,
> non aliter, quam qui aduerso uix flumine lembum
> remigiis subigit, si brachia forte remisit,
> atque illum in praeceps prono rapit alueus amni.
> (1.199–203)

> (Thus by fate all things run toward the worse, and are brought back collapsed; it is not otherwise than one who, by rowing, hardly manages his boat upstream; if he perhaps relaxes his arms, then at the same time the boat will toss him headlong into the river.)

Long recognized as one of the most deeply negative images in the *Georgics*, this scene makes explicit the sense of threat that undergirds the poem's didactic premise. Fate swirls around the human being, often bringing destruction and failure.

Yet the simple fact of continued human perseverance separates triumph from loss. In a similar way, the act of writing *The Petition for an Absolute Retreat* represents an attempt to go on creating despite serious losses and the threat of future instability. By addressing Fate in the very first line of her poem, Finch assigns a name to the disorienting events that transformed her from a political favorite to an outcast in her own country. In acknowledging the potency of these forces, she begins the process of resisting them.

The strongest force to appear in *The Petition* is the continual sweep of time: Finch looks constantly to the passing of the seasons to dictate the pace of her life, but she also reflects upon the "swiftly flying Time" Adam and Eve spent together before their fall. Near the middle of the poem, she laments the rapid progression of time between youth—"too soon outgrown"—and old age (141). All things move toward their end, she admits; even the "stubborn Oak / Which no Breezes can provoke" (142–143) eventually becomes decrepit and gnarled, overpowered finally by a forceful "Whirlwind" (145).

As the forces of time and weather sweep through the poem, they conjure up for Finch the memory of political destruction: her lament for the shrunken oak also suggests the fall of the Stuarts, for whom the Royal Oak was an important icon, its power increased by the story of Charles II's taking shelter in an oak tree at the battle of Worcester during the English civil war.[15] This image was a popular one among seventeenth-century poets, but Finch may also have found valuable the depiction of this tree in the *Georgics*:

> Forsitan et scrobibus quae sint fastigia quaeras.
> ausim uel tenui uitem committere sulco.
> altior ac penitus terrae defigitur arbos,
> aesculus in primis, quae quantum uertice ad auras
> aetherias, tantum radice in Tartara tendit.
> ergo non hiemes illam, non flabra neque imbres
> conuellunt: immota manet, multosque nepotes
> multa uirum uoluens durando saecula uincit.
> tum fortis late ramos et brachia tendens
> huc illuc, media ipsa ingentem sustinet umbram.
> (2.288–297)

> (And perhaps you will ask what depth there should be for the ditch? I would dare even to commit the vine to a furrow. But deeper in the ground is planted a tree, especially an oak, which stretches as much into the lofty winds as it does down into the underworld. Therefore not winter, nor blasts of wind, nor rain showers overpower it, enduring many ages of men rolling over. Then spreading its strong wide branches and boughs here and there, itself in the middle it sustains a great shadow.)

Here the sturdy trunk of the oak resists both the violence of storms and the passing of long stretches of time, the two forces Finch notes as having withered the oak in her own poem. Virgil's oak roots deeply into the ground, but extends equally high into the air, forming a bridge between the underworld below and the heavens above. This sustained and vivid praise naturally attracted the attention of Jacobite poets: Dryden made good use of this passage in his translation, explicitly connecting the sturdy nature of the oak—here "*Joves* own Tree"—to the strength of an ideal king:

> How deep they must be planted, woud'st thou know?
> In shallow Furrows Vines securely grow.
> Not so the rest of Plants; for *Joves* own Tree,
> That holds the Woods in awful Sov'raignty,
> Requires a depth of Lodging in the Ground;
> And, next the lower Skies, a Bed profound:
> High as his topmost Boughs to Heav'n ascend,
> So low his Roots to Hell's Dominion tend.
> Therefore, nor Winds, nor Winters Rage o'rethrows
> His bulky Body, but unmov'd he grows.
> For length of Ages lasts his happy Reign,
> And Lives of Mortal Man contend in vain.
> Full in the midst of his own Strength he stands,
> Stretching his brawny Arms, and leafy Hands;
> His Shade protects the Plains, his Head the Hills commands.
>   (2.395–410)

In Dryden's English, the ruler of trees, favored by the ruler of gods, represents absolute benevolence and intelligence. The triplet that concludes the passage accentuates the wide sweep of the oak's reign; "Full" and "Stretching," the tree cuts an imposing figure above the open and vulnerable "Plains." Both Virgil and Dryden reinforce the stability of the oak by first contrasting its roots with those of the vine, which extend only into a shallow furrow. This fundamental vulnerability necessitates the support of oaks or other hardy trees.

In her own poem, however, Finch exploits the poetic potential of the relationship between shallowly rooted vines and their sturdy supports: treating the oak as a bridge into the political past, she turns immediately to her memories of defeat by the powerful political forces that brought about swift and permanent political change. Rather than align herself directly with the Stuart oak, she couches her experience in an extended metaphor that emphasizes vulnerability:

> When a helpless Vine is found,
> Unsupported on the Ground,
> Careless all the Branches spread,
> Subject to each haughty Tread,

Bearing neither Leaves, nor Fruit,
Living only in the Root;
Back reflecting let me say,
So the sad *Ardelia* lay;
Blasted by a Storm of Fate,
Felt, thro' all the *British* State;
Fall'n, neglected, lost, forgot,
Dark Oblivion all her Lot;
(150–161)

These lines represent the lowest psychological point in *The Petition*. By describing herself as an "Unsupported" vine, Finch specifically invokes the agricultural practice of binding grapevines to sturdier trees so that they grow properly and bear abundant fruit. She reinforces the "helpless[ness]" of the vine with other deeply negative initial modifiers—"Careless," "Subject to," "Bearing neither." When, at the beginning of the poem, Finch writes that she would live carelessly in retreat, she means to contrast the simplicity and innocence of a rural home with the affectation and foppishness of city life. Here, however, carelessness signifies something much more harmful: the "Careless[ly] . . . spread" limbs suggest that the vine has been left untended, and therefore vulnerable to destructive forces.[16]

This passage may perhaps bring to mind the moment in Milton's *Paradise Lost* when the serpent first catches sight of Eve: "Herself, though fairest unsupported Flow'r, / From her best prop so far, and storm so nigh" (9.432–433).[17] These moments are linked both by the more general image of agricultural propping and by two specific verbal echoes—"unsupported" and "storm"—that reverberate through them. Other passages in *The Petition* also suggest that Finch was thinking about Milton's vision of Eden as she composed this poem, but *Paradise Lost* offers us at best only a partial set of terms for approaching the question of why Finch turns specifically to viticulture—the propping and care of grape vines—when remembering her own devastating losses. Crucially, the "Unsupported" and "Careless" condition of the vine also recalls Virgil's persistent interest in the tending of vineyards.[18]

Of all the plants treated in the *Georgics*, the vine receives some of the poet's most sustained attention. Occupying much of book 2, viticulture is also a primary point of focus in the opening lines of the poem:

Quid faciat laetas segetes, quo sidere terram
uertere, Maecenas, ulmisque adiungere uitis
conueniat, quae cura boum, qui cultus habendo
sit pecori, apibus quanta experientia parcis,
hinc canere incipiam.
(1–4)

(What makes the grain fields happy, when to turn the earth, Maecenas,
and bind the vines to the elms, what care of oxen, how to breed cattle,
how much experience have the economical bees, here I begin to sing.)

From their first appearance, vines represent solidarity. They require the support of
a larger tree—here an elm, though Virgil will later suggest an oak. Some translations render the Latin *conueniat* as "wed," invoking the classical trope in which
the intertwined vine and elm symbolize marriage.[19] Yet the vine represents a more
general sense of camaraderie as well; although the *Georgics* admit that some veg-
etation will spring up uncultivated, and that such plants do possess a particular
kind of hardiness, the poem also advises that a tree growing on its own offers little:
it will grow *infecunda*, or without fruit. Only cultivated orchards, where plants
grow together, will bring forth viable harvests. Lying flat, "Bearing neither Leaves,
nor Fruit, / Living only in the Root," Finch renders herself an isolated vine, one
strong enough to survive, but only in the barest sense. Although once cultivated,
this vine has been left untended, unfruitful, and useless.

The image of the unpropped vine has gone virtually undiscussed in work
on *The Petition*, likely because scholars have been more interested in the conclusion of the scene, in which the uplifting power of the women's friendship saves
Finch from despair.[20] Also not insignificant is the fact that Roger Lonsdale's important anthology of eighteenth-century women's poetry, published in 1989, included
only a truncated version of the poem; comprising the first 128 lines, this excerpt
included all the passages William Wordsworth praised in an essay of 1815, as well
as passages that suggest Finch's reading of Milton and Marvell, but stops well short
of both the section on the vine and the later passages in which Finch turns to
Roman history as a source for lessons on the futility of public ambition.

Yet by representing herself as an unpropped vine, Finch specifically invokes
the plant characterized by the *Georgics* as the one most viscerally connected to war
and history. In the Latin poem, the cultivation of grapes represents the memory
of conflict as well as the constant process of ordering destructive forces into a viable
and profitable crop. For Virgil, the vine is a nexus of war and peace: his *Georgics*
describe viticulture in military terms, as the farmers attack the unruly vines and
arrange them into orderly regiments. The task of handling vines responsibly does
not end with propping, however: the supported vines produce grapes in abundance,
but that fruit also makes the wine that the poem blames for impulsive madness
and violence (2.454–457). The vine thus represents discipline, moral uprightness,
and mutual support, but it also suggests the threat of chaos. Every step—propping,
reaping, vintning, consuming, and propping again the following season—demands

careful and responsible action. But if performed well, these actions give rise to a benevolent and valuable product, and diffuse the threat of degeneration and violence.

Recall that in Finch's poem, degeneration occurs suddenly and violently. The vine has not simply fallen away from its prop, but has been "Blasted by a Storm of Fate" (158). Fate, the same force Finch invokes in the first line of the poem, returns here with devastating power, tearing the vine away from its support. Finch finds in the violence of a storm an analogue for the frenetic behavior of those who live in the city, fueling the rages of factional politics. Read in relation to this passage, the whims of fashion in food or dress criticized in the opening passages of the poem now appear much more sinister—perhaps the same erratic energies are to blame for the political losses of Stuart sympathizers. Virgil, too, blames "Fate"—*fatis*—for the storms that undo the deliberate work of the farmer. He describes the devastating effects of violent rainstorms, whose winds rage as though in *proelia*, or battles, against one another. These storms occur *saepe*, or frequently: the war-like force of the storm regularly threatens to undermine the efforts of the farmer (1.316–326, 333–339). Yet Virgil offers a relatively consoling precept, *numquam imprudentibus imber/obfuit* (1.373–374), or, "The rain has never done harm without forewarning." Human beings, in other words, can learn to read the signs of an impending storm, and can act accordingly to reduce the damage done to the harvest.

By turning to the image of a vine attacked by the winds and rain of a storm, Finch links her poem subtly, yet meaningfully, with Virgil's insistence on continuous labor and learning as necessary for maintaining the vineyard. In *The Petition*, this maintenance derives from the mutual labor of friendship, a subject amenable to representation in terms of viticulture. The poem eventually presents Arminda as the prop Ardelia lacks in the wake of the "Storm of Fate," and Finch goes on to describe friendship as a crucial component of her retreat:

> *Friendship* still has been design'd,
> The Support of Human-kind;
> The safe Delight, the useful Bliss,
> The next World's Happiness, and this.
> Give then, O indulgent Fate!
> Give a Friend in that Retreat
> (Tho' withdrawn from all the rest)
> Still a Clue, to reach my Breast.
> Let a Friend be still convey'd
> Thro' those Windings, and that Shade!
> (192–201)

The initial couplet here recalls the vine one last time: Finch invokes *"Friendship"* as "The Support of Human-kind." Earlier, she had asked that we imagine a vine "Unsupported," and here she recalls the metaphor, transforming the negative modifier into its original, positive form. The sustaining force of friendship becomes like the tree that protects the vine, rendering it able to bear fruit. In characterizing friendship this way, Finch charges it with a more general and enduring stability. Figuring herself as a vine, Finch admits her own vulnerability. But praising her friend as a crucial source of support, one who "Warm'd anew her drooping Heart, / And Life diffus'd thro' every Part" (66–67), Finch imagines that together they will survive the most violent storms—whether they be natural disasters or political upheavals.

Yet to conjure up the vine is also to invoke one of the most striking images of war to appear in the *Georgics*: when Virgil explains the task of propping vines in long rows, he invokes the order and discipline of soldiers preparing for battle:

> sin tumulis accliue solum collisque supinos,
> indulge ordinibus; nec setius omnis in unguem
> arboribus positis secto uia limite quadret:
> ut saepe ingenti bello cum longa cohortis
> explicuit legio et campo stetit agmen aperto,
> derectaeque acies, ac late fluctuat omnis
> aere renidenti tellus, necdum horrida miscent
> proelia, sed dubius mediis Mars errat in armis:
> omnia sint paribus numeris dimensa uiarum;
> non animum modo uti pascat prospectus inanem,
> sed quia non aliter uiris dabit omnibus aequas
> terra, neque in uacuum poterunt se extendere rami.
> (2.276–287)

(But if on sloping mounds and hills, grant room for rows; nonetheless, place your trees so that each lane may be squared precisely: as often in great war when a long legion of troops unfolds and stands in the open field, the battle lines straight, and far and wide all the land shines with bronze, not yet mixed in horrible battle, but as dangerous Mars wanders in between their weapons: all should be measured in equal rows, not only to supply a foolish mind with a [pleasing] sight, but since not otherwise will the earth give strength equally to all, nor will they be able to extend their branches up into the air.)

The orderly shape of the vineyard offers more than aesthetic pleasure; arranged in rows, the vines grow straight and strong together. The military metaphor comes on suddenly; concluding a passage on the merits of various soil types, Virgil makes a hard turn, beginning, *ut saepe ingenti bello*—"as often in great war." With the short leap from the end of one line to the beginning of another, the vines have transformed into troops on the verge of battle. Now rather than clusters of grapes, they bear swords at the ready. Virgil constructs a pulsing image of anticipation, but then drops the poem abruptly back into the language of agricultural precepts, expelling the specter of war as quickly as he introduces it.

The ease of this shift between the language of battle and the language of agriculture suggests a fallen or marked quality to rural labor: no matter how peaceful the land seems at present, deep scars always run through it. Yet I also think that Virgil means us to read this image in reverse. On the page, vines can suddenly become soldiers, but soldiers can suddenly become vines, too. The farmer diffuses the threat of war, harnessing its discipline, its weapons, and its very energy, all in the service of peaceable labor. To read the poem in only one direction is to read incompletely: the *Georgics* offer no absolute triumph over conflict, nor a cynical conception of peace. Rather, the poem asks that we accept mutability and contingency as permanent components of the process of constructing a peaceful way of life.

Finch could have chosen any number of metaphors to portray the desolation and suffering she experienced after the Revolution of 1688. By invoking the vine, she dramatizes the danger of living without support, but also the inherently political nature of living among others. In the classical poem, the propped vine represents strength, but it also represents a soldier standing with his troop, poised for war. The military resonances of the image perhaps strengthen the effect of Catherine's name, "Arminda," which shares a root with the Latin word *arma*—weapons—and resembles *armanda*, a future passive participle that suggests the act of arming someone for battle. These etymological resonances connect the poem's representation of two friends, one a vulnerable vine and the other a stabilizing prop, even more clearly with the militaristic valences of the *Georgics*. Given these links, the image of the vine in Finch's poem interrupts any easy dichotomies between peace and conflict: within the artificial world that constitutes *The Petition*, Ardelia and Arminda enjoy the peace they make, but their friendship is rendered in the contingent terms of both agriculture and war. Beyond the page, Catherine and Anne stand together as committed political allies, but their solidarity might be tested at any moment, and depends on the preservation of their mutual, perpetual commitment to Jacobitism, and, more fundamentally, to one another.

In the closing sections of *The Petition*, Finch turns toward the future, toward the outcome the speaker will enjoy when, having adopted a georgic sense of humility toward both the natural and supernatural forces working around her, she recalibrates the rhythms of her life according to the seasons, rather than too-easily changed political affiliations. As Finch confronts the problem of surviving under a hostile government, she admits the indelible marks made by history upon her life, but she seeks nevertheless to order that history, and to incorporate it into a peaceful life.

The poem concludes with an admonishment of public striving: contrasting her own need for peaceful retreat with the story of Crassus—who in the early stages of the Roman civil wars was propelled to his demise by an excess of "Ambition" (252)—Finch elevates the implications of her call for retreat. Refusing fame and glory as paths toward peace, she advises instead that human beings live more happily when, like Marvell's Fairfax, they maintain a sense of mindful proportion:

> Fitly might the Life of Man
> Be indeed esteem'd a Span,
> If the present Moment were
> Of Delight his only Share;
> If no other Joys he knew
> Than what round about him grew:
> (264–279)

Only by living in this way, "From a rightly govern'd Frame" (276), can the human being gain access to "things unutterable" (279)—mysteries not unlike those Virgil seeks to understand as he observes the stars, sun, and moon, the quaking of the earth, and the rolling of the seas. Attending only to "the present Moment," Finch treats this kind of focused attitude as the only one that can counter the ravages of time, and, more fundamentally, can help alleviate anxieties about the problems that either have passed or may come to be.[21]

In the final lines of the poem, Finch leaves "the Fair, the Gay, the Vain" to their own pursuits, granting

> Ev'ry one their sev'ral Wish;
> Whilst my Transports I employ
> On that more extensive Joy,
> When all Heaven shall be survey'd
> From those Windings and that Shade.
> (289–293)

From a position of retreat Finch gains wide poetic vision. Not unlike Virgil at the end of the *Georgics*, she situates herself beyond the world of political ambition. Both poets understand poetry itself as an alternate world, allowing for a different way of knowing, no matter how intensely it converses with politics. These poets are interested in *how* and *why* things happen, but they also understand the contingency haunting the outcome of the most deliberate and precise actions—even poetic creation. Both poets also consider how peace can be constructed and maintained, and understand the profound contingency that haunts even the most apparently stable worlds. Unlike the statesman or the conqueror, who strives to impose security from the top down, each poet envisions security as something built from the bottom up. The *Georgics* urge people in general, but poets in particular, to cultivate understanding and circumspection, and in the years following her expulsion from court life, Anne Finch took up this challenge. By reaching back into the *Georgics*, *The Petition for an Absolute Retreat* finds an apt image of defiance against the constantly rushing currents of time and fate. For Finch, the language of agriculture opens a channel through which to make sense of natural and political hostilities alike.

FINCH AND THE FORCE OF FABLE

By way of conclusion, I want now to provide an example of how a greater awareness of Finch's engagement with Virgilian georgic principles can help us better understand the intricacies of her poetry. A prolific writer and translator of fables, Finch famously used the form to respond to the political strife that persisted after the civil wars and that was exacerbated by both the Revolution of 1688 and the intense party politics that marked the reign of Queen Anne.[22] The published octavo volume of 1713 features most of her fables; among these appears "Jupiter and the Farmer," which immediately follows *The Petition for an Absolute Retreat*, and was also included in the folio manuscript largely completed during the 1690s. As she renders Jean de La Fontaine's "Jupiter et le métayer" into English, Finch moves the poem closer to the driving ethics of the *Georgics*, distancing it from the more obviously Judeo-Christian ending Fontaine had originally written for it.

Finch's fables have long been admired for their trenchant responses to political and social matters, and "Jupiter and the Farmer" is no different. Yet her translation engages with more than topical concerns: it reflects the crux of the *Georgics*, which offer agricultural life as a way to reconcile personal survival with the powerful constructive and destructive forces moving perpetually around the human being. As we have seen, within the world of Virgil's poem nature functions on a temporal and spatial scale not immediately apparent to people, who must labor both to understand its rhythms and to organize their lives in response to natural events. These conditions mark a fallen age after the rule of Saturn, when the earth provided fruits unprovoked by pruning hooks or plows, but the poem does not blame humankind for ushering in this new, imperfect state.

Describing the transition away from the idyllic age of Saturn, Virgil makes this state of hardship and lack brutally clear:

> pater ipse colendi
> haud facilem esse uiam uoluit, primusque per artem
> mouit agros, curis acuens mortalia corda
> nec torpere graui passus sua regna ueterno.
> ante Iouem nulli subigebant arua coloni;
> ne signare quidem aut partiri limite campum
> fas erat; in medium quaerebant, ipsaque tellus
> omnia liberius nullo poscente ferebat.
>
> (1.121–128)

(The father himself did not wish the way of cultivating to be easy, and first through art moved the fields, by care sharpening mortal intellects, and did not suffer his reign to be lethargic in heavy sloth. Before Jove no farmers subjugated the fields, nor even to mark or divide the field with a boundary was allowed; they sought common space, and the land itself brought forth all things more freely, demanding nothing.)

This passage contrasts sharply with the ideal of noble and pleasant labor that many eighteenth-century writers sought to articulate in their own georgic poems. Here, the survival of human beings depends on their ability to harness and manipulate the resources latent in the earth. Whereas the age of Saturn provided for them—they needed only to pluck the fruits the earth offered—the age of Jupiter grants them the raw materials for success, accompanied closely by the stark possibility of failure. In the *Georgics* Virgil makes very few promises about the chances of achieving a prosperous life as a farmer; he is careful to offer only history and precepts—often couched in future-tense, subjunctive, or imperative verbs—leaving open the question of whether anyone will heed them. Success requires effort—to learn, and to act based on that knowledge. A farmer who makes no effort to work in relation to nature, either because he thinks it too easy or too difficult to control, faces certain failure.

In both its French and English iterations, the fable relates an episode in which the king of the gods intends to let a plot of land, the current care of which he has entrusted to Mercury. This premise recalls Virgil's vision of the Iron Age, in which land was no longer communally enjoyed, but divided into parcels. "Jupiter et le Métayer" and "Jupiter and the Farmer" both subscribe to a similar ethic. The version by La Fontaine moves quickly past this initial premise: its first line tells us that Jupiter had land to let, the second relates how Mercury was charged with advertising it, and from there the poem describes the failures of the prideful farmer who imagines himself more knowledgeable than the gods. The fable as rendered by Finch, however, expands the opening scene:

> When Poets gave their God in *Crete* a Birth,
> Then *Jupiter* held Traffick with the Earth,
> And had a Farm to Lett: the Fine was high,
> For much the Treas'ry wanted a Supply,
> By *Danaë*'s wealthy Show'r exhausted quite, and Dry.
>
> (1–5)

Finch mentions nothing of Mercury until the sixth line, but she also nearly triples the amount of space allotted for Jupiter, adding the image of the "Poets." She situates poetic history before mythology, implying that poetic efforts gave rise to the gods themselves. She does not rejoin La Fontaine until the third line, writing "And had a Farm to Lett" to render *Jupiter eut jadis une ferme à donner*. Nothing in the French supports the middle line, in which the god holds "Traffick with the Earth." Locating her fable at the very beginning of the reign of Jupiter, Finch underscores the imposition of arduous agricultural responsibility.

In Finch's words, because Mercury has "rack'd the Rent" (7), interested parties remain few and far between. At last, one volunteer appears, though he proves to be quite prideful, accepting the lease only on the condition that

> if at his Desire
> All Weathers tow'rds his Harvest may conspire;
> The Frost to kill the Worm, the brooding Snow,
> The filling Rains may come, and *Phoebus* glow.
>
> (12–15)

Rather than learn to read weather patterns and soil types, this farmer seeks absolute control over his newly leased land, thinking he can order nature better than the gods themselves. Despite his hubristic demands, however, the gods agree, and he proceeds to work, though now "anxious in his Mind," since the other tenants, submitting to the rule of Jupiter, pace their efforts differently. Nonetheless, the prideful farmer

> Now asks a Show'r, now craves a rustling Wind
> To raise what That had lodg'd, that he the Sheaves may bind.
> The Sun, th'o'er-shadowing Clouds, the moistning Dews
> He with such Contrariety does chuse;
> So often and so oddly shifts the Sene,
> Whilst others Load, he scarce has what to Glean.
>
> (19–25)

As expected, he fails wretchedly while his neighbors prosper. Although granted all the necessary raw materials, he lacks the circumspection and patience of a good farmer. He also assumes an absolute dichotomy between submission and authority; misunderstanding the responsibilities of agricultural labor, he demands omnipotence. Yet the georgic mode insists that the successful farmer not attend only to his own will, making changes "so often and so oddly"; instead, he must align his choices with the rhythms of nature. In teaching attention to signs and processes, the georgic shows how each stage of labor makes future tasks possible at the same time that it has been made possible by past ones. Unsatisfied with the terms of this relationship, however, the farmer as rendered by both La Fontaine and Finch seeks dominion over the land, with disastrous results.

In La Fontaine's fable, the final lines suggest a religious moral, transforming the poem into a general lesson on the importance of faith in "Providence":

> Que fait-il? il recourt au monarque des dieux;
>   Il confesse son imprudence,
> Jupiter en usa comme un maître fort doux.
>   Concluons que la Providence
>   Sait ce qu'il nous faut, mieux que nous.[23]

(What does he do? He appeals to the king of the gods; he confesses his imprudence, Jupiter as usual is a very gentle master. Let us conclude that Providence knows what we need, better than we.)

The French fable leaves agricultural imagery behind, concluding with a gesture that separates human and divine knowledge, as well as human and divine agency. The divine will provide, suggests the tale, and human beings need only receive the fruits of Providence.

Finch's translation, however, remains firmly rooted in the language of farming and of the Greco-Roman gods:

> O *Jupiter!* with Famine pinch'd he cries,
> No more will I direct th' unerring Skies;
> No more my Substance on a Project lay,
> No more a sullen Doubt I will betray,
> Let me but live to Reap, do Thou appoint the way.
>   (26–30)

Finch makes a series of choices here that move the fable away from La Fontaine. She adds a first-person apostrophe where the French poet relies on a question and a brief reflection, both in the third person. In his final two lines, La Fontaine uses first-person plural pronouns; when combined with the question and its answer, this closing gesture includes his readers, welcoming them into the community of those who understand the moral lesson of the fable. Finch, on the other hand, allows the farmer to speak; the accumulation of lines beginning with "No more" makes his error explicit: he has known the power to control nature, but his human mind is too small for the task. The final line brings relief: "No more" gives way to "Let me," as the farmer promises to follow the rhythms decreed by Jupiter, who will "appoint the way" to successful labor.

More significantly, though, the English rendition moves toward the *Georgics*, which also emphasize respect for divine omnipotence, but focus on the possible successes or failures of an individual farmer. Perhaps the strongest connection to the *Georgics* lies in Finch's choice of the phrase "with Famine pinch'd" to describe the miserable farmer. Her alteration of La Fontaine here conjures up the final image in Virgil's long description of all the difficulties Jupiter imposes upon humanity:

> tum uariae uenere artes. labor omnia vicit[24]
> improbus et duris urgens in rebus egestas.
> (1.145–146)

The twentieth-century translation of these lines by H. T. Rushton Fairclough also refers to the way hardship—induced by the sweeping power of natural forces—"pinches" the human laborer:

> and art followed hard on art. Toil triumphed over every obstacle,
> unrelenting Toil,
> and Want that pinches when life is hard.

Of course, Fairclough was translating more than two centuries after Finch was turning fables from French to English. Yet the major translations of the *Georgics* completed in the century before Finch began writing seriously all preserve the severity of the labor *improbus et duris urgens*—pressing sternly and unrelentingly—that marks the life of the farmer:

> Then diuerse occupations and trades came up in use,
> For ceaslesse labour maistreth and overcomes all things,
> And so doth preasing pouertie and need in cases hard.
> Abraham Fleming, 1589[25]

Then th'arts were found; for all things conquer'd
By restlesse toyle, and hard necessity.

Thomas May, 1628[26]

Then Arts began; fierce toyl through all things breaks,
And urgent want strange projects undertakes.

John Ogilby, 1654[27]

And various Arts in order did succeed,
(What cannot endless Labour urg'd by need?)

John Dryden, 1697[28]

Ogilby's "fierce toil," May's "restlesse toyle," and Fleming's "preasing pouertie" all capture the severity of the hardship imposed upon the farmer by his fundamental state of want—only Dryden's translation softens the image, relegating "Labour" to a parenthetical line and modifying it with the cognate "urg'd." Moreover, Dryden stands alone in splitting the couplet in half, granting a full line for the subject of arts, followed by a full line for labor, as if to suggest that the two entities complete and balance one another—although the parenthetical line, which reads as an aside, undercuts this balance, with the result that the "Arts" receive more emphasis. The other translators attempt no such equilibrium: Fleming expands the images of toil and lack, spreading them across two of the three ponderous fourteeners he uses to render Virgil's two hexameters. Ogilby and May write with a similar sense of proportion, each allotting about a quarter of the couplet for arts and leaving the rest for labor. The three earlier translations ring far less positively than Dryden's; his lines suggest a small celebration of the birth of the arts, whereas the others lament their arduous origin. Despite such disparate tones, however, these translations make explicit the lack that motivates the farmer; the fable's protagonist only comes to understand this fundamental condition by ruining his harvest.[29]

At every turn, the *Georgics* emphasize the extreme forces resisting the farmer, and make explicit the gravity of agricultural efforts: the successful farm should be organized according to a deep awareness of both the predictable and unpredictable ways of nature. The farmer who fails to acknowledge the potency of this vast system, striving instead to rule it with the power of a god, reaps nothing but famine. Virgil and his translators all stress the pain of hunger and other hardships that inspire creation and compel the farmer to complete backbreaking work throughout the year. When Finch's farmer appeals to the heavens "with *Famine* pinch'd," he speaks from the realm of Virgilian georgic, which everywhere points to the dire consequences of pride and ignorance.

In the final line of the fable, Finch's farmer pleads, "Let me but live to Reap, do Thou appoint the way," having fully accepted the rule of Jupiter. One valid way to read this line would be to understand it as an expression of religious piety not unlike the statement made by La Fontaine at the end of his fable. Finch would not be the first writer to refer allegorically to the Christian God by substituting the Greco-Roman Jupiter, and it would surely be a mistake to claim that she turns wholly away from the Christian implications of the fable. Moreover, the *Georgics* are rife with commands to be mindful of rural deities who wield great powers to support or undermine the efforts of the farmer. Yet Finch quite clearly alters the French original: the English poem remains squarely within the realms of mythology and agriculture, and makes none of the overtly Christianizing leaps suggested by "Providence." As a result, I find equally valid a reading of this line that reflects a georgic ethic, one that advises submitting to and working in concert with a natural system that transcends the human capacity to impose order. By reconsidering his role as one who reaps rather than one who commands, the formerly foolish farmer relinquishes his hope of ruling nature himself, and agrees to labor in relation to the terms ordained by Jupiter. The Christianized French version reduces the human being quite dramatically for the sake of reinforcing the awesome and totalizing power of God; the Virgilian georgic mode, on the other hand, allows for a more intensive meditation on the possibilities and limits of human agency. Both systems admit the power of supernatural forces, but the georgic world invites greater focus on the processes by which human figures negotiate the conditions of their environments.

In rewriting the ending in a way that so dramatically diverges from La Fontaine, Finch imbues the fable with several simultaneous meanings. She gestures toward Stuart mythology—with all its visions of the monarch as an omnipotent, ordering figure—by casting Jupiter as a benevolent tyrant in whom the prideful farmer ought to have placed his faith. She also assumes a poetic stance significantly different from the one inhabited by La Fontaine: her ending elides the voice of the poet, who concludes the French version by relating a moral. Instead of adding a couplet to gloss the fable, Finch trusts the poem to communicate meaning without blatant editorializing by its speaker. Finally, although her ending can be understood to arrive at more or less the same religious lesson as La Fontaine's original, it makes much more explicit the farmer's acceptance of the fact that he must labor according to the natural rhythms ordained by Jupiter. In Finch's English, "Jupiter and the Farmer" enters a space not solely defined by religious faith: like the *Georgics*, this fable wonders at the immense system of causes and effects operating in terms not always clear to human beings, but which must nevertheless be learned for the sake of survival.

In establishing this relationship between human beings and potent natural forces, the *Georgics* construct a malleable ethic that can be applied to many contexts in which the terms of lasting peace are not readily apparent. I suspect that both Finch and Virgil recognized that the relationship between the farmer and nature could help to explain and resolve more general problems. By reading signs in the wind, learning causes and effects, and accepting that larger forces—both benevolent and malevolent—will always be in play, the seventeenth-century political outsider could begin to understand how to make a new life for herself, whereas the ancient political favorite could begin to weigh both the victories and injustices wrought by the central powers at Rome. In either context, the first and most important action is to read the environment, seeking to comprehend its short- and long-range patterns. Read in this light, "Jupiter and the Farmer" is one of Finch's most thoroughly georgic efforts. The changes she makes to La Fontaine's French bring her version more immediately into alignment with the Virgilian aim of coming to understand the causes of things: in demanding control over the order of things, the fable's farmer suffers abject failure.

In the same year that Finch published her *Poems*, Alexander Pope produced *Windsor-Forest*, a panegyric celebrating the Treaty of Utrecht and the consequent end of the War of the Spanish Succession. Although *Windsor-Forest* reflects Pope's own knowledge of the *Georgics*, it does not share with *The Petition for an Absolute Retreat* a deep, Virgilian sense of the uncertainties and contingencies that always accompany peace. Yet Pope was not only thinking about Virgil; he also borrowed from *Cyder*, a georgic poem written by John Philips and published five years earlier. As the first formal English imitation of the *Georgics*, *Cyder* is often thought to begin the story of the eighteenth-century georgic. More accurately, however, Philips's poem stands as a hinge between poets who found in Virgil's *Georgics* a way of expressing political uncertainty, and poets who appreciated Virgil because his poems pleased an emperor.

NOTES

1. Barbara McGovern, *Anne Finch and Her Poetry: A Critical Biography* (Athens: University of Georgia Press, 1992), 17.
2. This and all subsequent quotations from the poetry of Anne Finch taken from the edition by Myra Reynolds, *The Poems of Anne, Countess of Winchilsea* (Chicago: University of Chicago Press, 1903). Jennifer Keith and Claudia Thomas Kairoff have generously made available to me their edition of *The Petition for an Absolute Retreat*, which I have consulted for this chapter, and which will appear in their forthcoming collection of Finch's poetry. I cite their notes on the poem as appropriate below, but for the sake of consistency, I have quoted from the Reynolds edition even when discussing *The Petition*.
3. In her commendatory poem on the translation, Mary, Lady Chudleigh—a relative of Hugh, Lord Clifford, to whom Dryden had dedicated the *Pastorals*—made a similar state-

ment about the value of the *Virgil* for the development of the English language: "Our Language like th'*Augean* Stable lay, / Rude and uncleans'd, till thou by Glory mov'd, / Th' *Herculean* Task didst undertake" (68–70) (*The Poems and Prose of Mary, Lady Chudleigh*, ed. Margaret J. M. Ezell [Oxford: Oxford University Press, 1993]).

4. Deborah Kennedy, *Poetic Sisters: Early Eighteenth-Century Women Poets* (Lewisburg, PA: Bucknell University Press, 2013), 32. Kennedy's point follows a similar one made by Charles Hinnant in *The Poetry of Anne Finch: An Essay in Interpretation* (Newark: University of Delaware Press, 1994), 136. In a recent article demonstrating the intense relationship between politics and translation—largely from French—in Finch's body of work, Jennifer Keith also acknowledges the Horatian strains in *The Petition* as part of a larger argument about the poet's responses to the traditionally masculine arena of classical translation ("The Reach of Translation in the Works of Anne Finch," *Philological Quarterly* 95, no. 3/4 [2016]: 467–493).

5. Virgil, *Georgics*, ed. Thomas, 1:88.

6. Richard F. Thomas finds the military language that Virgil applies to viticulture to betray reservations about what is achieved as a result of agricultural success (ibid., 20).

7. Keith and Claudia Thomas Kairoff note that this poem had to have been finished by about 1701 or 1702, since Finch included it in her folio manuscript. It was not published in print until it appeared in the *Poems* of 1713 (*The Cambridge Edition of the Works of Anne Finch, Countess of Winchilsea*, 2 vols., gen. ed. Jennifer Keith, Vol. 1, *Early Manuscript Books*, ed. Jennifer Keith and Claudia Thomas Kairoff, assoc. ed. Jean I. Marsden [Cambridge: Cambridge University Press, forthcoming May 2019. Keith numbers *The Petition for an Absolute Retreat* among those poems Finch used to "conve[y] her allegiance to the exiled Stuart family" ("Anne Finch's Aviary: or, Why She Never Wrote 'The Bird and the Arras,'" *Philological Quarterly* 88, nos. 1–2 [2009], 80).

8. Paula Backscheider, concurring with McGovern, has observed that Finch most likely derived her own poetic pseudonym, "Ardelia," from the friendship poetry of Katherine Philips (*Eighteenth-Century Women Poets and Their Poetry: Inventing Agency, Inventing Genre* [Baltimore: Johns Hopkins University Press, 2005], 180, 436n17). Catharine Gray ("Katherine Philips and the Post-Courtly Coterie," *English Literary Renaissance* 32, no. 3 [2002]: 426–451, and *Women Writers and Public Debate in 17th-Century Britain* [New York: Palgrave Macmillan, 2007]) has shown how the ostensibly private environments within which women were expected to move put them in particularly good position to create "new forms of collective public debate" (*Women Writers and Public Debate*, 2–3). Penelope Anderson (*Friendship's Shadows: Women's Friendship and the Politics of Betrayal in England, 1640–1705* [Edinburgh: Edinburgh University Press, 2012]) heightens the political stakes of classicized representations of friendship between women, and Amanda E. Herbert connects female friendship to the emergence of British identity across the eighteenth century (*Female Alliances: Gender, Identity, and Friendship in Early Modern Britain* [New Haven, CT: Yale University Press, 2014). Laura Tallon has demonstrated how her ekphrastic poems, especially those written to members of the Thynne family, trouble conventional notions of gender and the arts ("Ekphrasis and Gender in Anne Finch's Longleat Poems," *Eighteenth-Century Life* 40, no. 1 [2016]: 84–107).

9. Paul Alpers urges less emphasis on the golden age as a marker of the mode (*What Is Pastoral?* [Chicago: University of Chicago Press, 1996]). Ken Hiltner argues that the gradual dissipation of pastoral and concomitant rise of georgic resulted from British interest in representing colonial dominance (*What Else Is Pastoral?* [Ithaca, NY: Cornell University Press, 2011]).

10. Although not formally a didactic poem, *The Petition* enacts the same "coming into being" that Katharina Volk has observed in classical didactic poetry (*The Poetics of Latin*

Didactic: Lucretius, Vergil, Ovid, Manilius [Oxford: Oxford University Press, 2002], 13–16).

11. Ann Messenger characterizes *The Petition* as a prayer (*Pastoral Tradition and the Female Talent: Studies in Augustan Poetry* [Norwalk, CT: AMS Press, 2001], 70). Susan Lanser describes the poem as a "utopian" vision (*The Sexuality of History: Modernity and the Sapphic, 1565–1830* [Chicago: University of Chicago Press, 2014)], 117).

12. Although the word "Liberty" in this passage would ultimately come to signal such Whig ideals as diminished monarchial power, for the Jacobite Anne Finch it suggests a life lived wholly outside of recognizable state structures, at least so long as William III occupies the throne. For a broader treatment of Jacobitism and protective shade, see Wes Hamrick, "Trees in Anne Finch's Jacobite Poems of Retreat," *SEL* 53, no. 3 (2013): 541–563, especially 556. In their forthcoming edition of this poem, Keith and Kairoff point to the work of Paul Monod, whose *Jacobitism and the English People, 1688–1788* (Cambridge: Cambridge University Press, 1993) explains the ways in which the notion of liberty was also at times significant in Jacobite rhetoric.

13. Ann Messenger specifically connects the fruits of Marvell's poem "The Garden" to Finch's scene of abundance (*Pastoral Tradition*, 70).

14. Christine Perkell has emphasized the fact that the agricultural labor depicted by the *Georgics* bears little resemblance to the activities of large corporate farms, worked by slaves, that Virgil would have known in his own time. This blatant departure from contemporary fact suggests, for Perkell, that the poem loads the figure of the farmer with a great deal of symbolic or metaphorical meaning (*The Poet's Truth*, 29).

15. See Hamrick, "Trees," as well as Nicolle Jordan, "'Where Power Is Absolute': Royalist Politics and the Improved Landscape in a Poem by Anne Finch, Countess of Winchilsea," *The Eighteenth Century* 46, no. 3 (2005): 255–275. For women's creative work in the planning and maintenance of real rural spaces, see Stephen Bending, *Green Retreats: Women, Gardens and Eighteenth-Century Culture* (Cambridge: Cambridge University Press, 2013).

16. These lines recall a grisly scene of military defeat—couched in language that suggests strains of Jacobitism—in Dryden's *Alexander's Feast, or The Power of Musique,*

> He sung *Darius* Great and Good,
> > By too severe a Fate,
> Fallen, fallen, fallen, fallen,
> > Fallen from his high Estate
> > And weltring in his Blood:
> Deserted at his utmost Need,
> By those his former Bounty fed:
> On the bare Earth expos'd He lyes,
> With not a Friend to close his Eyes.
> > > (*Works*, 7:75–78)

17. Milton, *Complete Poems and Major Prose*, ed. Hughes.

18. Anthony Low (1985), Kevis Goodman ("'Wasted Labor'? Milton's Eve, the Poet's Work, and the Challenge of Sympathy," *ELH* 64, no. 2 [1997]: 415–446), and Louis L. Martz ("*Paradise Regained*: Georgic Form, Georgic Style," *Milton Studies* 42 [2002]: 7–25), among others, have offered comment on Milton's engagements with the *Georgics.*

19. See Virgil, *Eclogues. Georgics. Aeneid 1–6*, ed. Fairclough.

20. For instance, see McGovern, *Anne Finch*, 110, as well as Carol Barash, "The Political Origins of Anne Finch's Poetry," *HLQ* 54, no. 4 (1991), 344, and *English Women's Poetry, 1649–1714: Politics, Community, and Linguistic Authority* (Oxford: Oxford University Press, 1997), 280.

21. This idea resurfaces in at least two of Finch's fables: in "There's No To-Morrow"—the poem that immediately precedes *The Petition* in the volume of 1713—a man perpetually promises to marry his lover "To-morrow," but of course tomorrow exists only in the mind, so the wedding never occurs, and Finch observes wryly, "*The Tale's a Jest, the Moral is a Truth*" (16). In "The Hog, the Sheep, and Goat, Carrying to a Fair," the hog realizes during the journey that the farmer will shear the sheep and milk the goat, but butcher him. Finch concludes, "The Wretch who tastes his suff'rings late, / Not He, who thro' th'unhappy Future prys, / Must of the Two be held most Fortunate and Wise" (28–30). In both cases, the ethic expressed in *The Petition* takes a darkly comical turn, as Finch depicts the uncomfortable consequences of thinking beyond "the present Moment."

22. Confirming an earlier observation by Myra Reynolds, Backscheider notes that fables comprise about a third of Finch's total oeuvre, and argues for her mastery of the genre, which rivaled that of Dryden, Behn, Ogilby, and Prior (*Eighteenth-Century Women Poets*, 43). See also Gillian Wright, "The Birds and the Poet: Fable, Self-Representation and the Early Editing of Anne Finch's Poetry," *Review of English Studies* 64 (2013): 246–266. In *Fables of Power: Aesopian Writing and Political History* (Durham, NC: Duke University Press, 1991), Annabel Patterson demonstrates the profoundly political nature of the fable, observing that during the late seventeenth and early eighteenth centuries, "the story of the fable . . . is the story of party prejudice" (141). Jayne Elizabeth Lewis points out that Wordsworth's preference for Finch's nature poetry, a much smaller proportion of her output, contributed to disinterest in her fables generally (*The English Fable: Aesop and Literary Culture, 1651–1740* [Cambridge: Cambridge University Press, 1996], 131).

23. Jean La Fontaine, *Fables de La Fontaine*, ed. Francis Tarver (London: Libraire Hachette, 1898), 105–106. Ensuing translation my own.

24. Textual commentary varies on the conjugated form of *uincere* in this line; I have adhered to the edition by Richard F. Thomas, which follows the more dominant tradition of using the perfect-tense form *uicit*, rather than the present-tense form *uincit* that appears in the famous corresponding phrase in the *Eclogues*, *omnia uincit amor*, and in the Ruaeus *Georgics*. Some differences in the various translated versions can be attributed to this inconsistency. Thomas has suggested that the Roman poet "intends the reader to apply" the lines on burdensome toil "throughout the poem" (*Georgics* 17); they make clear the hardship that marks agricultural life, and counter the happy ideal of country labor. One of the most frequently quoted phrases in the *Georgics*, *labor omnia vicit* has sometimes been read as emblematic of the poem's driving ethics. Yet as Perkell has noted, the tradition of reading this phrase selectively—that is, without regarding the hexameter that follows it—has done a disservice to the larger poem. It is exactly this kind of indeterminate lineation, observes Perkell, that makes the *Georgics* so fascinating and yet so difficult: the poem frequently raises an ostensibly certain idea in one line, but then, as the syntax continues into the next hexameter, a qualification arises that casts all certainty aside (Perkell, Introduction to *The Poet's Truth*.).

25. Fleming, *The Bucoliks of Publius Virgilius Maro, prince of all Latine poets; otherwise called his pastorals, or shepeherds meetings. Together with his Georgiks or ruralls, otherwise called his husbandrie, conteyning foure books. All newly translated into English verse by A.F.* (London, 1589), sig. Bv.

26. Virgil, *Virgil's Georgicks Englished*, trans. May, 8.

27. Virgil, *Works of Publius Virgilius Maro Translated*, trans. Ogilby, 68. Ogilby revised these lines from his translation of 1649, which read there as follows: "Then came strange arts, *fierce labor all subdues*. / Inforc d [*sic*] by bold *Necessity*, and *Want*," (46). See also Chapter 2, n26.

28. Dryden, *Works*, 5:1.218–219.
29. Working in the more recent tradition of celebrating multiplicity in the *Georgics* rather than lamenting their lack of unity, William Batstone refuses an overtly positive or negative reading of Jupiter's decree; his edict brings "simultaneously victory and defeat, effort and the need for effort, artifice and the failure of artifice" ("Virgilian Didaxis: Value and Meaning in the *Georgics*," in *The Cambridge Companion to Virgil*, ed. Charles Martindale [Cambridge: Cambridge University Press, 1997; online ed. 2006], 137).

4

IMITATION

The *Georgics* and the Eighteenth Century

I N 1713, THE SAME YEAR in which Anne Finch published her collected *Poems*, Queen Anne's representatives signed the Peace of Utrecht, by which Britain gained the Asiento, or the exclusive right to export slaves from Africa to Spanish America. By this time, an England once violently divided had become, at least on paper, a more united Great Britain under the Act of Union (1707); with this agreement, the newly formed and formalized British state hoped to protect the Act of Settlement and buttress its strength on the global stage, an aim heightened by its concerns about the potency of France.[1] It had subsequently turned its gaze more fully outward in hopes of building an empire. As the eighteenth century progressed, English poets appeared to need the Virgilian georgic mode less and less: the imperial dream of a replicated Pax Romana fundamentally conflicts with the sense of uncertainty and contingency that haunts the *Georgics*. In the century following Dryden's translation, most poems on agricultural labor shifted their gaze toward the hope of empire, praising British farmers as a national point of pride—and of profit.

Standard literary history has long assumed that the formal English georgic poems of the eighteenth century uniformly reflect this burgeoning imperial certainty, and many eighteenth-century poems modeled on the *Georgics* do claim the products of British agricultural labor as important resources undergirding imperial and national power. But such poems do not converse with Virgil in any meaningful way; rather, the Roman poet presides over them as an authoritative symbol in the same way that a miniature bust of Beethoven adorns the top of young student's piano: as a commanding object meant to suggest the twin possibilities of greatness and timelessness. For many eighteenth-century poets, the looming figure of Virgil indicated that poetry, if linked to empire, could survive for millennia. Yet this idea depends upon a fundamental misreading of the poet as necessarily supportive of Roman ambition. Of course, this tradition of misreading did not always produce imperial poetry; some poets borrowed from Virgil a more general sense of authority. In Thomas Marriott's georgic poem *Female Conduct* (1759), for example, the didactic voice lectures with the aim of correcting women's behavior in a way that does not at all resemble Hesiod's gentle prodding of his recalcitrant brother, Virgil's self-effacing acknowledgment of his patron Maecenas, or Finch's caring address to her friend Catherine. For Marriott, the weight that history had heaped upon Virgil offered poetic credibility and a strong voice through which to impart his corrective precepts.

Yet the questions prompted by the *Georgics* did not disappear from British georgic poetry altogether. In order fully to appreciate its faint resonances, we must reconsider the poem that gave rise to nationalistic agricultural poetry in English. In this chapter, I shall suggest that *Cyder*, John Philips's poem of 1708, is less politically confident than has been assumed, and that it represents the point at which the Virgilian georgic mode and the formal georgic genre simultaneously meet and diverge. Composed to celebrate the union of Scotland with England and Wales, *Cyder* initiates the vogue for the patriotic English georgic. At the same time, however, it also indicates subtle hesitations about the power of a political document to impose unity.

The poems traditionally read as descendants of *Cyder* express belief in a fundamental British stability, grounded in agricultural productivity and central to a growing national and imperial identity. The most commonly acknowledged poem of this kind is *The Seasons*, by James Thomson. Itself a union of scientific, philosophical, political, and descriptive poetry, this poem has long been thought to exemplify British poets' engagement with Virgil's *Georgics*. Yet I submit that this work represents a distinct and permanent break from the poetry of uncertainty. In writing a descriptive poem rather than a didactic one, Thomson reinforces the fiction of a more unified British identity, as well as the associations of that identity with imperial power.[2] By the 1720s, when *Winter* first appeared, and certainly by the 1740s, when the final revisions were published, poems deeply interested in confronting faction and civil war—poems demanding a voice at once didactic and uncertain—had become irrelevant. Although the final defeat of the Jacobite cause at Culloden in 1745 was certainly not the last moment of political tension for the British, by midcentury it was indeed the case that the long shadow of civil war had receded enough to allow imperial interests to accelerate, and internal discord had paled in contrast to British conflicts with the French.

If the uncertain Virgilian georgic had begun to disappear from political poetry, and Virgil's forms were becoming crystallized markers of didactic poetry more broadly, then it may seem to be the case that eighteenth-century poets were not interested in staging the kind of dynamic conversations with ancient poetry that their late seventeenth-century counterparts had found valuable. But in the concluding section of this chapter, I propose one example of how Virgilian ambivalences persisted in midcentury georgic: *The Hop-Garden* (1752), by Christopher Smart. Smart offers only a shadowy vision of future peace; in his poem, nationalistic sentiments hardly guarantee the power to realize stability and tranquility. Although in this moment British agricultural poetry was generally moving away from dynamic engagements with Virgil's darker strains, *The Hop-Garden* demonstrates how untidy such transitions can be. Just as the dream of empire—whether under Augustus or a Hanoverian king—has always depended on glorious fictions, there have always been poets ready to expose them.

No neat genealogy can explain the afterlife of the *Georgics* in English poetry. Instead, the Virgilian georgic fractures into a glittering array of poetic shards, which lodge in distinct poems and shine in distinct ways. In a way, this turn reflects the idiosyncratic literary landscape of the eighteenth century, where we have come to understand that no genre or mode can seriously be understood in terms of purity and stability. Yet everywhere that compelling conversations with the *Georgics* endure, we shall certainly find explorations of loss, contingency, changeability, and uncertainty.

JOHN PHILIPS AND THE INMATE ORCHAT

The story of the didactic georgic in English often begins with *Cyder*, an early example of the nexus between nationalistic agricultural poetry and classical imitation.[3] Published in January 1708, the poem takes up the subject of apple cultivation, but it is widely known for celebrating the Act of Union, realized in the previous year.[4] *Cyder* was much anticipated, but also heavily parodied—John Gay's mocking response, *Wine*, appeared soon after. Yet despite its seeming triviality, *Cyder* represents an important hinge between the uncertain Virgilian georgic mode and the imitative English georgic genre, which we should understand to be connected to the Latin poem in only the most literal ways.

Although it includes several exhortatory passages on British unity, *Cyder* also exposes the differences between declaring and doing. The Union had officially created a single political entity, but Queen Anne had long faced difficult relations with the Scots, and such tensions could hardly be expected to dissipate immediately.[5] Early responses among the English and Scottish peoples were mixed; new economic opportunities could not fully ameliorate the disruption of each side's sense of its own history.[6] Accordingly, Philips's poem suggests that the political document, like the agricultural premises of the Latin *Georgics*, can only serve as a point of origin from which lasting peace and stability might proceed. By writing a didactic poem that spends a great deal of time on the practices of grafting apple trees, Philips emphasizes the contingency of the processes that may lead to unity. Moreover, in choosing to write a georgic poem, Philips adopts a genre already well known for its structural variety—a reputation derived primarily from Addison's *Essay on the Georgics* appended to Dryden's translation a decade earlier. Virgil's varied didactic poem offers to Philips a way of articulating multiplicity as a source of peaceable stability. In the early years of the eighteenth century, Virgilian, didactic, agricultural poetry opened up a conceptual space within which Philips could imagine the Union in terms otherwise obstructed by the lingering conventions of panegyric, which privileged the awesome power of the monarch to impose order. As *Cyder*'s didactic passages yoke together various digressions, Philips urges a vision of unity derived from the transformed energies of factionalism.

The common conflation of a broadly defined georgic poetics and British nationalism has precluded the question of why, exactly, Philips wrote a didactic poem on the topic of apple cultivation in response to the Act of Union. Such a question seems beside the point if we accept the georgic as a celebration of labor completed for the prosperity of the nation.[7] Alternatively, the question seems relatively trivial in light of the poem's topicality; one explanation would point to Philips's choice of subject as a natural result of his poem's connection to Tory Herefordshire, which was well known for its production of apple cider.[8] Both answers hold, but neither fully articulates the implications of the poem's theme.

If we add a more metaphorical reading to the topical ones long understood, then we can begin to see *Cyder* as a poem perched between two kinds of georgic. It reflects at once the new English georgic implicated in the development of a more unified British identity, as well as the older, Virgilian georgic motivated by an interest in the consequences of civil war and the contingency of national and imperial projects, which casts doubt upon declarations of stability. The world of Virgilian georgic seeks everywhere to negotiate the space between construction and destruction, peace and war, success and failure. *Cyder* shares these concerns, even as it initiates a form of poetry rightly deemed "imperial." Its didactic form allows it to articulate doubts about the effectiveness of declared unity and prosperity while simultaneously commemorating that declaration. In this way, Philips's georgic poem does not instigate a new literary trend, but rather unites two disparate conceptions of georgic poetry. The apple tree, simultaneously representing a hybrid history and a promising future, transcends topicality, and instead bears many meanings for this poem. By attending closely to some specific images in *Cyder*, I shall show here how they constitute the broader political meaning of the poem more powerfully than any of its topical references to politicians or locales. Philips does not describe grafting as a single operation that will necessarily guarantee a newly stable and permanently healthy crop, but rather as a continuous and contingent process. This model has obvious implications for the recent Union, but it also provides an alternative vision of political peace more generally, one that might counter the long history of disruption that Philips recounts in his poem.

As an agricultural didactic poem modeled closely on the *Georgics*, *Cyder* emphasizes the process of cultivating stability. Philips's specific choice to write a didactic poem on the subject of apple cultivation suggests a serious interest in, and ambivalence about, broader questions of peace, unity, and political power. Admittedly, *Cyder* does culminate in praise for Anne's political achievement— anticipating the idealism of Pope's *Windsor-Forest*—and a distinct strain of praise for British agriculture does indeed run through the poem; yet at every turn, its didactic stance undercuts the certainty of declared national unity supported by agricultural productivity. Like Virgil, Philips also understands his agricultural subject matter as a point of departure for conceiving of both lasting stability and the possibility of failure.

In the opening lines of *Cyder*, Philips implicitly claims Virgilian authority by recreating the Latin poet's initial series of subordinate clauses, at the same time that he explicitly claims Miltonic authority:[9]

> What Soil the Apple loves, what Care is due
> To Orchats, timeliest when to press the Fruits,
> Thy Gift, *Pomona*, in *Miltonian* Verse
> Adventrous I presume to sing;[10]

In "presuming" to sing, Philips sounds decidedly less confident than the Virgil who had been rendered by Dryden: "The Birth and Genius of the frugal Bee, / I sing, *Maecenas*, and I sing to thee" (1.5–6). Dryden's translation of the Latin phrase *hinc canere incipiam* ("from here I begin to sing") removes the sense of beginning and instead doubles the sound of the poet "sing[ing]." Earlier in the seventeenth century, Thomas May and John Ogilby had also rendered *hinc canere incipiam* as "I sing." Of course, neither Dryden nor the earlier translators misread the Latin poem, and throughout his English version Dryden generally preserves Virgil's ambivalences and hesitations. Perhaps this was a creative choice, possibly inflected or conflated with the *Aeneid*'s triumphant opening phrase *arma virumque cano* ("Arms and the man I sing"). Here, however, Philips suggests a degree of hesitation and daring that aligns the tone of his poem more closely with the contingent nature of Virgil's phrase *hinc canere incipiam*.

In a manner typical of an agricultural didactic poem, *Cyder* includes many subjunctive constructions; in an early passage, Philips urges balance between the farmer's hoped-for abundance and his knowledge of forces that threaten the young orchard:

> Who-e'er expects his lab'ring Trees shou'd bend
> With Fruitage, and a kindly Harvest yield,
> Be this his first Concern; to find a Tract
> Impervious to the Winds, begirt with Hills,
> That intercept the *Hyperborean* Blasts
> Tempestuous, and cold *Eurus* nipping Force,
> Noxious to feeble Buds:
>
> (1.20–26)

The *Georgics* everywhere implore the farmer to make choices grounded in humility, the quality most necessary for agricultural success. Philips makes a similar gesture here, suggesting that even the earliest stages of cultivation require an acute awareness of potential failure. More specifically, the farmer must recognize the "Noxious" power of the winds, and situate the orchard in appropriate relation to them. With this image, Philips allows that unstable foundations can ultimately give rise to stable conditions, but he also suggests that the memory of those threats will never dissipate completely. Forever situated so as to be protected from the winds, the orchard itself represents the necessary negotiation of destructive forces, and the healthy fruits that will spring forth as a result of this initial choice will therefore represent both a positive outcome and the thwarting of a decidedly negative one.

Before moving to explicitly didactic passages on how to graft one species onto another, Philips observes several forms of discord among plants, and proposes in them a natural analogue for human conflicts:

> The Prudent will observe, what Passions reign
> In various Plants (for not to Man alone,
> But all the wide Creation, Nature gave
> Love, and Aversion):
>   . . . Therefore, weigh the Habits well
> Of Plants, how they associate best, nor let
> Ill Neighbourhood corrupt thy hopeful Graffs
> (1.248–272)

With this passage, Philips situates human friendship and enmity within a broader, natural context, as if to say that a certain degree of attraction and repulsion ought to be accepted as a normal part of life. Then the metaphor shifts; Philips addresses the farmer directly, urging him to choose wisely his candidates for grafting. He charges humanity with the special power to make such decisions, and suggests that by blending species to make new ones, the artificial practice of grafting can produce trees that grow stronger and healthier than they would naturally. The best fruits, in other words, require "Art," or cultivation:

> Wouldst thou, thy Vats with gen'rous Juice should froth?
> Respect thy Orchats; think not, that the Trees
> Spontaneous will produce an wholsom Draught.
> Let Art correct thy Breed; from Parent Bough
> A Cyon meetly sever; after, force
> A way into the Crabstock's close-wrought Grain
> By Wedges, and within the living Wound
> Enclose the Foster Twig; nor over-nice
> Refuse with thy own Hands around to spread
> The binding Clay: Ee'r-long their differing Veins
> Unite, and kindly Nourishment convey
> To the new Pupil; now he shoots his Arms
> With quickest Growth; now shake the teeming Trunc,
> Down rain th'impurpl'd Balls, ambrosial Fruit.
> (1.273–286)

Here, Philips establishes a series of familial and corporeal metaphors to articulate the steps required for grafting: cut from the "Parent Bough," the "Foster Twig" enters the "living Wound" of the new tree. Once the two species begin to grow together, their "Veins / Unite," allowing the younger plant to receive "kindly Nourishment"; together these phrases suggest both familiar ideas about domestic bonds of kinship and the violence necessary for creating this new, unnatural lineage. This passage may also urge more than the acceptance of a new national identity; beginning with an image of a vat filled to the brim with profitable juices, Philips perhaps gestures toward the immediate economic benefits guaranteed by the Union, which had removed customs duties from trade within Great Britain.[11]

Moving from the specific work of grafting to the more general labors of the farmer, Philips emphasizes interconnectedness, and the presence of the great in the small:

> But the hidden Ways
> Of Nature wouldst thou know? how first she frames
> All things in Miniature? thy Specular Orb
> Apply to well-dissected Kernels; lo!
> Strange Forms arise, in each a little Plant

> Unfolds its Boughs: observe the slender Threads
> Of first-beginning Trees, their Roots, their Leaves,
> In narrow Seeds describ'd; Thou'lt wond'ring say,
> An inmate Orchat ev'ry Apple boasts.
>
> (1.350–358)

Philips presents a series of rounded shapes simultaneously larger and smaller than one another: first the "Specular Orb," or human eye, which inspects the apple seeds, which in themselves contain multitudes. As the spectator gazes on these "well-dissected Kernels," he should see in their tiny fibers the makings of whole trees, with branches extending upward and roots delving into the ground. Philips's poem, too, "first . . . frames / All things in Miniature." In this way, his poem—like Virgil's—does not simply lay agricultural metaphors over political meanings; rather, a Virgilian georgic poet begins with close attention to particulars and then looks outward, extrapolating larger patterns from smaller ones, and perceiving fluid processes where others might only see stable objects. Each state, from seed, to branch, to fruit, represents an end in itself and constitutes part of a larger cycle. Therefore, when Philips sees the apple, he also sees an "inmate Orchat," an image that works in two directions: backward, in that it reflects the process of cultivation that gave rise to it, but forward, too, in that it bears within the potential to give rise to more trees. The single apple, then, derives from an always-present multiplicity. For Philips, unity does not preclude heterogeneity.

In the same way that the "miniature" seed gives rise to the tree, this individual passage broadens into two larger sections of the poem. The first looks forward, urging the farmer to live according to a code of humility and industry. The second looks backward, attempting to reconcile the failures of history with present claims to stability. The first section is insistently didactic:

> Thus All things by Experience are display'd,
> And Most improv'd. Then sedulously think
> To meliorate thy Stock; no Way, or Rule
> Be unassay'd; prevent the Morning Star
> Assiduous, nor with the Western Sun
> Surcease to work; lo! thoughtful of Thy Gain,
> Not of my Own, I all the live-long Day
> Consume in Meditation deep, recluse
> From human Converse, nor, at shut of Eve,
> Enjoy Repose; but oft at Midnight Lamp
> Ply my brain-racking Studies, if by chance
> Thee I may counsel right; and oft this Care
> Disturbs me slumbring. Wilt thou then repine

To labour for thy Self? and rather chuse
To lye supinely, hoping, Heav'n will bless
Thy slighted Fruits, and give thee Bread unearn'd?
(1.359–374)

Whereas in the earlier passage "Nature" presents "All things in Miniature," here the human being must learn to see and comprehend them "by Experience." Again, the poem enacts a simultaneous forward and backward movement; the word "Experience" works in both directions, as it both "display[s]" and "improve[s]." One reader has insisted that by "Experience" Philips means "experiment," suggesting scientific trial and error.[12] This meaning, now obsolete, was indeed current at the time and remained so nearly until the nineteenth century, and clearly applies here. Yet the ostensibly more modern meaning of "experience," or "the actual observation of facts or events, considered as a source of knowledge," has been in use since the fourteenth century.[13] I detect both meanings in this case; by experience, or knowledge gleaned in the past and applied in the present, the farmer—and by extension, the human being in general—can improve his efforts. At the same time, forward-looking experiment, or trial, creates new knowledge. The one suggests contemplation, while the other suggests activity; a similar tension surfaces as the poet first describes his "brain-racking Studies" in the service of broad wisdom, but then turns to his reader, imploring him not to "lye supinely" and expect a harvest "unearn'd," but rather to "prevent the Morning Star," or arrive in the fields before the dawn. Philips suggests that both poetic and agricultural work depend on knowledge and reflection combined with action, since both benefit from the combination of past experience and fresh experimentation. Yet this passage also appears to propose that the poet ought to sing, or teach, but that it remains for the farmer to read and act; herein lies the crux of the didactic stance, which leaves a distinct gap between a vision articulated by the poet and its realization carried out by the laborer—a gap between the knowledge of how to complete a task and the act of executing it. The agricultural didactic enforces everywhere the continuation of labor, but also the continuation of learning, in order to create more effective ways of laboring.

This ethic extends to history in the poem's second book, where Philips contemplates the discord that arose from unity, and the potential unity that might arise from discord. Philips recounts the long history of conflict plaguing England in the centuries before the Union. In lines recalling John Denham's *Cooper's Hill*, he praises Edward III as an upright and peaceable king, but also remembers him as the point of origin from which arose the long dispute between the houses of York and Lancaster:

Thrice glorious Prince! whom, Fame with all her Tongues
For ever shall resound. Yet from his Loins
New Authors of Dissention spring; from him
Two Branches, that in hosting long contend
For Sov'ran Sway;

(2.594–598)

Philips's effusive tone disintegrates into lament as he envisions the warring factions descended from Edward. Whereas the poem celebrates grafting as a beneficial practice precisely because it joins disparate species, it points to the Wars of the Roses as conflicts derived from an opposite process, in which enemies spring from a common origin.

As book 2 continues, English history as told by Philips becomes a narrative of peace achieved and ruptured, but concludes in the present moment, during the reign of Queen Anne, when the British finally have the opportunity to foster lasting stability. In contrast to Edward, who bred discord from unity, and the several rulers who struggled against faction after him, Queen Anne appears as a monarch capable of creating unity from multiplicity:

James descends,
Heav'ns chosen Fav'rite, first *Britannic* King.
To him alone, Hereditary Right
Gave Power supreme; yet still some Seeds remain'd
Of Discontent; two Nations under One,
In Laws and Int'rest diverse, still persu'd
Peculiar Ends, on each Side resolute
To fly Conjunction; neither Fear, nor Hope,
Nor the sweet Prospect of a mutual Gain,
Cou'd ought avail, 'till prudent ANNA said
Let there be UNION; strait with Reverence due
To Her Command, they willingly unite,
One in Affection, Laws, and Government,
Indissolubly firm; from *Dubris* South,
To Northern *Orcades*, Her long Domain.

(2.630–644)

Scholars frequently note the echo of "Let there be UNION" in Alexander Pope's *Windsor-Forest*, published in celebration of the Treaty of Utrecht:

At length great ANNA said—Let Discord cease!
She said, the World obey'd, and all was *Peace*!

(327–328)[14]

This link between the poems achieved the status of a commonplace long ago. *Windsor-Forest* has often been included in accounts of eighteenth-century georgic poetry because it, like *The Seasons*, does not assume a didactic stance but nevertheless owes many structural and lexical debts to Virgil. In these passages, both poems exalt Queen Anne as an idealized, nearly divine power with enough political influence to both declare and achieve unity—or, in the later poem, international peace. Yet for hundreds of lines, *Cyder* has been teaching us to see ostensibly stable objects—the apple plucked from a hybrid tree, or here, the declaration of British unity—as both reflections and components of larger processes. Despite its obvious engagement with Virgil, *Windsor-Forest* does not proceed as a didactic poem, and as Pat Rogers has shown in two exhaustive books, it occupies a firm place in the tradition of Stuart iconography, mythology, and panegyric, all of which take a keen interest in images of the golden age returned. In the poem's final moments, the forest's trees are harvested and manufactured into ships, ready to carry British goods around the world: Pope's sweeping panegyric translates the peace of the golden age into a vision of global trade. Later georgics are rooted more firmly here than they are in Virgil.

Cyder may flirt with such idealism, but it remains securely attached to the Virgilian georgic mode, which refuses the dream of regression and accepts instead a deep awareness of the vast distance between the declaration and the realization of stability. *Cyder* certainly suggests hope; by contrasting Edward with Anne—who has perhaps, but not yet certainly, created a hardier state by grafting Scotland and Wales onto England—Philips expresses the hope that this new source of national strength will not re-create past disappointments. Pope's model of peace assumes the creation of a new, stable foundation, and therefore may prove as illusory as an opulent court masque. Philips's poem, however, offers a Virgilian georgic peace, which accepts a constant negotiation of heterogeneous energies. In many passages, Philips depicts or warns of failure, but does so most movingly near the beginning of his second book: "A thousand Accidents the Farmer's Hopes / Subvert, or checque; uncertain all his Toil" (2.46–47). At its core, farm labor is an expression of hope, and even when assiduously achieved, the results of this work always remain vulnerable to events that cannot be prevented.

Philips tempers this dark vision, however, by reconfiguring British heterogeneity as a potential strength, rather than a threat; in this way, his poem should not be read as an extended allegory or metaphor, or as a baldly topical piece of Tory propaganda, but as a sustained argument for conceiving of multiplicity as an important component of political unity. Like the figure of Nature in his poem, Philips "first . . . frames / All things in Miniature." In 1708, Philips could look back upon centuries of English history and lament how frequently "was Peace in vain / Sought for by Martial Deeds, and Conflict stern" (2.547–548). Yet Philips enfolds such sorrowful memories into his larger didactic agricultural poem, and like Marvell, Dryden, and Finch before him, envisions lasting peace not as a golden age returned, but as a state of perpetual cultivation.

FROM DIDACTIC TO DESCRIPTIVE

If the story of the formal English georgic often begins with *Cyder*, then it just as often culminates in *The Seasons*.[15] Yet *The Seasons* bears little resemblance to the Virgilian georgic. James Thomson's poem has long been recognized as a work steeped in the classical tradition and especially rife with passages that allude to or imitate Virgil.[16] But *The Seasons* diverges from the *Georgics* in at least one major way: it adopts an observational and descriptive stance, not a didactic one articulated primarily in precepts.[17] Studies of the poem have tended to dismiss this formal distance from the *Georgics*,[18] but these differences indicate fundamentally disparate conceptions of peace.

Writing several decades after the initial publication of *The Seasons*, John Aikin—physician, writer, and younger brother of Anna Laetitia Barbauld—praises Thomson for abandoning the didactic stance:

> But it is in that truly excellent and original poem, Thomson's *Seasons*, that we are to look for the greatest variety of genuine observations in natural history, and particularly in that part of it which regards the animal creation. And here I shall just remark, that the merited success of this piece has proved a refutation of those critics who deny that description can properly be the sole object of a poem, and would only admit its occasional introduction as part of a narrative, didactic, or moral design. . . . I mean not here to enter at large into a disquisition concerning didactic poetry; but only to suggest a comparison between the result of Thomson's unconfined plan, scarcely less extensive than nature itself, and that of some other writers, not inferior in genius, who thought it necessary to shackle themselves with teaching an art, or inculcating a system.[19]

Aikin eventually softens his criticism, admitting that Virgil was not really aiming to teach. But in order to promote the descriptive, he demotes the didactic, dismissing it—as scholars would centuries later—as a formal feature to be taken or left, or worse, as a "shackle" on the imaginations of otherwise skilled poets. In any case, for Aikin, teaching detracts from poetic achievement.

With this formal shift, however, *The Seasons* ceases to communicate the contingency suggested by the didactic form of Philips's poem. For Virgil writing in the wake of the Roman Civil Wars, and for Philips contemplating the meaning of the Union, didactic agricultural poetry offers a space in which to contemplate the creation of stable states—and to question the very claim to stability. Each poet finds value in the language of cultivation because the rhythms of agricultural work underscore the urgency of well-timed and continuous labor. The farmer who ceases to act ceases to thrive; such is the fate as well, these poets urge, of the makers of peace. Both poets choose the didactic frame to align their work with an earlier tradition of authoritative writers, but they share another motivation, too. Despite the centuries that separate their poems, Virgil and Philips find in the agricultural didactic a way of articulating the uncertainty that attends the transition from factional division to national unity—a transition that makes possible the realization of empire. Both the *Georgics* and *Cyder* perch precariously on the verge of this realization, depending as much upon experience as experiment to imagine the future.

The descriptive quality of *The Seasons*, therefore, suggests a significantly different set of conditions. *The Seasons* has long been read as a poem of empire; I have no quarrel with that interpretation, but want to emphasize that this association is exactly the quality that divorces the poem from the conception of Virgilian georgic that I have been articulating, here and in earlier chapters. Both Thomson and Philips engage with Virgil's *Georgics*, but only Philips shares with the Roman poet an interest in communicating political uncertainty at the level of form. Of course, factional politics persisted into and beyond Thomson's career, but by the 1720s the terms of the debate had changed dramatically. A Great Britain that could seriously consider itself an imperial power would no longer have found it necessary to address the concerns that motivated Virgil. By writing a poem related by an observer rather than a teacher, Thomson takes for granted the conditions that sustain the foundations of empire. In other words, whereas the georgic as I understand it maintains a keen interest in the creation of stability, the poetry of rural description assumes that stability, however imperfect or troubled, as a fundamental premise. Despite its frequent allusions to passages in the *Georgics*, *The Seasons* marks the realization of a distinctly British kind of georgic poetry, not a Virgilian one. For this poem, and for the united Britain it envisions, agricultural imagery increasingly connoted the structures of global economic power. By the middle decades of the eighteenth century, emphasis had shifted toward the value of agricultural commodities, and therefore the language of farm labor could no longer support the analogical valence I believe operates in the *Georgics* and in English poetry written in response to the civil wars and their consequences.

As the early verse paragraphs of *Spring* begin to tumble forth, Thomson vacillates between invocation and description: after beseeching the spring to emerge from "the Bosom of yon dropping Cloud"[20] and appealing to the grace of the Countess of Hertford, Thomson describes the early signs of the changing season, largely indicated by the first steps of the farmer into his fields. He conjures up Virgilian georgic by calling upon natural forces to complement human labor, and then swiftly argues for the poem's relevance—even for those unaccustomed to work:

> BE gracious, HEAVEN! for now laborious Man
> Has done his Part. Ye fostering Breezes blow!
> Ye softening Dews, ye tender Showers, descend!
> And temper All, thou world-reviving Sun,
> Into the perfect Year! Nor, ye, who live
> In Luxury and Ease, in Pomp and Pride,
> Think these lost Themes unworthy of your Ear:
> Such Themes as these the *rural* MARO sung
> To wide-imperial *Rome*, in the full Height
> Of Elegance and Taste, by *Greece* refin'd.
>   (*Spring* 48–57)

This passage, from the edition published in 1746—the main source for James Sambrook's standard edition of 1981—diverges in a small but significant way from earlier iterations that appeared in the editions printed between 1728 and 1738:

> 'Twas such as these the *Rural Maro* sung
> To the full *Roman* Court, in all it's height
> Of Elegance and Taste.

In the later version, Thomson claims kinship with those poets who appealed to the tastes of imperial Rome, but conflates the period in which Virgil was writing his *Georgics* and possibly reading them aloud to Octavian—a time still deeply scarred by the Roman civil wars—with the era of Augustan power fully realized. In other words, whereas the earlier version might plausibly suggest the period during which Virgil composed the *Georgics*, the later lines situate Virgil anachronistically, claiming that he "sung" rural poetry "To wide-imperial Rome," despite the fact that he completed his agricultural poems two years before Rome entered its imperial period.

Although such a poet as John Dryden had seen the ambiguities in the works of the Roman poet quite clearly, doubting the comprehensiveness of his allegiance to Augustus, in general the dominant association of Virgilian poetry with imperial achievement would persist well into the twentieth century, when classicists began to sense more fully the strains of anti-imperial sentiment in the *Aeneid*. We should not be surprised, then, that despite the Latin poem's anachronistic portrayal of Roman agriculture, the deep uncertainties it betrays about the future of Rome, and its distinct tendency to focus on labor rather than its fruits, Thomson would nevertheless find in the *Georgics* a foundation upon which to unite agricultural productivity and imperial supremacy.

The verse paragraph that follows famously realizes this union:

> Ye generous Britons, venerate the Plow!
> And o'er your Hills, and long withdrawing Vales,
> Let Autumn spread his Treasures to the Sun,
> Luxuriant, and unbounded! As the Sea,
> Far thro' his azure turbulent Domain,
> Your Empire owns, and from a thousand Shores
> Wafts all the Pomp of Life into your Ports;
> So with superior Boon may your rich Soil,
> Exuberant, Nature's better Blessings pour
> O'er every Land, the naked Nations cloath,
> And be th' exhaustless Granary of a World!
> (67–77)

The agricultural world depicted here departs from the Virgilian realm of deep uncertainty, replacing it with confident security. The image of "th' exhaustless Granary" suggests a perpetual supply of food at home and a surplus of profitable produce to be sold abroad. Thomson betrays no concern about the possibility of agricultural failure. In his introduction to the poem, Sambrook makes a related point, writing that Thomson's invocation of Virgil "elevate[s] the ordinary labours of the field"; he finds in this agricultural imagery an "implication . . . that the local harmony between the husbandman, his team, and his land is the foundation of the larger harmony of a wide mercantile empire which has cultural links with ancient Rome."[21] The idea of empire absorbs the language and imagery of the georgic, dispensing with images of process—arduous agricultural work—and replacing them with images of products. This shift bears an analogy with the shift suggested between the didactic and the descriptive: whereas one takes up the subject of *how*, the other concerns itself with *what*. It assumes the existence of something to be described, whereas the didactic lives outside the real, in a subjunctive, abstract space.

Although *The Seasons* does connect rural life to peace, it does so in a way that recalls the dream of the golden age.[22] The poem laments the ravages of civil war, but insists on a now deeply embedded British wholeness, which supports peace through national strength and wealth. Thomson approaches this peace by observing a shepherd and his sheep:

Around him feeds his many-bleating Flock,
Of various Cadence; and his sportive Lambs,
This way and that convolv'd, in friskful Glee,
Their Frolicks play. And now the sprightly Race
Invites them forth; when swift, the Signal given,
They start away, and sweep the massy Mound
That runs around the Hill; the Rampart once
Of iron War, in ancient barbarous Times,
When disunited BRITAIN ever bled,
Lost in eternal Broil: ere yet she grew
To this deep-laid indissoluble State,
Where *Wealth* and *Commerce* lift the golden Head;
And, o'er our Labours, *Liberty* and *Law*,
Impartial, watch, the Wonder of a World!
                                    (*Spring* 835–848)

Although Thomson shares with Virgil an interest in the history of the land, here the English poet suggests that the "once" violent past has been transformed into the present "deep-laid" and "indissoluble" Britain, resounding with what Thomson will later refer to as "the various voice / Of rural Peace" (917–918). Thomson places the violent "once" and the peaceable "now" onto a linear timeline: aligning the poem with Whig tropes, he suggests that past faction has been replaced by present unity, and that with every passing day Britain moves further from times of war. Yet even at the time of the poem's initial publication, Whig factions were struggling with one another for political dominance. In contrast to this idealism, the *Georgics* suggest a more fluid temporal relationship between past war and present peace, one that gestures toward continued negotiations of warlike energies. For instance, rural laborers dredge up the memories and materials of battle with their plows, and the poet makes soldiers of vines, and vines of soldiers. Thomson, however, describes peace in terms of perfection, in the most basic sense of the word: he imagines it as thoroughly made. By extension, *The Seasons* presents Britain itself as a stable and identifiable object—a "Wonder" to be seen and admired.

Admittedly, *The Seasons* is a Virgilian poem in that it gestures toward and rewrites much of the Roman author's poetry; it is also true that the poem blends history, myth, poetry, and scientific knowledge in a manner akin to that of the *Georgics*. Perhaps most basically, it seems like a Virgilian georgic poem because it is organized into four books, each of which treats a portion of the agricultural year—despite the fact that this chronological scheme more immediately recalls Pope's *Pastorals* and Spenser's *Shepheardes Calender* than the thematically arranged *Georgics*. Yet by abandoning the didactic stance, *The Seasons* turns decisively away from the poetry of uncertainty, and rests upon the ideological foundations of a relatively unified Britain, poised to accelerate an imperial program.

A more productive way to understand the relationship between *The Seasons* and the *Georgics* might be to imagine Thomson's poem as an extended dramatization of Virgil's Lucretian wish, expressed in the middle of his poem, to know the causes of things—of *all* the workings of the universe. Literary history often proceeds as a series of interlocking expansions and contractions: Virgil compresses the *Iliad* into two books of his *Aeneid*, in which Aeneas relates the Trojan War to Dido; Dante expands the single books depicting excursions into the underworld in Virgil and Homer to create his *Inferno*. Thinking along these lines, we might imagine *The Seasons*—a poem that betrays deep respect for and fascination with scientific knowledge—as a four-book version of Virgil's passage on the *felix*, or happy person, who knows the causes of things. In this way, *The Seasons* is not itself a georgic poem, but rather a poem made possible by the *Georgics*.

Within the world of *The Seasons*, the idea of a unified and powerful British empire matters more than the actual state of affairs at home or abroad; although Thomson's vision of Britain is exuberant, it is also highly idealized. The fiction of a unified British identity depended heavily on the idea of an enemy abroad. Indeed, Linda Colley begins her sweeping book on the making of British identity during the eighteenth century by reminding us of the almost constant wars between Britain and France between 1689 and 1815.[23] As a result, Thomson and other georgic poets exploited the genre for its patriotic potential. Robert Dodsley and John Dyer, for instance, were particularly eager to offer the French as an easy foil for the British in their georgic poems, boasting about what they claimed was a fundamental state of peacefulness in their own nation. In *The Fleece* (1757), which appeared not long after the commencement of the Seven Years' War but two years before the celebrated victories of 1759, Dyer relishes the opportunity to insult the "trifling Gaul, / Effeminate" (1.149–150), whom he deems unfit to thrive in the foggy English countryside. The morally minded Dodsley claimed in his georgic *Agriculture* (1753) that "the streams of wealth / And plenty flow" (1.22–23) at home, where the English are permanently prepared to deploy their weapons and warhorses against the French:

> Should e'er insidious France again presume
> On Europe's freedom, such [steeds], tho' all averse
> To slaughtering war, thy country shall present
> To bear her Hero to the martial plain,
> Arm'd with the sword of justice.
>
> (2.523–527)

Dyer thinks similarly, characterizing France as a perpetual aggressor:

> So may distress, and wretchedness, and want,
> The wide felicities of labor learn:
> So may the proud attempts of restless Gaul
> From our strong borders, like a broken wave,
> In empty foam retire.
>
> (1.8–12)

As it progresses, his poem suggests an even more forcefully patriotic attitude than Dodsley's; time and again, Dyer criticizes the climates of foreign lands as too extreme, and praises the temperate weather in England as fit not only for raising sheep, but also for developing a powerful and replicable national identity. *The Fleece* concludes with a prideful double vision of a British empire, poured like a liquid around the globe and charged with clothing the world's peoples in its wool:

> 'Tis her delight
> To fold the world with harmony, and spread
> Among the habitations of mankind,
> The various wealth of toil, and what her fleece,
> To clothe the naked, and her skillful looms,
> Peculiar give.
>
> (4.664–669)

In both poems, agriculture grounds the larger imperial project; rather than follow Virgil in speaking through the language of rural labor to contemplate the processes that give rise to stability, writers of formal georgic poems take the agricultural premises literally, celebrating the products of British agricultural labor as central components of a rapidly crystallizing sense of national identity and global dominance.

Yet despite the enthusiasm running through his patriotic georgic, Dyer was no blind champion of empire; nearly two decades earlier, he had published *The Ruins of Rome* (1740), which reflected his artistic and architectural studies in Italy during the 1720s.[24] In the poem, Dyer laments the demise of the Roman Empire, now "Fall'n, fall'n, a silent Heap" (16), but he also acknowledges its enduring power as an idea: "Lo the resistless Theme, Imperial *Rome*" (15).[25] As a "resistless theme," Rome perpetually invites translation and rewriting, and inspires new artistic creations; in this way, its ruins endure as raw materials for further contemplation and manipulation. Yet they also literalize the overwhelming power of time, which eventually wears down even the most impressive human achievements. These ideas run counter to those undergirding many midcentury English georgics, which look perpetually forward to new imperial glories built on ever-stronger economic foundations. Mistakenly convinced that Virgil meant in his *Georgics* to impart a vision of imperial potency and rural bliss, poets perhaps did not often think to use the georgic genre to communicate political doubt, even though they were not otherwise insensitive to the distance between the fiction and the reality of the imperial project.

At least one poet, however, did explicitly join his uncertainties about war and peace to his interest in writing agricultural didactic poetry. In the middle of the eighteenth century, shortly after the end of the War of the Austrian Succession (1740–1748) and the defeat of the final Jacobite rebellion, Christopher Smart published a georgic poem that indicated much less confidence about the prospect of lasting stability. *The Hop-Garden* lacks the exuberance of *The Seasons* and frequently betrays distinct strains of self-doubt. Smart was a better student of the classics than Thomson, but never achieved the same degree of public appreciation, nor did he enjoy the aristocratic patronage that supported much of his contemporary's career. A writer scorned by the elite for his hack work and derided by readers of light verse for his more erudite poetry, and a man who struggled to please his financially shrewd employer and father-in-law, John Newbery,[26] Smart was perhaps more inclined than Thomson to detect and expose the darker corners of British claims to imperial glory.

AFTER THOMSON: CHRISTOPHER SMART, *THE HOP-GARDEN*, AND THE END OF GEORGIC PEACE

By the mid-eighteenth century, didactic poetry still offered a connection to Virgil, and therefore to an illustrious tradition of creative achievement. Yet after Philips, the didactic georgic lost much of its capacity to communicate meaning through its form. In fact, the English georgic became instead the genre most amenable to the division between form and content, since this poetry of instruction could be applied in earnest to nearly any subject.[27] By the end of the eighteenth century, the English scientific georgic had moved so far away from Virgil that John Aikin could plausibly suggest that the Roman poet himself had been mistaken in choosing a subject largely unfit for didactic poetry. In 1795, in an essay published with an edition of *The Art of Preserving Health*, Aikin argues that in contrast to the agricultural subjects treated in the *Georgics*, Armstrong's medical subject matter has been more "happily calculated for didactic poetry."[28] In describing the value of georgic writing, Aikin makes the conventional gestures of reverence to Virgil, but ultimately criticizes the poet for mishandling his subject:

> For no unprejudiced reader will deny, that in many of the preceptive passages, notwithstanding the variety of resources he employs to elevate them into poetry, he is overpowered by his subject, and chained, as it were, to the earth he is laboring;—while, on the other hand, as a teacher of the art, he is frequently so obscure, as to have embarrassed the whole race of agricultural and literary critics since his time. It may also be observed, that had he extended his views further into the philosophical part of his subject, and made a full use of the moral and physical variety it was capable of affording, he would not have found it necessary to wander into digressions so remotely connected with his proposed topics, as scarcely to be justified by any reasonable claim of poetic licence.[29]

In criticizing Virgilian "digressions" and "poetic licence," Aikin gestures toward ancient and contemporary debates over the literary value and scientific accuracy of the *Georgics*. Yet whereas Aikin's critical stance descends from Joseph Addison's *Essay*, which distinguished didactic form and agricultural content, he diverges from his predecessor in finding fault with the ultimate structure and content of the *Georgics*. In separating the didactic frame from the subject of farming, however, both writers move English georgic poetry further away from its Virgilian origins.

Many poets writing in the later decades of the eighteenth century contributed to this ever-widening gulf between didactic forms or frames and scientific contents. One of the most blatant articulations of this shift appears in James Grainger's preface to his georgic poem, *The Sugar-Cane* (1764), which he hoped would be appreciated for its scientific accuracy:

> Soon after my arrival in the West-Indies, I conceived the design of writing a poem on the cultivation of the Sugar-Cane. My inducements to this arduous undertaking were, not only the importance and novelty of the subject, but more especially this consideration; that, as the face of this country was wholly different from that of Europe, so whatever hand copied its appearances, however rude, could not fail to enrich poetry with many new and picturesque images.
>
> I cannot, indeed, say I have satisfied my own ideas in this particular: yet I must be permitted to recommend the precepts contained in this Poem. They are the children of Truth, not of Genius; the result of Experience, not the productions of Fancy.[30]

With *The Sugar-Cane*, Grainger intends to communicate realistic descriptions of a natural environment little known to readers at home in Britain. He emphasizes his own labor as an observer, having taken up the "arduous" task of transforming information into poetry. Whereas other poems derive from "Genius" and "Fancy,"

"Truth" and "Experience" inform this poem; Grainger privileges observation, introducing himself as both a poet and a natural historian. He suggests here that a tired British poetic landscape requires "enrich[ment]," and such sentiments left the way wide open for Romantic writers to claim their own new and exciting powers to enrich. Yet perhaps the lifelessness that Grainger detected occurred not because there was nothing left to write about in England, but because poets had become deaf to the power of the didactic form *itself* to make meaning.

Surprisingly, much of the recuperative work on the georgic has tended to accept and replicate the terms whereby Aikin and Grainger—and even, at times, the Romantics—conceived of the genre. Yet important exceptions exist, and although it is true that georgic writers more or less accepted Addison's conception of the genre as elevating low subjects to high art, they did not do so slavishly. Christopher Smart, for instance, used the notion of the georgic as a poetics of elevation to reflect upon his own abilities as a young poet. Moreover, Smart includes in his georgic poem a vision of peace far darker than Virgil's. In many ways, Smart's poem *The Hop-Garden: A Georgic in Two Books*, fulfills Addison's vision of georgic poetry: it raises low subjects to the heights of good poetry, and it attends to the realistic details of agricultural labor. Yet it also retains some traces of the conversation about the nature of lasting peace that often occupied the minds of poets writing during the difficult years of transition from the seventeenth to the eighteenth century.

This poem, first published in 1752, has hardly been overvalued by scholars or poets,[31] and indeed Smart sometimes loses control of the verse as it careens into overelaborate diction, but he also undertakes a serious engagement with questions of history, creativity, and most significantly for this book, peace. Smart was an enthusiastic participant in the tradition of poetic imitation—the opening lines of *The Hop-Garden* evoke both Virgilian and Miltonic poetry.[32] Yet as in the *Georgics* and *Cyder*, the didactic stance and agricultural focus of *The Hop-Garden* necessarily bring with them the double languages of hope and uncertainty. To engage explicitly with the processes of agricultural labor is, for Smart, simultaneously to confront the possibility of poetic and political failure.

The Hop-Garden treats the subject of hop cultivation in Kent. Like Virgil, however, Smart uses this topic as a point of departure for other considerations. From its earliest moments, *The Hop-Garden* is also a poem about poetry, dramatizing the poet's aspirations toward meaningful literary achievement, as well as his acceptance of the lower georgic register as the safest course. Early in the poem, Smart invokes the muse that guided Sir Philip Sidney, but quickly abandons any hope of having his prayer answered:

> Had I such pow'r, no peasants toil, no hops
> Shou'd e'er debase my lay: far nobler themes,
> The high atchievements of thy warrior kings
> Shou'd raise my thoughts, and dignify my song.
> But I, young rustic, dare not leave my cot,
> For so enlarg'd a sphere—ah! muse beware,
> Lest the loud larums of the braying trump,
> Lest the deep drum shou'd drown thy tender reed,
> And mar its puny joints: me, lowly swain,
> Every unshaven arboret, me the lawns,
> Me the voluminous Medway's silver wave,
> Content inglorious, and the hopland shades!
> (1.22–33)[33]

Smart betrays a qualified relationship with the georgic here; although eventually he accepts the "inglorious" subject of rustic labor, he first expresses his preference for the "nobler themes" of epic. Unlike Milton, Smart accepts a middle flight, casting himself as a "young rustic," and remaining safely within what he deems the safer sphere of the agricultural world, since the "braying trump" and "deep drum" of heroic war might overpower his poetic capabilities. Of course, in making these gestures, Smart also aligns himself with the midcareer Virgil in two ways: first, he echoes the end of the *Georgics*, where the poet describes himself *ignobilis oti*—at lowly leisure—while Caesar wages publicly glorious war. Second, he recalls Virgil's doubts about his own epic aims, expressed near the mathematical middle of the *Georgics*; in this passage, Virgil points to the natural and agricultural worlds as fit substitutes should he fail as a writer of epic. Smart acknowledges this connection with his own footnote appended to the poem, quoting the Latin lines.

Despite having acquiesced to the georgic, Smart appears to forget his vow of ingloriousness rather quickly, launching the language of his poem into an overwhelmingly aestheticized register. This language can sound strange at best, and offensive at worst, to twenty-first-century ears more accustomed to quieter, smaller poetic gestures. Smart addresses his newfound comrades, "Yeomen, and countrymen," as "Egregious shepherds of unnumber'd flocks," some of whom live "in fair Madum's vale / Imparadis'd, blest denizens" (1.34, 36, 38–39). We might be tempted to dismiss such language as merely ostentatious or derivative; and indeed, Smart seems to be reveling in the ornamental possibilities here, importing the word "imparadis'd" from *Paradise Lost* (4.506), and replicating Milton's affinity for prefixes and etymological puns—"egregious" derives from the Latin *grex/gregis*, or "flock." But the hyperbolic language here is also perhaps a response to Addison's own characterization of georgic poetry as the ideal middle mode, one to be praised primarily for its capacity to make art from the unbeautiful stuff of rustic life. If Smart seems to have traveled beyond the pale of good poetry here, I think it possibly a purposeful overstep that challenges Addison's judgments: the ostensibly heightening power of the georgic collapses here into something that better resembles mock- than pre-epic poetry.

Yet this very threat of collapse provides the most important link between the agricultural subject matter and broader concerns about literary achievement. A poem that follows the rhythms of the agricultural year is very nearly guaranteed to arrive at a conclusion: however lengthy its digressions, an agricultural didactic must describe each stage of labor, from selecting turf to sowing seeds, to tending crops, and finally to reaping the harvest. Like the author of the *Georgics* and his imitators, Smart often propels *The Hop-Garden* forward by noting that the time has come to move on: "Thus much be sung of picking—next succeeds / Th' important care of curing" (2.190–191). In this way, unlike the more varied landscape of pastoral song, or the massive undertakings of epic poetry, the georgic provides a predictably secure framework upon which to display verbal artistry. At the same time, however, an agricultural poem always implicitly acknowledges failure: to speak as a teacher is to be unsure that the lessons will be heeded; to speak of construction is to suggest the threat of destruction; to speak of maintenance is to admit the possibility of lapse. This inherent tension between success and failure marks the agricultural didactic poem as a source of exceptionally apt terms for thinking about poetic creation.

In the poem's second book, which describes the reaping of the crops sown in the first book, Smart again explores the bounds of poetic achievement. After a long rewriting of Virgil's meditation on the signs of an impending storm, Smart shifts to the new day that follows, calling for the return of "Justice" and "Fair Prudence" as the farmhands return to their labors, "for not without / A certain method cou'dst thou rule the mob / Irrational" (2.155, 156–157). Smart most immediately means the "mob" of disorderly workers, but the next shift in the poem suggests he is thinking of poetic prudence, too:

> Now see the crew mechanic might and main
> Labour with lively diligence, inspir'd
> By appetite of gain and lust of praise:
> What mind so petty, servile, and debas'd,
> As not to know ambition? Her great sway
> From *Colin Clout* to Emperors she exerts.
> To err is human, human to be vain.
> 'Tis vanity, and mock desire of fame,
> That prompts the rustic, on the steeple top
> Sublime, to mark the outlines of his shoe,

And in the area to engrave his name.
With pride of heart the churchwarden surveys,
High o'er the belfry, girt with birds and flow'rs,
His story wrote in capitals: "'Twas I
That bought the font; and I repair'd the pews."
With pride like this the emulating mob
Strive for the mastery—who first may fill
The bellying bin, and cleanest cull the hops.
                              (2.160–177)

In this section of the poem, Smart rounds out the set of aesthetic questions that
have been propelling *The Hop-Garden*: whereas earlier he expressed epic hopes but
settled for georgic, over the course of the poem he has continued to chase the spec-
ters of Milton and Virgil, translating and imitating the classical poet while creating
verbal links to the English one. Here, Smart considers his own potential "appetite
of gain and lust of praise": although the passage suggests that pride may plague
anyone, "From *Colin Clout* to Emperors," its examples repeatedly point to writing
or marking as the primary symbols of self-exultation. The "rustic" indicates his
labor by "engrav[ing] his name," and the "churchwarden" celebrates his own work
by marking out his "story . . . in capitals." By the time we reach the "emulating
mob" who "Strive for mastery," Smart seems to be on the verge of criticizing poets,
imitating their forebears, who would claim original and ultimate achievement. As
the line turns across the phrase, "fill / The bellying bin," we come to understand
that Smart has returned to the harvest scene, but his implicit criticism of poetic
pride persists. Such gestures of uncertainty and self-criticism should compel us to
read with a keener eye Smart's conversation with his literary forebears. His poem
teeters precariously on the verge of farce, but within this vertiginous passage lies
a meditation on the contingency of all poetic attempts.

This recognition of contingency leads Smart to negotiate another layer of
meaning: *The Hop-Garden* speaks through the double concerns of agricultural and
poetic labor to consider political problems, too. In perhaps the most striking echo
of Milton in the poem, Smart praises the hop as a symbol of golden-age peace
under Queen Elizabeth, but admits that in earlier ages it was "Shun'd" as "an interdicted plant" (1.182–183).[34] Milton uses the same adjective more than once to
describe the tree of knowledge in *Paradise Lost*: in book 7 the narrator reminds us
that "*Adam* or his Race" have been "Charg'd not to touch the interdicted Tree"
(7.45–46), and earlier, Eve sees in her Satanic dream "the Tree / Of interdicted
knowledge" (5.51–52).[35] These links suggest that the very status of the hop as a
worthy poetic subject is contingent; in this way, the connection to *Paradise Lost*
heightens the sense of potential failure that already burdens the poem.

The transformation of the hop from prohibited plant to prized crop is bound up with questions of peace:

> In those blest days when great Eliza reign'd
> O'er the adoring nation, when fair peace
> Or spread an unstain'd olive round the land,
> Or laurell'd war did teach our winged fleets
> To lord it o'er the world, when our brave sires
> Drank valour from uncauponated beer;
> Then th' hop (before an interdicted plant,
> Shun'd like fell aconite) began to hang
> Its folded floscles from the golden vine,
>
> (1.176–184)

Here, the hop appears as part of a golden age maintained under the auspices of Queen Elizabeth; a few lines later Smart will contrast this age of peace and fairly sold beer with those of the Saxon king Hengist, who used a poison drink and his seductive daughter to usurp the throne of Vortigern, criticized as a "voluptuous" ruler who "the toils of war, / Neglected" (1.192–194). The relationships among peace, war, and kingship are striking here: Smart suggests military discipline as a fundamental part of upright governance—a surprising contrast with the meditations on peace in the other poems I have discussed in this and earlier chapters. Consider again the lines on the peace of Elizabeth's age; despite his inclusion of olives and the golden hop, Smart constructs a rather unwieldy "either/or" formulation in the third and fourth lines, rendered even more confusing by the triple initial rhyme that results from the alignment of "O'er," and two instances of "Or." Elizabeth's reign "O'er" England, a time when the ostensibly unifying force of "fair peace" is split between the "either" implied by the first "Or"—"Or spread an unstain'd olive round the land"—and the "or" of the second line—"Or laurell'd war did teach our winged fleets." In a sense, peace here can take *either* the form of widespread tranquility signified by the olive, *or* the form of military activity. The division of these two states into separate lines reinforces their separation; but the echoing sound of "or"—which extends into "laurell'd war," "lord," "our," and "valour"—unites them.

Perhaps the aural intricacy of this moment suggests broader ambivalence on the part of the poet; he seems to be working out exactly what he means by peace, but finds it difficult to settle on a single vision. This sense of doubleness returns at the transition from the first to the second book. Book 1 concludes with a praise of medieval Kent, to whose citizens William the Conqueror, "like Caesar, deign'd to yield" (1.421). This history of resilience and autonomy might hopefully extend into future battles waged by the "sons" of "Cantium" (1.426, 423), but

>   till then
> With olive, and with hop-land garlands crown'd,
> O'er all thy land reign Plenty, reign fair Peace.
>   (1.427–429)

As in the earlier passage, here the hop joins the olive in signaling widespread peace, and Smart draws his first book to a close with this triumphant and decisive gesture. The opening lines of book 2, however, find the poet despairing lost peace:

> O'er the wild world, like Noah's dove, in vain
> I seek the olive peace, around me wide
> See! see! The wat'ry waste—In vain, forlorn
> I call the Phoenix fair Sincerity;
> Alas!—extinguish'd to the skies she fled,
> And left no heir behind her.
>   (2.9–14)

We soon learn that these despairing words lament the death of "Mr. Theophilus Wheeler of Christ-College, Cambridge," who was born in Kent and died at eighteen.[36] In contrast to the sweeping, prideful claim of peace at the end of book 1, here the peace lost is personal and emotional. Yet Smart promptly returns to the language of political discord as the poem turns from the death of a friend to the reaping of the harvest. This scene of labor teems with energy: "from the great metropolis . . . rush / Th' industrious vulgar" who "like Prudent bees" gather the hops (2.57–58). The workers are apt to become rowdy and disorganized, and as a result to threaten the final stages of the agricultural cycle. Smart describes the force that orders them in terms that recall both *Cyder* and *Windsor-Forest*. In the passage that follows, he names his sister, Marianne, the queen of the laborers:

>   Oft her command
> Has sav'd the pillars of the hopland state,
> The lofty poles from ruin, and sustain'd,
> Like ANNA, or ELIZA, her domain,
> With more than manly dignity. Oft I've seen,
> Ev'n at her frown the boist'rous uproar cease,
> And the mad pickers, tam'd to diligence,
> Cull from the bin the sprawling sprigs, and leaves
> That stain the sample, and its worth debase.
>   (2.91–99)

Here Smart joins his own earlier homage to Queen Elizabeth with a faint echo of the lines on Anne in the poems by Philips and Pope, with the word "cease" perhaps suggesting a slightly stronger link to *Windsor-Forest*. In any case, these lines lighten the political tones of the earlier poems; Marianne resembles the queens insofar as she exerts an ordering power over the riotous reapers, but instead of civil war the "mad pickers" risk "stain[ing]" the hop husks with the juices of their leaves. Although perhaps the risk of economic loss is one to consider seriously, the effects of the language in this passage are more humorous than they are seriously political. Addison had praised the georgic for its capacity to heighten, but for Smart the georgic framework functions in two directions rather than one: the georgic can heighten farm labor to the language of monarchial power, but by doing so it suggests that monarchial power can be read in lower agricultural terms as well.

The playful rendering of politics in this passage jars with the darker one that concludes the poem. In the same way that Virgil, Milton, and Philips kept in view the political problems of their own periods while also reaching backward into literary history, Smart uses the final sections of his poem to criticize the nearly perpetual wars with France that England waged over the course of the eighteenth century. Having followed the chronology of the agricultural task to its predictable end, Smart first brings the main action of his poem to a conclusion:

> What then remains unsung? unless the care
> To stack thy poles oblique in comely cones,
> Lest rot or rain destroy them—'Tis a sight
> Most seemly to behold, and gives, O Winter!
> A landskip not unpleasing ev'n to thee.
>
> (2.237–241)

The only task that "remains unsung," or not yet turned into poetry, is the ordering of the stakes that will support next year's crop. Although apparently Addisonian in its aestheticizing of the "comely cones," beautiful even to "Winter" himself, this passage also suggests contingency and threat. At the same time that the passage asks us to see the poles as objects of beauty, it also adds a characteristically Virgilian subjunctive construction—"Lest rot or rain destroy them"—that betrays the utilitarian, protective value of the stack. Any agricultural task can be made beautiful by the poet, but neither Virgil nor Smart can erase the threat of decay and destruction that motivates the farmer's action. This miniature dramatization of contingency returns with sweeping force in the final two verse paragraphs, both marked by a jarringly negative turn suggesting that no true peace will be possible for England in the near future.

Following a catalogue of praises for various inhabitants and locales associated with Kent, Smart adopts a defensive, isolationist stance:

> Oh that Britannia, in the day of war,
> Wou'd not alone Minerva's valour trust,
> But also hear her wisdom! Then her oaks
> Shap'd by her own mechanics, wou'd alone
> Her island fortify, and fix her fame;
> Nor wou'd she weep, like Rachael, for her sons,
> Whose glorious blood, in mad profusion,
> In foreign lands is shed—and shed in vain.
> (2.285–292)

Suddenly, a poet who has been celebrating English labor turns his subject more immediately toward questions of war and militarism. Recall that the medal struck for the Treaty of Utrecht urged us to see elements of Anne, Minerva, and Britannia in the central figure on its reverse side. Here, Smart separates the Greek from the British goddess, casting the national deity as a student with much to learn from her more experienced teacher. In calling for only those military efforts that would "fortify" Britain, Smart also beseeches the nation not to seek war.

In the final verse paragraph, however, Smart abandons these hopes, concluding *The Hop-Garden* with a poignant acquiescence to the enmity between Britain and France:

> Now on fair Dover's topmost cliff I'll stand,
> And look with scorn and triumph on proud France.
> Of yore an isthmus jutting from this coast,
> Join'd the Britannic to the Gallic shore;
> But Neptune on a day, with fury fir'd,
> Rear'd his tremendous trident, smot the earth,
> And broke th' unnatural union at a blow.—
> "'Twixt you and you, my servants and my sons,
> Be there (he cried) eternal discord—France
> Shall bow the neck to Cantium's peerless offspring,
> And as the oak reigns lordly o'er the shrub,
> So shall the hop have homage from the vine."
> (2.294–304)

The verse paragraph begins with temporal ambiguity: the speaker declares that he *will* stand on the cliffs of Dover *now*. Read alone, the line appears to occupy an impossible future-present tense, but it makes more sense in relation to the subjunctive plea in the earlier section, where the speaker wishes that Britain *would* heed the wisdom of Minerva, and satisfy itself with strong defenses rather than military aggressions. If that situation should arise, *then* the speaker would be able to look upon France "with scorn and triumph." These conditional constructions underscore the distance between Smart's defensive stance and contemporary political realities. No explicit mention of active war appears in the closing moments of the poem, but Smart's criticism is no less trenchant for being implicit.

At this point, the speaker fades away completely, and the sea god Neptune speaks the final lines. The language of agricultural realities cedes here to that of mythology, prophecy, and history, all of which mix rather strangely. Deforming the triumphant lines of *Windsor-Forest* spoken by Father Thames, reversing the scene of calmed seas in the first book of the *Aeneid*, and perhaps distantly echoing Dido's curse on Aeneas, the god commands "eternal discord," which appears to mean perpetual war, but then Neptune orders that France will eventually "bow" to England—and, more specifically, to Kent. This poem, so interested in its own development, concludes in a stunningly distanced way, abandoned by its primary speaker and consumed with disorienting grammatical structures. Perhaps Smart holds these lines at arm's length because they betray a deeply negative vision of unending battle decreed by the gods. Careful readers have observed in the last line here an echo of the conclusion Philips wrote for *Cyder*, in which the apple liquor "shall . . . triumph o'er the Vine" (2.669).[37] I would add, however, that at the same time that this poem gestures toward the earlier one, it also establishes an important internal link: the final word, "vine," recalls "vain," which concluded the earlier verse paragraph. With this near-rhyme, Smart reinforces the wastefulness of the war with France, perhaps considering external violence too high a price for internal unity. The inherently positive tenor of an agricultural poem treating the stages of a successful harvest takes an ironic turn when it is made to confront the destructiveness of war. At the end of *The Hop-Garden* Smart refuses to join agricultural and political peace. Instead, he simply falls silent.

Despite the earnest assertions of eighteenth-century agricultural specialists, the fundamental lessons of Virgil's poem were not limited to farm work. Writing in terms of agricultural success and failure, Virgil was trying to teach others to accept that things can always transform into other things. Failure—be it agricultural, poetic, or political—always looms. Yet so too does success. If all things derive from the same material foundations, then the implements of war can be recast into implements of peace: the sword can be formed once again into the scythe. Not all English writers who modeled their poems on the *Georgics* perceived these lessons, but those who did created a rich afterlife for an important ancient poem. More importantly, they offer to us a special point of access to long-standing ideas about the forces of destruction and construction. When we read these poets through Virgil, and Virgil through these poets, we become aware of a powerful conversation in which writers have dared to hope that we might, through continuous and arduous labor, create lasting peace.

NOTES

1. See Linda Colley, *Britons: Forging the Nation, 1707–1837*, rev. ed. (New Haven, CT: Yale University Press, 2005), 322. Colley notes that nearly perpetual war with France created in eighteenth-century Britain "a semblance of unity" that sometimes mitigated the tensions that persisted within and among England, Scotland, and Wales.

2. Suvir Kaul regards *The Seasons* as "an encyclopedia of nationalist desire." *Poems of Nation, Anthems of Empire: English Verse in the Long Eighteenth Century* (Charlottesville: University of Virginia Press, 2000), 147.

3. Pat Rogers has argued for heightened "politiciz[ation]" of the georgic under Philips's pen, and subsequently under Pope's, as the result of both writers' "introducing a more extensive stock of nationalist materials" ("John Philips, Pope, and Political Georgic," *Modern Language Quarterly* 66, no. 4 [December 2005]: 414–415).

4. Extending the work of Anthony Low, who understands the georgic mode as fundamental to moralistic nation-building, many scholars have derived their arguments about the poem from its association with the Act of Union, continuing a long tradition of locating *Cyder* at the inception of a distinctly British form of georgic. See especially Rachel Crawford, "English Georgic and British Nationhood," *ELH* 65, no. 1 (1998): 124.

5. See Winn, *Queen Anne*, 345–350, 427–436.

6. Colley, *Britons*, 12–13.

7. See for instance Juan Christian Pellicer, "Celebrating Queen Anne and the Union of 1707 in Great Britain's First Georgic," *Journal for Eighteenth-Century Studies* 37, no. 2 (2014): 220.

8. Rogers, "John Philips, Pope, and Political Georgic," 418–419. Pellicer describes *Cyder* as "a promotional publication for a leading minister who was just preparing a major ministerial coup," and who needed to count on the support of precisely the people strategically praised in Philips's poem" ("Harleian Georgic from Tonson's Press: The Publication of John Philips's *Cyder*, 29 January 1708," *The Library: The Transactions of the Bibliographical Society* 7, no. 2 [2006]: 192). In *Poetry, Enclosure, and the Vernacular Landscape, 1700–1830* (Cambridge: Cambridge University Press, 2002), Crawford offers a thorough account of the Herefordshire landscape and the poem's role in Britain's "nationalizing process" (127).

9. Philips's formal and allusive debts to Virgil and Milton have been exhaustively documented by Juan Christian Pellicer. See his edition of *Cyder,* co-edited with John Goodridge (Cheltenham: Cyder Press, 2001); "John Philips (1676–1709)"; "The Georgic at Mid-Eighteenth Century and the Case of Dodsley's 'Agriculture,'" *Review of English Studies* 54 (2003): 67–93; "Harleian Georgic from Tonson's Press"; "Reception, Wit, and the Unity of Virgil's *Georgics*," *Symbolae Osloenses* 82 (2007): 90–115; "Corkscrew or Cathedral? The Politics of Alexander Pope's *Windsor-Forest* and the Dynamics of Literary Kind," *Huntington Library Quarterly* 71, no. 3 (2008): 453–488; "Celebrating Queen Anne." For Philips and Milton, see also Dustin Griffin, "The Bard of Cyder-Land: John Philips and Miltonic Imitation," *Studies in English Literature, 1500–1900* 24, no. 3 (1984): 441–460.

10. This and all subsequent quotations of Philips's poem from *The Poems of John Philips*, ed. M. G. Lloyd Thomas (Oxford: Basil Blackwell, 1927).

11. Colley, *Britons*, 39; Winn, *Queen Anne*, 427–436.

12. Pellicer, "Celebrating Queen Anne," 220–221.

13. *Oxford English Dictionary*, s.v. "experience, n."

14. Rogers notes that an earlier version of Pope's poem hewed even more closely to the phrasing here ("John Philips, Pope, and Political Georgic," 432).

15. Crawford describes the poem as "perhaps the most fundamental English georgic of all time" (*Poetry, Enclosure, and the Vernacular Landscape*, 94).

16. Thomson, *The Seasons*, ed. James Sambrook (Oxford: Clarendon Press, 1981), provides exhaustive notes and commentary tracing allusions to Virgil and other classical writers. See also Ralph Cohen, *The Unfolding of "The Seasons"* (Baltimore: Johns Hopkins Press, 1970), 12; and Patricia Meyer Spacks, *The Varied God: A Critical Study of Thomson's "The Seasons"* (Berkeley: University of California Press, 1959), 183.

17. *The Seasons* has not been universally read as a descriptive poem; Cohen, arguing for its unities as derived from Thomson's spiritual commitments, understands it as a work of religious didacticism (*The Unfolding*, 3).

18. Pellicer suggests that "*The Seasons*, despite its lack of a perceptive element . . . showed most fully how British poets might elevate contemporary scientific and agricultural topics in an entirely serious manner" ("The Georgic at Mid-Eighteenth Century," 70). In his edition of *The Seasons*, Sambrook makes a similar gesture, writing that "*The Seasons* is not prescriptive in quite Virgil's way" (xxv); he emphasizes its descriptive quality as a major source of praise from writers of the Romantic period (xxix–xxx), noting specifically the "eye" that surveys the world of the poem (xxi). See also Goodman, *Georgic Modernity and British Romanticism*, chap. 2, and Philip Connell, "Newtonian Physico-Theology and the Varieties of Whiggism in James Thomson's *The Seasons*," *HLQ* 72, no. 1 (2009): 1–28.

19. John Aikin, *An Essay on the Application of Natural History to Poetry* (London, 1777), Eighteenth-Century Collections Online, 57–59.

20. This and all subsequent quotations from Thomson, *The Seasons*, ed. Sambrook.

21. Ibid., xxvi.

22. Thomson builds his model of peace upon what Ralph Cohen has deemed "a typical eighteenth-century cluster of peace, prosperity, patriotism, and plenty," where "the estates are the sources of wealth and the basis for Britain's power" (*The Unfolding*, 7).

23. Colley, *Britons*, 1.

24. Belinda Humphrey, "Dyer, John," in *Oxford Dictionary of National Biography* (Oxford University Press, 2004; online ed.).

25. Dyer, *The Ruins of Rome. A poem* (London, 1740).

26. Karina Williamson, "Smart, Christopher (1722–1771)," in *Oxford Dictionary of National Biography* (Oxford University Press, 2004; online ed.).

27. In *English Poetry of the Eighteenth Century, 1700–1789* (Harlow, UK: Longman, 2003), David Fairer articulates the richness of eighteenth-century georgic, as well as its readiness to allow "freer reworkings and extension to different topics" (90).

28. John Armstrong, *The Art of Preserving Health. By John Armstrong, M.D. To which is prefixed A Critical Essay on the Poem, by J. Aikin, M.D.* (London, 1795), 6.

29. Ibid., 5.

30. James Grainger, *The Sugar-Cane: a poem. In four books* (London, 1764), preface.

31. See Moira Dearnley, *The Poetry of Christopher Smart* (London: Routledge and Kegan Paul, 1968), xiv.

32. Betty Rizzo articulates the poet's aesthetic commitments; in addition to imitation and emulation, Rizzo observes sustained interest in "compact concision," "vigor of attack," and "comprehension or complete inclusiveness." ("Christopher Smart's Poetics," in *Christopher Smart and the Enlightenment*, ed. Clement Hawes [New York: St. Martin's Press, 1999], 121.) In *Christopher Smart's English Lyrics: Translation in the Eighteenth Century* (Surrey, UK: Ashgate, 2014) Rosalind Powell traces Smart's imitation and emulation of classical, biblical, and other English writers.

33. *The Poetical Works of Christopher Smart,* vol. 4, *Miscellaneous Poems English and Latin,* ed. Karina Williamson (Oxford: Clarendon Press, 1987).

34. Smart recalls here early resistance to beer made with hops, a plant that originated on the Continent and was therefore sometimes deemed unpatriotic—or even illegal—to consume from the fifteenth to the seventeenth centuries. Henry VI was reputed to have "vehemently resisted the use of hops," and during his reign a citizen of Kent was charged with adding hops to beer (Ian Spencer Hornsey, *A History of Beer and Brewing* [Cambridge: Royal Society of Chemistry, 2003], 319, 314).

35. Milton, *Complete Poems and Major Prose.*

36. Smart appends his own note identifying Wheeler; Williamson adds further information in *The Poetical Works of Christopher Smart.*

37. Ibid., 419n.

THE WORD "GEORGIC" HAS NOT OFTEN been known to summon visions of peace and war, loss and resilience, or mutability and contingency. For most of the poets in this book, however, the language of agricultural struggle offers a way of comprehending the difficulties of their worlds. In a sense, these poets are united by their losses: Dryden and Finch found themselves jettisoned to the political margins, and although Marvell and Philips never suffered the same overt rejections, they both understood the fragile nature of stability, especially when that stability has been declared and spectacularly celebrated. It is true that a deep gulf of time and a vast range of other poetic experiments and traditions stand between any of these poets and the ancient Roman Virgil. Yet theirs was a culture steeped in translated, imitated, and rewritten Roman poetry, and during the Restoration and early eighteenth century, to write poems on agriculture was necessarily to invoke the *Georgics*.

We have perhaps not detected the extent of eighteenth-century engagements with this poem because we have too often associated Virgil's middle poem with the hope of empire. We have also tended to trust eighteenth-century poets, like Thomson, who were a little too willing to conflate the authority of Roman emperors with the poetry written before their definite rise. The British were eager to borrow the power of an ancient empire, and in their view the best way to do this was to connect themselves to its art and culture. As a result, the Virgil who appeared in middle and later eighteenth-century British poetry was often treated as little more than a lifeless ornament, tacitly adorning imperial art. Yet the living Virgil would hardly have recognized this version of himself; from the opening of the *Eclogues* forward, he had asked difficult questions about the role of poetry in a world marked by conquest and governed by strong men, and—as Dryden might surmise—had he been living in the seventeenth century, he would likely have asked similar questions under Cromwell or William of Orange.

The ominous and ambiguous *Georgics* were especially appealing to English poets whose lives had unfolded such that they were moved to doubt the capacity of central powers to impose and perpetuate peace. Responding to intense disappointment or profound uncertainty—or both—each of these poets envisions a peaceful future in which stability holds because it is perpetually cultivated. The work of the poet becomes like the work of the farmer. Both must struggle in order to create, and both must admit the inexorable forces always working around and against them. These forces range from the simple possibility of creative inadequacy to the much more dramatic possibility that deteriorating political stability will impede not only their work, but also their lives.

In the fourth book of the *Georgics*, Virgil relates how the divine intellect, or *diuinae mentis* (220), of bees renders them capable of building a whole civilization—they live in a kind of city, obey common laws, and even wage wars. The *Georgics* proceed by developing one subject from the seeds of another: here, the early passages on the bees' society give rise to a narrative about the beekeeper Aristaeus, who beseeches the gods for help after his colony suddenly and inexplicably dies. His mother, Cyrene, answers his lamentations by bringing him instructions from Neptune: in order to understand why the colony sickened, Aristaeus must capture Proteus, an all-knowing god with infinite powers to change his shape. Having succeeded in restraining Proteus, Aristaeus learns that his agricultural misfortune derives from an offense; he attempted to rape Eurydice on the night of her wedding to Orpheus, and as a result unwittingly initiated the events that led to the deaths of both. Realizing that what seemed a chance misfortune actually resulted from his own wrongdoing, Aristaeus learns that he must perform a ritual sacrifice—*petens pacem*, or "seeking peace" (535)—to appease the nymphs he has offended. Miraculously, upon completion of the sacrifice new bees spring from the bodies of heifers he slaughters.

It is fitting that this ever-shifting poem, rife with images of mutability and always moving between genres, adopts the changeable Proteus as its most powerful teacher. All the lessons of the earlier books—humility, responsibility, effort, understanding—culminate in this final narrative, where the *Georgics* envision the making of peace as a transformative process. Significantly, uncertainty stalks the equilibrium Aristaeus achieves; the scene of his atonement necessarily recalls the memory of his crime, and his peace persists in the perpetual present of the poem as we experience it. When Virgil speaks in the lines following this scene, he makes no guarantee of future happiness either for Aristaeus or for himself; instead, he steers the poem back to the present, where he sings at a distance from the victorious Octavian.

The sense of mutability that runs through this poem and the ones that converse with it suggests that war is an undeniable element of past days and a probable aspect of future events. The labor that marks the Virgilian georgic world and determines the success of the farm recasts everyday life as a constant reformulation of violent energy, and a constant attempt to counter destructive forces with creative ones. Writers translate, imitate, and allude to the *Georgics* for many reasons, but I have been endeavoring here to urge our attention more directly toward the georgic's history of engaging with history—or more specifically, of engaging with war—as it constructs a model of vigilant and active peace. The Virgilian georgic mode unites ideal and action, labor and product, and insists always that we see the one in the other.

In this book, I have sought to illuminate one historical period in which poets were conversing actively with the lessons of the *Georgics*, but these engagements also appear in works of art created before and after the century that followed the English civil wars. I hope that other scholars will find more instances where artists call for a georgic peace raised from the ground up and consistently maintained. Although I have been primarily concerned with poetry, others might also look to the novel, where examples abound. Consider just one example of the ground to be tilled there: about a third of the way through Thomas Hardy's novel of 1874, *Far from the Madding Crowd*, several of its main characters undertake the yearly task of shearing sheep, and in one striking passage, the narrator contemplates tools and weapons together: "Peace and war kiss each other at their hours of preparation, sickles, scythes, shears, and pruning-hooks mingling with swords, bayonets, and lances, in their common necessity for point and edge."[1] Like Virgil, Hardy troubles the boundary between peace and war by noting their common material foundations. Instead of depicting a single scythe recast as a sword, however, this sentence unravels into a heaping pile of implements: these are the objects of peace and war, which are locked in such close proximity that they "kiss." This word captures the striking and immediate mutability of these two states: when the sheep shearer sharpens his blade, he unwittingly flirts with the possibility of violence, since he holds in his hand a tool that can hardly be distinguished from a weapon until he begins to use it for work rather than for war. With this single sentence, Hardy also recalls an idea that unites the poems of Virgil, Marvell, Dryden, Finch, and Philips: very often, the threat of violence does not lurk in the distance or linger at the horizon. It comes from within, inhabiting places we might be tempted to assume will remain peaceful because they are quiet, or far from the city, or green. But the Virgilian georgic in all its iterations asks us to remain perpetually willing to work for peace, since it admits the protean nature of stability.

Dryden, Marvell, Finch, and Philips detected these values in the georgic, and a great responsibility now falls upon us to see them as well, particularly because the same questions of lasting peace persist into the present day. Conflicts worldwide demonstrate that viable peace derives from constant efforts, and that complacency breeds violence. In an essay published in the *New York Times* on 15

May 2014, Colum McCann called for perpetual attention to peace in Northern Ireland, where he feared efforts to sustain it were faltering; his words have only become more apt since their first publication:

> It is, of course, naïve to expect total reconciliation. Some grievances are so deep that the people who suffered them will never be satisfied. But the point is not satisfaction—the point is that the present is superior to the past, and it has to be *cultivated* as such. . . . Once upon a time, there were bullets in the back of the head. There were car bombs along South Leinster Street. There were young girls getting tarred and feathered in the flatlands of Belfast. That's not happening anymore. But just because it's not happening now, doesn't mean it will not happen again. To lose the process now would be an international crime that reaches backward and forward both. [my emphasis]

McCann recognizes that peace requires continuous cultivation, and that the success or failure of this process has implications extending "backward and forward both." This temporal simultaneity recalls the two-faced deity whose temple was chosen by the Romans to represent peace: Janus, god of middleness, of doorways, and of guardianship. He looks backward, at the memory of what was, at the same time that he gazes forward, toward what will be. His body—the part that walks and works—remains between, linking the double foci of the mind, and rooting past and future in the present. As Virgil's middle work—perched between pastoral song and epic war—the *Georgics* fully inhabit this sense of middleness, as do the poets in this book. They ask us to consider the volatile space between war and peace, and to recognize the significance of cultivation as necessary for lasting stability. They offer us no golden age returned: instead, they instruct us in the ways of making peace. As we move ever further into the future, we would do well to heed this ancient call.

NOTE

1. Thomas Hardy, *Far from the Madding Crowd* (1874; repr., London: Penguin Books, 2003), 114.

Although this is a book about work, many people have made the writing of it far more pleasant than toilsome. Mrs. Whittington encouraged me to take Latin, and taught me much more than verb tenses and ablative absolutes: she is one of the most gifted teachers I have known, and I can only hope to match her example in the classroom. At the University of Rochester, James Longenbach taught me how to read poems and how to talk about them with other people. At Boston University, I could not have asked for a wiser, more encouraging, or more dedicated mentor than James Winn, who first suggested that I think about the *Georgics* and English poetry, and who has offered unstinting support to this project through its many transformations. I am also grateful to have studied under Erin Murphy, who always imparts astute commentary and judicious advice. A fellowship from the Boston University Center for the Humanities, as well as conversation with the seminar participants there, were invaluable for the development of this book. At the College of the Holy Cross, my colleagues are some of the most generous academics I have known to date; special thanks are due to Christine Coch, Maurice Géracht, Shawn Maurer, Jonathan Mulrooney, Paige Reynolds, and Aaron Seider. I am indebted as well to the students who took my course on georgic and pastoral during the spring of 2017; their energy and intelligence were intensely motivating. Thanks to Greg Clingham, Miriam Wallace, Kate Parker, Pam Dailey, and the readers at Bucknell University Press; their thoughtful and diligent work has made this a better book, as have the keen eyes of Kristen Bettcher and Barbara Goodhouse. I have for many years been grateful for the friendship and encouragement of Devin Byker, Reed Gochberg, Kelsey Graham, Joyce Kim, Sierra Laventure-Volz, Kate Nielsen, and Laura Tallon. Mick, Maureen, and Lauren Schoenberger have always been immensely supportive and truly kind, and I am grateful to them in ways beyond articulation here. Finally, Greg Chase has heard the ideas in this book articulated aloud more than anyone on earth, and I am continually astounded by his indefatigable patience and steadfastness.

Acheson, Katherine O. "Military Illustration, Garden Design, and Marvell's 'Upon Appleton House.'" *English Literary Renaissance* 41, no. 1 (2011): 146–188.

Addison, Joseph. *A Translation of All Virgil's Fourth Georgick, except the Story of Aristeus*. In *The Miscellaneous Works of Joseph Addison*, edited by A. C. Guthkelch. London: G. Bell and Sons, 1914. Literature Online. Cambridge: Chadwyck-Healey, 2000.

Addison, Joseph and Richard Steele. *The Guardian*, edited by John Calhoun Stevens. Lexington: The University Press of Kentucky, 1982.

Aikin, John. *An Essay on the Application of Natural History to Poetry*. London, 1777. Eighteenth Century Collections Online.

Alpers, Paul J. *What Is Pastoral?* Chicago: University of Chicago Press, 1996.

Anderson, Frances E. *Christopher Smart*. New York: Twayne, 1975.

Anderson, Penelope. *Friendship's Shadows: Women's Friendship and the Politics of Betrayal in England, 1640–1705*. Edinburgh: Edinburgh University Press, 2012.

Anselment, Raymond A. "Clarendon and the Caroline Myth of Peace." *Journal of British Studies* 23, no. 2 (1984): 37–54.

Armstrong, John. *The Art of Preserving Health. By John Armstrong, M.D. To which is prefixed A Critical Essay on the Poem, by J. Aikin, M.D.* London, 1795. Eighteenth Century Collections Online.

Ayres, Philip. *Classical Culture and the Idea of Rome*. Cambridge: Cambridge University Press, 1997.

Backscheider, Paula. *Eighteenth-Century Women Poets and Their Poetry: Inventing Agency, Inventing Genre*. Baltimore: Johns Hopkins University Press, 2005.

Barash, Carol. "Dryden, Tonson, and the Patrons of *The Works of Virgil* (1697)." In *John Dryden: Tercentenary Essays*, edited by Paul Hammond and David Hopkins, 174–239. Oxford: Oxford University Press, 2000.

———. *English Women's Poetry, 1649–1714: Politics, Community, and Linguistic Authority*. Oxford: Oxford University Press, 1997.

———. "The Political Origins of Anne Finch's Poetry." *HLQ* 54, no. 4 (1991): 327–351.

Barnard, John. "Dryden's *Virgil* (1697): Gatherings and Politics." *The Papers of the Bibliographical Society of America* 109, no. 1 (2015): 131–139.

Baswell, Christopher. *Virgil in Medieval England: Figuring the "Aeneid" from the Twelfth Century to Chaucer*. Cambridge: Cambridge University Press, 1995.

Batstone, William. "Virgilian Didaxis: Value and Meaning in the *Georgics*." In *The Cambridge Companion to Virgil*, edited by Charles Martindale. Cambridge: Cambridge University Press, 1997. Online edition, Cambridge Companions Online, 2006.

Bending, Stephen. *Green Retreats: Women, Gardens and Eighteenth-Century Culture*. Cambridge: Cambridge University Press, 2013.

Bolton, Edmund. *Hypercritica, or, A Rule of Judgement, for Writing or Reading our Histories*. 1618. In *Ancient Critical Essays Upon Poets and Poesie*, edited by Joseph Haslewood. London: Robert Triphook, 1815. Literature Online. Cambridge: Chadwyck-Healey, 1999.

Brooks, Cleanth. "Criticism and Literary History: Marvell's Horatian Ode." *Sewanee Review* 55, no. 2 (1947): 199–222.

Brower, Reuben A. "Lady Winchilsea and the Poetic Tradition of the Seventeenth Century." *Studies in Philology* 42, no. 1 (1945): 61–80.

Bucknell, Clare. "The Mid-Eighteenth-Century Georgic and Agricultural Improvement." *Journal for Eighteenth-Century Studies* 36, no. 3 (2013): 335–352.

Bush, Douglas. "Marvell's 'Horatian Ode.'" *Sewanee Review* 60, no. 3 (1952): 363–376.

Caldwell, Tanya. "Honey and Venom: Dryden's Third *Georgic.*" *Eighteenth-Century Life* 20, no. 3 (1996): 20–36.

———. "John Denham and John Dryden." *Texas Studies in Literature and Language* 46, no. 1 (2004): 49–72.

———. *Time to Begin Anew: Dryden's "Georgics" and "Aeneis.*" Lewisburg, PA: Bucknell University Press, 2000.

———. *Virgil Made English: The Decline of Classical Authority*. New York: Palgrave Macmillan, 2008.

Chalker, John. *The English Georgic: A Study in the Development of a Form*. Baltimore: Johns Hopkins Press, 1969.

Chernaik, Warren. *The Poetry of Limitation: A Study of Edmund Waller*. New Haven, CT: Yale University Press, 1968.

———. "Waller, Edmund (1606–1687)." In *Oxford Dictionary of National Biography*. Oxford University Press, 2004; online ed., 2011.

Chudleigh, Mary. *The Poems and Prose of Mary, Lady Chudleigh*. Edited by Margaret J. M. Ezell. Oxford: Oxford University Press, 1993.

Cleary, Scott M. "Slouching toward Augusta: Alexander Pope's 1736 'Windsor Forest.'" *SEL* 50, no. 3 (2010): 645–663.

Cohen, Ralph. *The Unfolding of "The Seasons.*" Baltimore: Johns Hopkins Press, 1970.

Colie, Rosalie. *"My Ecchoing Song": Andrew Marvell's Poetry of Criticism*. Princeton, NJ: Princeton University Press, 1970.

Colley, Linda. *Britons: Forging the Nation, 1707–1837*. Rev. ed. New Haven, CT: Yale University Press, 2005.

Connell, Philip. "Newtonian Physico-Theology and the Varieties of Whiggism in James Thomson's *The Seasons.*" *HLQ* 72, no. 1 (2009): 1–28.

Copeland, Rita. *Rhetoric, Hermeneutics and Translation in the Middle Ages*. Cambridge: Cambridge University Press, 1991.

Corse, Taylor. *Dryden's "Aeneid": The English Virgil*. Newark: University of Delaware Press, 1991.

Crawford, Rachel. "English Georgic and British Nationhood." *ELH* 65, no. 1 (1998): 123–158.

Crump, M. Marjorie. *The Epyllion from Theocritus to Ovid*. Oxford: Basil Blackwell, 1931.

———. *Poetry, Enclosure, and the Vernacular Landscape, 1700–1830*. Cambridge: Cambridge University Press, 2002.

Dalzell, Alexander. *The Criticism of Didactic Poetry: Essays on Lucretius, Virgil, and Ovid*. Toronto: University of Toronto Press, 1996.

Davis, Paul. "'But slaves we are': Dryden and Virgil, Translation and the 'Gyant Race.'" *Translation and Literature* 10, no. 1 (2001): 110–127.

———. "'Dogmatical' Dryden: Translating the *Georgics* in the Age of Politeness." *Translation and Literature* 8, no. 1 (1999): 28–53.

———. "Dryden and the Invention of Augustan Culture." In *The Cambridge Companion to John Dryden*, edited by Steven N. Zwicker. Cambridge: Cambridge University Press, 2004.

———. *Translation and the Poet's Life: The Ethics of Translating in English Culture, 1646–1726*. Oxford: Oxford University Press, 2008.

Dearnley, Moira. *The Poetry of Christopher Smart*. London: Routledge and Kegan Paul, 1968.

De Bruyn, Frans. "Eighteenth-Century Editions of Virgil's *Georgics*: From Classical Poem to Agricultural Treatise." *Lumen* 24 (2005): 149–163.

———. "From Virgilian Georgic to Agricultural Science: An Instance in the Transvaluation of Literature in Eighteenth-Century Britain." In *Augustan Subjects: Essays in Honor of Martin C. Battestin*, edited by Albert J. Rivero. Newark: University of Delaware Press, 1997.

———. "Reading Virgil's *Georgics* as a Scientific Text: The Eighteenth-Century Debate between Jethro Tull and Stephen Switzer." *ELH* 71, no. 3 (2004): 661–689.

Dodsley, Robert. *Trifles*. London: J. Dodsley, 1777. Literature Online. Cambridge: Chadwyck-Healey, 1992.

Donovan, Fiona. *Rubens and England*. New Haven, CT: Yale University Press, 2004.

Downes, Kerry. "Rubens's 'Peace and War' at the National Gallery." *Burlington Magazine* 121, no. 915 (1979): 397–398.

Dryden, John. *The Letters of John Dryden with Letters Addressed to him*. Edited by Charles E. Ward. Durham, NC: Duke University Press, 1942.

———. *The Works of John Dryden*. Edited by H. T. Swedenberg et al. 20 vols. Berkeley: University of California Press, 1956–2000.

Dubrow, Heather. "Guess Who's Coming to Dinner? Reinterpreting Formalism and the Country House Poem." *Modern Language Quarterly* 61, no. 1 (2000): 59–77.

Durling, Dwight Leonard. *The Georgic Tradition in English Poetry*. New York: Columbia University Press, 1935.

Dyer, John. *The Poetical Works of Mark Akenside and John Dyer*. Edited by Robert Aris Willmott. London: George Routledge, 1855. Literature Online. Cambridge: Chadwyck-Healey, 1992.

———. *The Ruins of Rome. A poem*. London, 1740. *Eighteenth Century Collections Online*.

Erskine-Hill, Howard. *The Augustan Idea in English Literature*. London: Edward Arnold, 1983.

Ezell, Margaret. *The Patriarch's Wife: Literary Evidence and the History of the Family*. Chapel Hill: University of North Carolina Press, 1987.

———. *Writing Women's Literary History*. Baltimore: Johns Hopkins University Press, 1993.

Fairer, David. *English Poetry of the Eighteenth Century: 1700–1789*. Longman Literature in English Series. Harlow, UK: Longman, 2003.

———. "Georgic." In *The Oxford Handbook of British Poetry, 1660–1800*. Oxford: Oxford University Press, 2016.

———. "'Where Fuming Trees Refresh the Thirsty Air': The World of Eco-Georgic." *Studies in Eighteenth Century Culture* 40 (2011): 201–218.

Farrell, Joseph P. *Vergil's "Georgics" and the Tradition of Ancient Epic: The Art of Allusion in Literary History*. Oxford: Oxford University Press, 1991.

Finch, Anne. *The Anne Finch Wellesley Manuscript Poems: A Critical Edition*. Edited by Barbara McGovern and Charles H. Hinnant. Athens: University of Georgia Press, 1998.

———. *The Poems of Anne, Countess of Winchilsea*. Edited by Myra Reynolds. Chicago: University of Chicago Press, 1903.

Fleming, Abraham. *The Bucoliks of Publius Virgilius Maro, prince of all Latine poets; otherwise called his pastorals, or shepeherds meetings. Together with his Georgiks or ruralls, otherwise called his husbandrie, conteyning foure books. All newly translated into English verse by A.F.* London, 1589. Early English Books Online.

Forrer, Leonard. "Roettiers (Roettier or Rotier), John (or Jan)." In *Biographical Dictionary of Medallists*, vol. 5. London: Spink and Son, 1912. Pp. 161–173. archive.org.

Fowler, Alastair. "The Beginnings of English Georgic." In *Renaissance Genres: Essays on Theory, History, and Interpretation*, edited by Barbara K. Lewalski. Cambridge, MA: Harvard University Press, 1986.

Franks, Augustus W., and Herbert A. Grueboer. *Medallic Illustrations of the History of Britain.* 2 vols. London: Trustees of the British Museum, 1885. *archive.org.*

Friedman, Donald M. *Marvell's Pastoral Art.* Berkeley: University of California Press, 1970.

Frost, William. "Dryden's Virgil." *Comparative Literature* 36, no. 3 (1984): 193–208.

Fujimura, Thomas H. "Dryden's Virgil: Translation as Autobiography." *Studies in Philology* 80, no. 1 (1983): 67–83.

———. "John Dryden and the Myth of the Golden Age." *Papers on Language and Literature* 11, no. 2 (1975): 149–167.

Fulford, Tim. *Landscape, Liberty and Authority: Poetry, Criticism and Politics from Thomson to Wordsworth.* Cambridge: Cambridge University Press, 1996.

———. "'Nature' Poetry." In *The Cambridge Companion to Eighteenth-Century Poetry,* edited by John Sitter. Cambridge: Cambridge University Press, 2001; online ed., 2006.

Gale, Monica R. *Virgil on the Nature of Things: The "Georgics," Lucretius, and the Didactic Tradition.* Cambridge: Cambridge University Press, 2000.

Gavin, Michael. "Critics and Criticism in the Poetry of Anne Finch." *ELH* 78, no. 3 (2011): 633–655.

Geymonat, Mario. "Capellae at the End of the Eclogues." *Harvard Studies in Classical Philology* 102 (2004): 315–318.

Gillespie, Katherine. *Domesticity and Dissent in the Seventeenth Century: English Women's Writing and the Public Sphere.* Cambridge: Cambridge University Press, 2004.

Gillespie, Stuart. *English Translation and Classical Reception: Towards a New Literary History.* Oxford: Wiley-Blackwell, 2011.

Gilmore, John. *The Poetics of Empire: A Study of James Grainger's "The Sugar-Cane."* New Brunswick, NJ: Athlone Press, 2000.

Goodman, Kevis. *Georgic Modernity and British Romanticism: Poetry and the Mediation of History.* Cambridge: Cambridge University Press, 2004.

———. "'Wasted Labor'? Milton's Eve, the Poet's Work, and the Challenge of Sympathy." *ELH* 64, no. 2 (1997): 415–446.

Goodridge, John. *Rural Life in Eighteenth-Century English Poetry.* Cambridge: Cambridge University Press, 1995.

Grainger, James. *The Sugar-Cane: a poem. In four books.* London, 1764. Eighteenth Century Collections Online.

Gray, Catharine. "Katherine Philips and the Post-Courtly Coterie." *English Literary Renaissance* 32, no. 3 (2002): 426–451.

———. *Women Writers and Public Debate in 17th-Century Britain.* New York: Palgrave Macmillan, 2007.

Greene, Thomas M. "The Balance of Power in Marvell's 'Horatian Ode.'" *ELH* 60, no. 2 (1993): 379–396.

Griffin, Dustin. "The Bard of Cyder-Land: John Philips and Miltonic Imitation." *Studies in English Literature, 1500–1900* 24, no. 3 (1984): 441–460.

———. *Regaining Paradise: Milton and the Eighteenth Century.* Cambridge: Cambridge University Press, 1986.

Guyer, Sara. *Reading with John Clare: Biopoetics, Sovereignty, Romanticism.* New York: Fordham University Press, 2015.

Haber, Judith. *Pastoral and the Poetics of Self-Contradiction: Theocritus to Marvell.* Cambridge: Cambridge University Press, 1994.

Hammond, Paul. *Dryden and the Traces of Classical Rome.* Oxford: Oxford University Press, 1999.

———. "Dryden's Virgilian Kings." *The Seventeenth Century* 29, no. 2 (2014): 153–171.

———. "The Integrity of Dryden's Lucretius." *Modern Language Review* 78 (1983): 1–23.

————. *The Making of Restoration Poetry.* Cambridge: D. S. Brewer, 2006.

Hammond, Paul, and David Hopkins, eds. *John Dryden: Tercentenary Essays.* Oxford: Oxford University Press, 2000.

Hamrick, Wes. "Trees in Anne Finch's Jacobite Poems of Retreat." *SEL* 53, no. 3 (2013): 541–563.

Hardy, Thomas. *Far from the Madding Crowd.* 1874. Reprint, London: Penguin Books, 2003.

Harrison, S. J. "Some Views of the *Aeneid* in the Twentieth Century." In *Oxford Readings in Vergil's "Aeneid,"* edited by S. J. Harrison. Oxford: Oxford University Press, 1990.

Haynes, Kenneth. "Dryden: Classical or Neoclassical?" *Translation and Literature* 10, no. 1 (2001): 67–77.

Heinzelman, Kurt. "Roman Georgic in the Georgian Age: A Theory of Romantic Genre." *Texas Studies in Literature and Language* 33, no. 2 (1991): 182–214.

Herbert, Amanda E. *Female Alliances: Gender, Identity, and Friendship in Early Modern Britain.* New Haven, CT: Yale University Press, 2014.

Hesiod. *Works and Days.* Translated by David W. Tandy and Walter C. Neale. Berkeley: University of California Press, 1996.

Hiltner, Ken. *What Else Is Pastoral?* Ithaca, NY: Cornell University Press, 2011.

Hinnant, Charles H. *The Poetry of Anne Finch: An Essay in Interpretation.* Newark: University of Delaware Press, 1994.

Hirst, Derek, and Steven N. Zwicker. *Andrew Marvell: Orphan of the Hurricane.* Oxford: Oxford University Press, 2012.

————. "High Summer at Nun Appleton, 1651: Andrew Marvell and Lord Fairfax's Occasions." *Historical Journal* 36, no. 2 (1993): 247–269.

Hobbes, Thomas. *Leviathan.* Edited by A. P. Martinich and Brian Battiste. Peterborough, Ontario: Broadview, 2011.

Holland, Hugh. *A Cypres Garland. For the Sacred Fore-head of our Late soueraigne King Iames.* London: Simon Waterson, 1625. Literature Online. Cambridge: Chadwyck-Healey, 1992.

Hone, Joseph. "Isaac Newton and the Medals for Queen Anne." *Huntington Library Quarterly* 79, no. 1 (Spring 2016): 119–148.

Hooker, Helene M. "Dryden's Georgics and English Predecessors." *Huntington Library Quarterly* 9 (1946): 273–310.

Hopkins, David. *Conversing with Antiquity: English Poets and the Classics, from Shakespeare to Pope.* Oxford: Oxford University Press, 2010.

Horace. *Odes and Epodes.* Rev. ed. Edited by Paul Shorey and Gordon J. Laing. Chicago: Benjamin H. Sanborn, 1919.

Hornsey, Ian Spencer. *A History of Beer and Brewing.* Cambridge: Royal Society of Chemistry, 2003.

Hughes, Anthony. "Naming the Unnameable: An Iconographical Problem in Rubens' 'Peace and War.'" *Burlington Magazine* 122, no. 924 (1980): 157–163.

Humphrey, Belinda. "Dyer, John." In *Oxford Dictionary of National Biography.* Oxford University Press, 2004; online ed.

Hunter, J. Paul. "Formalism and History: Binarism and the Anglophone Couplet." *Modern Language Quarterly* 61, no. 1 (2000): 109–129.

Hutchinson, G. O. *Hellenistic Poetry.* Oxford: Oxford University Press, 1988.

Irvine, Robert P. "Labor and Commerce in Locke and Early Eighteenth-Century English Georgic." *English Literary History* 76, no. 4 (2009): 963–988.

Jameson, Fredric. *The Political Unconscious: Narrative as a Socially Symbolic Act.* Ithaca, NY: Cornell University Press, 1981.

Johnson, Samuel. *Samuel Johnson: The Major Works.* Edited by Donald Greene. Oxford: Oxford University Press, 2009.

Jordan, Nicolle. "'Where Power Is Absolute': Royalist Politics and the Improved Landscape in a Poem by Anne Finch, Countess of Winchilsea." *The Eighteenth Century* 46, no. 3 (2005): 255–275.

Kallendorf, Craig. *The Other Virgil: "Pessimistic" Readings of the "Aeneid" in Early Modern Culture*. Oxford: Oxford University Press, 2007.

Kaul, Suvir. *Poems of Nation, Anthems of Empire: English Verse in the Long Eighteenth Century*. Charlottesville: University of Virginia Press, 2000.

Keenlyside, Heather. "Personification for the People: On James Thomson's *The Seasons*." *ELH* 76, no. 2 (2009): 447–472.

Keith, Jennifer. "Anne Finch's Aviary: or, Why She Never Wrote 'The Bird and the Arras.'" *Philological Quarterly* 88, no. 1–2 (2009): 77–102.

———, gen. ed. *The Cambridge Edition of the Works of Anne Finch, Countess of Winchilsea*. 2 vols. Vol. 1, *Early Manuscript Books*, edited by Jennifer Keith and Claudia Thomas Kairoff, associate editor Jean I. Marsden. Cambridge: Cambridge University Press, forthcoming May 2019.

———. "'Pre-Romanticism' and the Ends of Eighteenth-Century Poetry." In *The Cambridge Companion to Eighteenth-Century Literature*, edited by John Sitter. Cambridge: Cambridge University Press, 2001; online ed., 2006, 271–290.

———. "The Reach of Translation in the Works of Anne Finch." *Philological Quarterly* 95, no. 3/4 (2016): 467–493.

Kennedy, Deborah. *Poetic Sisters: Early Eighteenth-Century Women Poets*. Lewisburg: Bucknell University Press, 2013.

Kennedy, D. F. "Shades of Meaning: Virgil, *Ecl.* 10.75–77." *Liverpool Classical Monthly* 8 (1983): 124.

Knoppers, Laura Lunger. *Constructing Cromwell: Ceremony, Portrait, and Print, 1645–1661*. Cambridge: Cambridge University Press, 2000.

La Fontaine, Jean. *Fables de La Fontaine*. Edited by Francis Tarver. London: Libraire Hachette, 1898. *archive.org*.

Lanser, Susan S. *The Sexuality of History: Modernity and the Sapphic, 1535–1830*. Chicago: University of Chicago Press, 2014.

Legouis, Pierre. *Andrew Marvell: Poet, Puritan, Patriot*. Oxford: Clarendon Press, 1965.

Leishman, J. B. *The Art of Marvell's Poetry*. New York: Minerva Press, 1968.

Lewalski, Barbara K. *The Life of John Milton: A Critical Biography*. Oxford: Blackwell, 2000.

Lewis, Jayne Elizabeth. *The English Fable: Aesop and Literary Culture, 1651–1740*. Cambridge: Cambridge University Press, 1996.

Lipking, Lawrence. "The Gods of Poetry: Mythology and the Eighteenth-Century Tradition." In *Augustan Subjects: Essays in Honor of Martin C. Battestin*, edited by Albert J. Rivero. Newark: University of Delaware Press, 1997.

Lonsdale, Roger, ed. *Eighteenth-Century Women Poets*. Oxford: Oxford University Press, 1989.

Low, Anthony. *The Georgic Revolution*. Princeton, NJ: Princeton University Press, 1985.

Lutz, Alfred. "'The Deserted Village' and the Politics of Genre." *Modern Language Quarterly* 55, no. 2 (1994): 149–168.

Lyne, R.O.A.M. "Vergil and the Politics of War." In *Oxford Readings in Vergil's "Aeneid,"* edited by S. J. Harrison. Oxford: Oxford University Press, 1990.

Mack, Maynard. *The Garden and the City*. Toronto: University of Toronto Press, 1969.

Magurn, Ruth Saunders, ed. *The Letters of Peter Paul Rubens*. Evanston, IL: Northwestern University Press, 1991.

Marcus, Leah. *The Politics of Mirth: Jonson, Herrick, Milton, Marvell, and the Defense of Old Holiday Pastimes*. Chicago: University of Chicago Press, 1986.

Markley, Robert. "'Gulfs, Deserts, Precipices, Stone': Marvell's 'Upon Appleton House' and the Contradictions of 'Nature.'" In *The Country and the City Revisited: England and the Politics of Culture, 1550–1850*, edited by Gerald MacLean, Donna Landry, and Joseph P. Ward. Cambridge: Cambridge University Press, 1999.

Martin, Gregory. *The Flemish School circa 1600–circa 1900*. National Gallery Catalogues. London: National Gallery, 1970.

Martindale, Charles. "Reception—a New Humanism? Receptivity, Pedagogy, the Transhistorical." *Classical Receptions Journal* 5, no. 2 (2013): 169–183.

Martz, Louis L. "*Paradise Regained*: Georgic Form, Georgic Style." *Milton Studies* 42 (2002): 7–25.

Marvell, Andrew. *The Poems of Andrew Marvell*. Rev. ed., edited by Nigel Smith. Harlow, UK: Pearson Longman, 2007.

McCann, Colum. "Ireland's Troubled Peace." *New York Times*, 15 May 2014. https://www.nytimes.com/2014/05/16/opinion/irelands-troubled-peace.html.

McGovern, Barbara. *Anne Finch and Her Poetry: A Critical Biography*. Athens: University of Georgia Press, 1992.

McKillop, Alan Dugald. *The Background of Thomson's "Seasons."* Reprint, Hamden, CT: Archon Books, 1961.

———, ed. Introduction to *James Thomson: The Castle of Indolence and Other Poems*. Lawrence: University Press of Kansas, 1961.

McRae, Andrew. *God Speed the Plough: The Representation of Agrarian England, 1500–1660*. Cambridge: Cambridge University Press, 1996.

Messenger, Ann. *Pastoral Tradition and the Female Talent: Studies in Augustan Poetry*. Norwalk, CT: AMS Press, 2001.

Miles, Gary. *Virgil's Georgics: A New Interpretation*. Berkeley: University of California Press, 1980.

Milton, John. *Complete Poems and Major Prose*. Edited by Merritt Y. Hughes. New York: Macmillan, 1957.

———. *The Riverside Milton*. Edited by Roy Flannagan. Boston: Houghton Mifflin, 1998.

Monod, Paul. *Jacobitism and the English People, 1688–1788*. Cambridge: Cambridge University Press, 1993.

Morgan, Llewelyn. *Patterns of Redemption in Virgil's Georgics*. Cambridge: Cambridge University Press, 1999.

Morris, David B. "Virgilian Attitudes in Pope's 'Windsor Forest.'" *Studies in Literature and Language* 15, no. 2 (1973): 231–250.

Mulcaster, Richard. *The First Part of the Elementarie Which Entreateth Chefelie of the right writing of our English tung*. London: Thomas Vautroullier, 1582. Literature Online. Chadwyck-Healey, 1999.

Nappa, Christopher. *Reading after Actium: Vergil's "Georgics," Octavian, and Rome*. Ann Arbor: University of Michigan Press, 2005.

Nelson, Stephanie. *God and the Land: The Metaphysics of Farming in Hesiod and Virgil*. Oxford: Oxford University Press, 2008.

Netzley, Ryan. *Lyric Apocalypse: Milton, Marvell, and the Nature of Events*. New York: Fordham University Press, 2015.

The New Oxford Annotated Bible. 3rd ed., edited by Michael D. Coogan et al. Oxford: Oxford University Press, 2001.

Norbrook, David. *Writing the English Republic: Poetry, Rhetoric and Politics, 1627–1660*. Cambridge: Cambridge University Press, 1999.

O'Brien, Karen, "Imperial Georgic: 1660–1789." In *The Country and the City Revisited: England and the Politics of Culture, 1550–1850*, edited by Gerald MacLean, Donna Landry, and Joseph P. Ward. Cambridge: Cambridge University Press, 1999.

O'Loughlin, M. J. K. "'This Sober Frame: A Reading of 'Upon Appleton House.'" In *Andrew Marvell: A Collection of Critical Essays*, edited by George deF. Lord. Englewood Cliffs, NJ: Prentice-Hall, 1968.

Orgel, Stephen. *The Illusion of Power*. Berkeley: University of California Press, 1975.

Palme, Per. *Triumph of Peace: A Study of the Whitehall Banqueting House*. Stockholm: Almqvist and Wiksell, 1956.

Patey, Douglas Lane. "Anne Finch, John Dyer, and the Georgic Syntax of Nature." In *Augustan Subjects: Essays in Honor of Martin C. Battestin*, edited by Albert J. Rivero. Newark: University of Delaware Press, 1997.

Patterson, Annabel. *Fables of Power: Aesopian Writing and Political History*. Durham, NC: Duke University Press, 1991.

———. *Marvell: The Writer in Public Life*. Harlow, UK: Longman, 2000.

———. *Pastoral and Ideology: Virgil to Valéry*. Berkeley: University of California Press, 1987.

———. "Pastoral versus Georgic: The Politics of Virgilian Quotation." In *Renaissance Genres: Essays on Theory, History, and Interpretation*, edited by Barbara K. Lewalski. Cambridge, MA: Harvard University Press, 1986.

Pellicer, Juan Christian. "Celebrating Queen Anne and the Union of 1707 in Great Britain's First Georgic" *Journal for Eighteenth-Century Studies* 37, no. 2 (2014): 217–227.

———. "Corkscrew or Cathedral? The Politics of Alexander Pope's *Windsor-Forest* and the Dynamics of Literary Kind." *Huntington Library Quarterly* 71, no. 3 (2008): 453–488.

———. "The Georgic at Mid-Eighteenth Century and the Case of Dodsley's 'Agriculture.'" *Review of English Studies* 54 (2003): 67–93.

———. "Harleian Georgic from Tonson's Press: The Publication of John Philips's *Cyder*, 29 January 1708." *The Library: The Transactions of the Bibliographical Society* 7, no. 2 (2006): 185–198.

———. "John Philips (1676–1709): Life, Works, and Reception." Doctoral thesis, University of Oslo, 2002.

———. "Reception, Wit, and the Unity of Virgil's *Georgics*." *Symbolae Osloenses* 82 (2007): 90–115.

Perkell, Christine G. "Pastoral Value in Vergil." In *Poets and Critics Read Vergil*, edited by Sarah Spence. New Haven, CT: Yale University Press, 2001.

———. *The Poet's Truth: A Study of the Poet in Virgil's Georgics*. Berkeley: University of California Press, 1989.

Philips, John. *The Poems of John Philips*. Edited by M. G. Lloyd Thomas. Oxford: Basil Blackwell, 1927. Literature Online. Cambridge: Chadwyck-Healey, 1992.

———. *Cyder: A Poem in Two Books (1708)*. Edited by John Goodridge and Juan Christian Pellicer. Cheltenham: Cyder Press, 2001.

Pooley, Roger. "The Poets' Cromwell." *Critical Survey* 5, no. 3 (1993): 223–234.

Pope, Alexander. *The Twickenham Edition of the Poems of Alexander Pope*. Edited by John Butt. 11 vols. New Haven, CT: Yale University Press, 1961–1969.

Powell, Rosalind. *Christopher Smart's English Lyrics: Translation in the Eighteenth Century*. Surrey, UK: Ashgate, 2014.

Power, Henry. "Virgil, Horace, and Gay's Art of Walking the Streets." *Cambridge Quarterly* 38, no. 4 (2009): 338–367.

Putnam, Michael C. J. "Vergil's *Aeneid*: The Final Lines." In *Poets and Critics Read Vergil*, edited by Sarah Spence. New Haven, CT: Yale University Press, 2001.

———. *Virgil's Poem of the Earth: Studies in the Georgics*. Princeton, NJ: Princeton University Press, 1979.

Quint, David. *Epic and Empire: Politics and Generic Form from Virgil to Milton*. Princeton, NJ: Princeton University Press, 1993.

Rabb, Thomas K. *The Struggle for Stability in Early Modern Europe*. Oxford: Oxford University Press, 1975.

Rasmussen, Mark, ed. *Renaissance Literature and Its Formal Engagements*. New York: Palgrave, 2002.

Rawson, Claude, and Aaron Santesso, eds. *John Dryden (1631–1700): His Politics, His Plays, and His Poets*. Newark: University of Delaware Press, 2004.

Raylor, Timothy. "Waller's Machiavellian Cromwell: The Imperial Argument of 'A Panegyrick to My Lord Protector.'" *Review of English Studies* 56, no. 225 (2005): 386–411.

Reeve, L. J. *Charles I and the Road to Personal Rule*. Cambridge: Cambridge University Press, 1989.

Rizzo, Betty. "Christopher Smart's Poetics." In *Christopher Smart and the Enlightenment*, edited by Clement Hawes. New York: St. Martin's Press, 1999.

Rogers, Pat. "John Philips, Pope, and Political Georgic." *Modern Language Quarterly* 66, no. 4 (2005): 411–442.

———. *Pope and the Destiny of the Stuarts: History, Politics, and Mythology in the Age of Queen Anne*. Oxford: Oxford University Press, 2005.

———. *The Symbolic Design of Windsor-Forest: Iconography, Pageant, and Prophecy in Pope's Early Work*. Newark: University of Delaware Press, 2004.

Ronda, Margaret. "Georgic Disenchantment in American Poetry." *Genre* 46, no. 1 (2013): 57–78.

———. "'Work and Wait Unwearying': Dunbar's Georgics." *PMLA* 127, no. 4 (2012): 863–878.

Rosenthal, Lisa. "The Parens Patriae: Familial Imagery in Rubens's *Minerva Protects Pax from Mars*." *Art History* 12, no. 1 (1989): 22–38.

Rossi, Andreola. *Contexts of War: Manipulation of Genre in Virgilian Battle Narrative*. Ann Arbor: University of Michigan Press, 2004.

Røstvig, Maren-Sofie. *The Happy Man: Studies in the Metamorphoses of a Classical Ideal*. Oslo: Norwegian Universities Press, 1954–1958.

Sale, William M. *Samuel Richardson: Master Printer*. Ithaca, NY: Cornell University Press, 1950.

Salvaggio, Ruth. *Enlightened Absence: Neoclassical Configurations of the Feminine*. Urbana: University of Illinois Press, 1988.

Schuler, Robert M. "Francis Bacon and Scientific Poetry." *Transactions of the American Philosophical Society* 82, no. 2 (1992): 1–65.

Scott-Baumann, Elizabeth. *Forms of Engagement: Women, Poetry, and Culture, 1640–1680*. Oxford: Oxford University Press, 2013.

Segal, Charles P. "The Achievement of Vergil." Rev. of *Virgil: A Study in Civilized Poetry* by Brooks Otis. *Arion* 4, no. 1 (1965): 126–149.

———. "'Aeternum per Saecula Nomen,' the Golden Bough and the Tragedy of History: Part I." *Arion* 4, no. 4 (1965): 617–657.

———. "'Aeternum per Saecula Nomen,' the Golden Bough and the Tragedy of History: Part II." *Arion* 5, no. 1 (1966): 34–72.

———. "Orpheus and the Fourth Georgic: Vergil on Nature and Civilization." *American Journal of Philology* 87, no. 3 (1966): 307–325.

———. "'Tamen Cantabitis, Arcades': Exile and Arcadia in 'Eclogues One and Nine.'" *Arion* 4, no. 2 (1965): 237–266.

Shakespeare, William. *King Lear*. The Arden Shakespeare, edited by R. A. Foakes. London: Cengage Learning, 1997.

Sharpe, Kevin. *The Personal Rule of Charles I*. New Haven, CT: Yale University Press, 1992.

Sherbo, Arthur. "Virgil, Dryden, Gay, and Matters Trivial." *PMLA* 85, no. 5 (1970): 1063–1071.

Sitter, John. "Creating a National Poetry." In *The Cambridge Companion to Eighteenth-Century Poetry*, edited by John Sitter. Cambridge: Cambridge University Press, 2001.

Smart, Christopher. *The Poems of the Late Christopher Smart*. London: Smart and Cowslade, 1791. Literature Online. Cambridge: Chadwyck-Healey, 1992.

———. *The Poetical Works of Christopher Smart*. Vol. 4, *Miscellaneous Poems English and Latin*. Edited by Karina Williamson. Oxford: Clarendon Press, 1987.

Smith, Courtney Weiss. *Empiricist Devotions: Science, Religion, and Poetry in Early Eighteenth-Century England*. Charlottesville: University of Virginia Press, 2016.

Smith, Nigel. *Andrew Marvell: The Chameleon*. New Haven, CT: Yale University Press, 2010.

———. *Literature and Revolution in England, 1640–1660*. New Haven, CT: Yale University Press, 1997.

Snyder, Susan. *Pastoral Process: Spenser, Marvell, Milton*. Stanford: Stanford University Press, 1998.

Sowerby, Robin. *The Augustan Art of Translation: Augustan Translation of the Classics*. Oxford: Oxford University Press, 2006.

———. "Augustan Dryden." *Translation and Literature* 10, no. 1 (2001): 51–66.

Spacks, Patricia Meyer. *Reading Eighteenth-Century Poetry*. Chichester, UK: Wiley-Blackwell, 2009.

———. *The Varied God: A Critical Study of Thomson's "The Seasons."* Berkeley: University of California Press, 1959.

Stechow, Wolfgang. *Rubens and the Classical Tradition*. Cambridge, MA: Harvard University Press, 1968.

Steiner, Thomas R., and Suzanne Langer. "Precursors to Dryden: English and French Theories of Translation in the Seventeenth Century." *Comparative Literature Studies* 7, no. 1 (1970): 50–81.

Stephens, John Calhoun, ed. *The Guardian*. Lexington: University Press of Kentucky, 1982.

Tallon, Laura. "Ekphrasis and Gender in Anne Finch's Longleat Poems." *Eighteenth-Century Life* 40, no. 1 (2016): 84–107.

Tarrant, R. J. "Poetry and Power: Virgil's Poetry in Contemporary Contexts." In *The Cambridge Companion to Virgil*, edited by Charles Martindale. Cambridge: Cambridge University Press, 1997. Online edition, Cambridge Companions Online, 2006.

Tate, Nahum. "The Ode for New-Year's-Day 1697–8. Set to Musick by *Dr. Blow*." Literature Online. Cambridge: Chadwyck-Healey, 2000.

Theodorakopoulos, Elena. "Closure: The Book of Virgil." In *The Cambridge Companion to Virgil*, edited by Charles Martindale. Cambridge: Cambridge University Press, 1997. Online edition, Cambridge Companions Online, 2006.

Thibodeau, Philip. *Playing the Farmer: Representations of Rural Life in Vergil's Georgics*. Berkeley: University of California Press, 2011.

Thomas, Richard F. *Reading Virgil and His Texts: Studies in Intertextuality*. Ann Arbor: University of Michigan Press, 1999.

———. *Virgil and the Augustan Reception*. Cambridge: Cambridge University Press, 2001.

Thomson, James. *The Seasons*. Edited by James Sambrook. Oxford: Clarendon Press, 1981.

Toohey, Peter. *Epic Lessons: An Introduction to Ancient Didactic Poetry*. London: Routledge, 1996.

Vergara, Lisa. *Rubens and the Poetics of Landscape*. New Haven, CT: Yale University Press, 1982.

Virgil. *Aeneid*. Translated by Theodore C. Williams. Boston: Houghton Mifflin, 1901. Perseus Digital Library. Edited by Gregory R. Crane. Tufts University. http://www.perseus.tufts.edu.

———. *Bucolics, Aeneid, and Georgics of Vergil*. Translated by J. B. Greenough. Boston: Ginn, 1900. Perseus Digital Library. Edited by Gregory R. Crane. Tufts University. http://www.perseus.tufts.edu.

———. *Virgil*. Translated by H. T. Rushton Fairclough. Rev. ed., edited by G.P. Goold. 2 vols. Cambridge, MA: Harvard University Press, 1986.

———. *Georgics*. Edited by R.A.B. Mynors. Oxford: Clarendon Press, 1990.

————. *Georgics*. Edited by Richard F. Thomas. 2 vols. Cambridge: Cambridge University Press, 1988.

————. *The Georgics of Virgil*. Translated by David Ferry. New York: Farrar, Straus and Giroux, 2006.

————. *P. Vergili Maronis opera: The Eclogues and Georgics*. Edited by George Long and A. J. Macleane, with commentary by John Conington. London: Whittaker, 1858.

————. *Virgil's Georgicks Englished*. Translated by Thomas May. London, 1628. Early English Books Online.

————. *The Works of Publius Virgilius Maro*. Translated by John Ogilby. London, 1649. Early English Books Online.

————. *The Works of Publius Virgilius Maro Translated, adorn'd with Sculpture, and illustrated with Annotations*. Translated by John Ogilby. London, 1654. Early English Books Online.

————. *The Works of Virgil, in Latin and English*. Translated by Christopher Pitt. London: R. Dodsley, 1753. Literature Online. Cambridge: Chadwyck-Healey, 1993.

Volk, Katharina. *The Poetics of Latin Didactic: Lucretius, Vergil, Ovid, Manilius*. Oxford: Oxford University Press, 2002.

————, ed. *Vergil's Georgics*. Oxford: Oxford University Press, 2008.

Voltaire. *Candide, ou, L'optimisme*. Edited by A. Morize. Paris: Hachette, 1913. The ARTFL Project. University of Chicago. http://artfl-project.uchicago.edu.

Wagner-McCoy, Sarah. "Virgilian Chesnutt: Eclogues of Slavery and Georgics of Reconstruction in *The Conjure Tales*." *ELH* 80, no. 1 (2013): 199–220.

Wallace, Andrew. "Virgil and Bacon in the Schoolroom." *ELH* 73, no. 1 (2006): 161–185.

Waller, Edmund. *The Poems of Edmund Waller*. Edited by G. Thorn Drury. 1893. Reprint, New York: Greenwood Press, 1968.

Watkins, Calvert, ed. *The American Heritage Dictionary of Indo-European Roots*. 2nd ed. Boston: Houghton Mifflin Harcourt, 2000.

Weinbrot, Howard. *Augustus Caesar in "Augustan" England*. Princeton, NJ: Princeton University Press, 1978.

Werlin, Julianne. "Marvell and the Strategic Imagination: Fortification in *Upon Appleton House*." *Review of English Studies* 63 (2012): 370–387.

West, Michael. "Dryden's Ambivalence as a Translator of Heroic Themes." *Huntington Library Quarterly* 36, no. 4 (1973): 347–366.

White, Christopher. *Rubens and His World*. New York: Viking Press, 1968.

Wilkinson, L. P. *The Georgics of Virgil: A Critical Survey*. Cambridge: Cambridge University Press, 1969.

Williams, Raymond. *The Country and the City*. Oxford: Oxford University Press, 1975.

Williamson, Karina. "Smart, Christopher (1722–1771)." In *Oxford Dictionary of National Biography*. Oxford University Press, 2004; online ed. 2004.

Winn, James. *John Dryden and His World*. New Haven, CT: Yale University Press, 1987.

————. "'Like Her Britannia's Self': Mythology and Politics in the Life of Queen Anne." *Swift Studies* 30 (2015): 31–70.

————. *The Poetry of War*. Cambridge: Cambridge University Press, 2008.

————. *Queen Anne: Patroness of Arts*. Oxford: Oxford University Press, 2014.

————. "'Thy Wars Brought Nothing About': Dryden's Critique of Military Heroism." *The Seventeenth Century* 21, no. 2 (2006): 364–382.

Woolf, D. R. "Bolton, Edmund Mary (*b*. 1574/5, *d*. in or after 1634)." In *Oxford Dictionary of National Biography*. Oxford University Press, 2004; online ed., 2004.

Worden, Blair. *Literature and Politics in Cromwellian England: John Milton, Andrew Marvell, Marchamont Nedham*. Oxford: Oxford University Press, 2007.

Wright, Gillian. "The Birds and the Poet: Fable, Self-Representation and the Early Editing of Anne Finch's Poetry." *Review of English Studies* 64 (2013): 246–266.

Yoshinaka, Takashi. *Marvell's Ambivalence: Religion and the Politics of Imagination in Mid-Seventeenth-Century England*. Woodbridge, UK: Boydell and Brewer, 2011.

Zwicker, Steven N. *Dryden's Political Poetry: The Typology of King and Nation*. Providence, RI: Brown University Press, 1972.

———. *Politics and Language in Dryden's Poetry: The Arts of Disguise*. Princeton, NJ: Princeton University Press, 1984.

———. "Politics and Literary Practice in the Restoration." In *Renaissance Genres: Essays on Theory, History, and Interpretation*, edited by Barbara K. Lewalski. Cambridge, MA: Harvard University Press, 1986.

ABOUT THE AUTHOR

MELISSA SCHOENBERGER is an assistant professor of English at the College of the Holy Cross in Worcester, Massachusetts, where she specializes in Restoration and eighteenth-century poetry.